# Biometrics: Advanced Id

## Springer

*London*
*Berlin*
*Heidelberg*
*New York*
*Barcelona*
*Hong Kong*
*Milan*
*Paris*
*Singapore*
*Tokyo*

Julian Ashbourn

# Biometrics:
## Advanced Identity Verification

**The Complete Guide**

 Springer

Julian Ashbourn

ISBN 1-85233-243-3  Springer-Verlag London Berlin Heidelberg

British Library Cataloguing in Publication Data
Ashbourn, Julian
  Biometrics : advanced identify verification : the complete
  guide
  1.Biometry 2.Identification 3.Identification – Data
  processing
  I.Title
  570.1'5195
  ISBN 1852332433

Library of Congress Cataloging-in-Publication Data
Ashbourn, Julian, 1952-
    Biometrics : advanced identify verification : the complete guide / Julian Ashbourn.
      p. cm.
    Includes index.
    ISBN 1-85233-243-3 (alk. paper)
      1. Pattern recognition systems. 2. Biometry. 3. Identification—Automation. 4.
    Computer vision. I. Title.
  TK7882.P3 A84 2000
  006.4—dc21

                                                    00-044026

Typesetting: Camera ready by author
Printed and bound at the Athenæum Press Ltd., Gateshead, Tyne & Wear
34/3830-543210  Printed on acid-free paper  SPIN 10748993

*This book is dedicated to Joanna, a gifted author,*
*artist, naturalist and remarkable human being*
*whose like rarely walks on this earth.*

Very special thanks to David Sidlauskas for his background information and for being a true pioneer, to John Daugman for his foreword and for being a true innovator and to Rosie, Sally and Karen at Springer Verlag for their enduring support, which is as much a part of this book as anything I have written.

Thanks also to all the unsung heroes of the international biometrics industry who have provided the author with many bright moments over the last decade and have unwittingly been the inspiration for this work.

Julian Ashbourn

# Foreword

Identifying a thing in terms of the properties that make it different from everything else is an old and venerable idea. Aristotle defined the "essence" (Gr. \epsilon \iota \delta \omicron \varsigma) of something as that quality distinguishing it from all other objects; Linnaeus built our botanical and zoological classification system from this principle; and Shannon's Theory of Information measures the informativeness of a message, in bits, entirely in terms of its improbability or uniqueness.

The quest of biometrics is to find the particular within the universal. Nearly all people have faces, eyes, hands, and fingers; detecting these universal human traits helps to distinguish a person from a tree, but serves little to distinguish among individual persons. For that task, one needs to find unique aspects of (say) a facial feature configuration or a fingerprint which are more particular than universal. Not only must there be great variability in such features amongst different individuals (else the features wouldn't be unique), but also there must be little or no variability in those same features for a given person over time and conditions (else they wouldn't be reliable). Everything in the science behind biometric technologies hinges upon the relative sizes of these two variabilities: the between-person and the within-person variability.

Traditional methods of establishing or confirming the identity of an unknown person have relied either upon some secret knowledge that he uniquely should have (such as a password or a PIN number), or upon an object that he uniquely should possess (such as a key, a token, or a card). Passwords date back at least to the Roman centurions, and special tokens at least to the Bronze Age. But testing for secret knowledge or special possessions can only confirm that the knowledge or possession is present, not that a rightful owner is present. It is in order to establish a more fundamental link between an identity and a particular body, through its unique appearance or behavior, that automated biometric pattern recognition techniques are being developed and tested.

The growing need for effective biometric identification is widely acknowledged. Famous cases of "identity theft" have emerged recently, and current estimates of credit card fraud based on falsely claimed identity reach several billions of dollars annually. Even more urgently, the rapid adoption of and increasing economic dependence upon electronic commerce and transactions create systemic vulnerabilities to impersonation on a scale that remains poorly appreciated, just as vulnerability to Internet viruses, and their cost, was misunderstood. Commenting on such emerging "information warfare" risks,

Whitfield Diffie (co-author of the Diffie-Hellman security protocol) has written that: "Society's dependence on electronic commerce will make this the target of first resort in future conflicts, continuing the 20th century trend toward involvement of civilian populations." But we should not imagine that high-stakes roles for biometrics are entirely new. The Old Testament reports the slaughter of 42,000 persons who failed a biometric test that remains under development today: voice identification. The Gileadites sought to track down escaped Ephraimites and to identify them as such by testing whether they pronounced "shibboleth" with a "s-" instead of a "sh-" sound. (All Gileadite readers of this foreword will know that "sh-" is the correct pronunciation.) We read in Judges 12:5-6, "Then said the men of Gilead unto him, Say now Shibboleth: and he said Sibboleth: for he could not frame to pronounce it right. Then they took him, and slew him at the passages of the Jordan: and there fell at that time of the Ephraimites forty and two thousand." This Biblical example illustrates a "phenotypic" biometric: one based upon features or behaviors that are acquired through experience and development, as opposed to a "genotypic" biometric which measures genetically determined traits. Examples of the latter include gender, blood group, and DNA sequence; examples of the former include fingerprints, iris patterns, and signature. Some biometrics are both: facial appearance changes dramatically with age and with expressions, and is thus phenotypic, but it is also very strongly genotypic as illustrated by monozygotic (identical) twins and even by family members sharing only half their genes. Many people consider DNA sequence to be the ultimate biometric, but the fact that one person in about 120 has a monozygotic twin means that the false match rate of a DNA biometric in the population at large cannot be much lower than one percent. The intrusiveness of acquiring a DNA sample is obviously a further limitation (although it must cheerfully be admitted that nearly half of the human race constantly seeks to provide a sample of its DNA to the other half). Elusive, non-scientific factors such as perceived intrusiveness and public acceptability are crucially important in the practical success of biometric systems, as Julian Ashbourn's work so ably shows.

Although the mathematical decisiveness of biometric decision-making depends ultimately just on the combinatorial complexity of the biometric, i.e. the number of degrees-of-freedom spanned by the variability of the chosen feature across the population, its actual success in deployment will depend equally on implementation and application issues that require careful consideration. The biometric literature to date has focused largely on scientific and mathematical issues underlying the pattern recognition and decision-making, leaving a vacuum in these other areas. In contrast, Julian Ashbourn's work both prior to and including this book has made much-needed contributions to understanding, gauging, managing, and improving how humans interact with devices, perceive their experiences, learn from them, and influence design. As such, this book has much to offer to all in the biometrics field, whether they be vendor, user, integrator, assessor, or researcher.

John Daugman

Cambridge

# About the author

After studying both art and electronics in his native England, Julian Ashbourn has enjoyed a varied career across several industries including professional audio, security electronics and information technology. He has travelled to many countries including America, Africa, Saudi Arabia, Australia, Germany, France, Luxembourg, Netherlands, Belgium and Ireland in the context of systems design, troubleshooting and general project management.

He was one of the first people to successfully integrate biometric technology and has had an input to a diverse range of biometric systems including border control, prison visitor systems, physical access control and many others. He has developed several software utilities including the innovative BioTrack series - the first applications to present biometric functionality in a familiar and easy to use 32 bit Windows format.

The author of many technical papers and popular biometric articles, he has presented at conferences around the world and was for many years a key contributor to the Association for Biometrics, providing a voice for biometrics in Europe and further afield. He has contributed to both TV and radio broadcasts on the subject and was responsible for the highly regarded Avanti international biometric journal.

With a broad range of interests including art, music, ancient history and emerging technology, his unique and down to earth approach coupled with considerable personal experience acts as a beacon to both light the way forward and dispel myths and misconceptions surrounding this fascinating technology.

# Preface

Biometrics bring a new dimension to individual identity verification. They allow the process to be automated and unsupervized where applicable whilst providing levels of accuracy and consistency that simply cannot be guaranteed by traditional methods relying solely on human interpretation. However, biometric verification is not infallible and its implementation requires an understanding of both the technology and the human interface with the technology, if success is to achieved. Careful consideration must be given to all aspects of biometric systems design including the user interface, the technical architecture, the environment in which it is to be deployed and all the background processes necessary for a particular situation. Only then can we be sure of a successful implementation of the technology.

Whilst biometrics may be seen by some as a new or emerging technology, there have in fact been a large number of biometric systems installed around the world during the last decade. Continuing technological developments in other areas such as communications and microprocessors coupled with an increasingly global society will provide more opportunities to integrate biometric verification into other processes for the benefit of both administrations and users.

This book provides an in depth grounding in the subject of biometrics for all those interested in identity verification, whether they be a potential end user of the technology such as a large corporation or government department, or a professional practitioner such as a consultant or systems integrator. It will also provide a valuable source of reference for the academic researcher or student of biometrics who will find a great deal of practical information to start them off on their particular voyage of discovery. Indeed, there is something in this book for everyone, even if they are of a non technical persuasion and are simply interested in biometrics as an exciting branch of 21$^{st}$ century science and technology.

The book is arranged as a series of logical self contained sections which are perhaps best read sequentially, although this is not essential. An experienced reader may choose to go directly to a chapter of interest.

Julian Ashbourn

# Contents

# 3. Biometric methodologies

## 3.1 Fingerprints

## 3.2 Hand geometry

## 3.3 Iris scanning

## 3.4 Retina scanning

## 3.5 Facial recognition

## 3.6 Voice verification

## 3.7 Signature verification

## 3.8 Other biometric techniques

# 4. Identification, verification and templates

## *4.1 Identification and verification - the distinction*

## *4.2 Template management*

## *4.3 Performance criteria*

## *4.4 Additional performance criteria*

## *4.5 Total system performance*

# 5. Implementing biometrics

## *5.1 Understanding the requirement*

## *5.2 Understanding the users*

## *5.3 Understanding the environment*

## *5.4 Putting the system together*

## *5.5 Installation issues*

# 7. Moving on

## 7.1 A biometric world

## 7.2 Biometrics in business

## 7.3 Overall conclusions

# 8. Running a biometric pilot scheme

## 8.1 Setting the objectives

## 8.2 Choosing the project team

## 8.3 Choosing the technology

## 8.4 Working with vendors

## 8.5 The test environment

## 8.6 Marketing and communications

## 8.7 The enrolment center

# 1. Where it all began

Khasekem could feel the heat of the sandy path even through his sandals as he walked under the burning morning sun down the gentle sloping hill towards the dock at Aswan. His thoughts turned to his student days at Heliopolis in lower Egypt, where he had stayed at the house of his uncle Sebekkhu. Sebekkhu was a man of learning and Khasekem was much indebted to his uncle for both his kindness and continual guidance throughout his training as a scribe at Heliopolis.

His first official post had been to copy some of the records appertaining to the construction of the great pyramid of Khufu which had been completed in the year of Khasekem's birth. From this he knew that the pyramid was designed to be 288 cubits tall with a base of 452 cubits square and required in excess of 2.5 million blocks of stone, each one precisely cut and identified as to its exact position within the construction. He also knew that over 1600 talents of silver had been spent on food for the workforce which at times approached 100,000 men, many of whom were from farming communities and were glad to have the opportunity to work on the project during the inundation periods in which their land was often flooded for 10 weeks or more. The food and shelter provided as a result of the pyramid construction was particularly welcome at this time. Khasekem had noted that there were many issues around accurate identification of these individuals.

Other men, particularly the skilled stonemasons would work on the project full time, many of them at remote quarry sites such as Aswan. This presented a logistical challenge of some note, as provisions were gathered and stored in a number of areas and then transported across land to various docking points on the Nile from which they would be transported by ship to Aswan. All provisions had to be accounted for and registered in the central records. It was Khasekem's good work in understanding and accurately copying these records that had won him his current post as assistant to the chief administrator at Aswan whose name was Tafnekht.

Khasekem's role was in the administration and provision of food to the workforce, a key element in the overall smooth running and success of the project. His dream was that through hard work and diligence in this position, he might one day be presented to the great Pharaoh Khaefre who was known to take a direct interest in the project and often commended outstanding workmanship and administration when brought to his attention.

The ships which docked at Aswan were typically of 100 cubits length and looked magnificent as they approached around the curve of the mighty river just north of the settlement. Khasekem never got tired of watching these graceful giants approach the dock in a frenzy of activity as sails were lowered and ropes thrown to the shore while the oarsmen and pilot skilfully manoeuvred the vessel into position. On the inward journey they brought wheat, barley and other provisions for the storehouse under Tafnekht's authority, before being loaded with stone blocks ready for shipment back to the pyramid site at Gizeh. Khasekem had to ensure that all provisions were correct and accounted for before issuing Tafnekht's seal on the return documentation. This was an important part of his job, but most of his time was spent on the administration of the provision of supplies to the working men.

Each man was granted an allowance of 1.5 khars per month to be made up of mostly wheat with a proportion of barley. A khar was measured in the standard hekat jar size with 16 hekats making 1 khar. The allowance usually comprized of 20 hekats of wheat plus 4 hekats of barley per man per month and an arrangement was made whereby each man would be allocated to a specific day of the month when he would be spared his usual duties in order that he may collect his month's provision from the storehouse, subject to Khasekem being satisfied as to the man's true identity and legitimate right to claim the allowance on that day. This had previously been a somewhat contentious issue as it had been discovered that some individuals had tried to claim an allowance twice in one month by claiming another identity or indeed by maintaining two identities. Whilst the penalties for this fraudulent behavior were harsh if discovered, the incentive to do so was strong when such provisions could be bartered for other goods and services among the working community. In addition, with a typical workforce of around 700 at the quarry, it was not always easy to detect the impostor. These occurrences were rare but Tafnekht had given clear and strict instructions in the name of the Pharaoh that such behavior would not be tolerated.

Since his time at Aswan, Khasekem had been further developing the system used for identifying claimants whereby each individual had a record which stipulated his name, age, place of origin and precise occupation at the site. Khasekem had been systematically adding further detail to these records in order to accurately identify each individual. He did this by noting unique physical and sometimes behavioral characteristics for each individual and including them as part of the record. Thus, when a claimant presented himself and gave his name Khasekem would refer to the record for that individual and read the descriptive notes previously taken. For example, notes from a typical record would read as follows: Nechutes, son of Asos, aged forty, of middle size, sallow complexion, cheerful countenance, long face with straight nose and a scar upon the middle of his forehead. The detail within these records enabled Khasekem to accurately verify the identity of each claimant. In cases where there were few particularly distinctive features, an anatomical measurement would be made to supplement the record. This would typically be the distance between the tip of an outstretched thumb and the elbow, which would be somewhere around 1 cubit in an adult male of typical proportions. A measuring rod marked with divisions would be used to take and subsequently verify this measurement.

Khasekem arrived at the storehouse on this hot and sunny morning and was glad to get into the shade provided by the brick-built enclosure. After checking that all the staff were present and that the storehouse was secure he consulted his records to see who was due to collect their allowance on that day. There were in fact 23 men due to claim on this day and he arranged for all of their records to be brought to his room where the claimants would initially present themselves in an orderly manner. After checking that all the records were present and correct, he gave instructions for the first man to be allowed to enter and make his claim. Perabsen, a stout man with skin blackened by continued exposure to the sun, strode purposefully into the room and after making the customary greetings to Khasekem announced that he was Perabsen of Dendara working with the seventh team of masons on area 9 of the main quarry and was due to collect his allowance on that day. Khasekem quickly located the relevant record and read the details noted for Perabsen which suggested among other things that he was a sturdily built man of medium height with a dark complexion and a slight cast to one eye. In addition, it was noted that Perabsen had a particularly booming voice and slightly forward disposition. The description fitted absolutely and so Khasekem consulted the main ledger to check when this man was last granted an allowance. It was in fact a month to the day and so Khasekem, satisfied that all was in order, gave instructions for Perabsen to be supplied with his quota of provisions.

The next man entered and presented himself as Harkhuf of Philae working on the special consignment of limestone ordered for the important new works at Karnak. Khasekem observed that this man was limping noticeably and also had a finger missing from his left hand, presumably the result of some unfortunate accident as he seemed in otherwise good health and spirits. He seemed to remember noting such particulars previously and wondered whether this had been for this man, Harkhuf. Consulting the record for Harkhuf of Philae confirmed that these were indeed traits associated with this man, together with other details of complexion and facial features which left Khasekem in no doubt as to the true identity of the man standing before him. Once again, after checking the main ledger, Khasekem gave instructions to grant Harkhuf his allowance of provisions and called for the next man to come forward. Throughout the day, the other 21 men presented themselves and had their identity verified by Khasekem in a similar manner. After the last man had been supplied with his provisions, the storehouse was officially closed for the day and a seal carefully placed upon the main doors. Khasekem completed the entries in the main ledger and gave explicit instructions for the day's personal records to be placed securely back in the repository. Khasekem was satisfied that all was well and in perfect order and closed off the ledger for that day's transactions. Indeed, this had been the case for some time now as there had been no recent instances of fraudulent identity claims or misappropriation of provisions from the storehouse now that Khasekem's strict but fair administration was well and truly in place. This gave Khasekem some considerable satisfaction as he could see that his carefully considered process was achieving the objective.

Figure 1.1 Khasekem

Khasekem was in fact successfully employing biometric identity verification to enhance the processes around his particular working role. He did not have the benefits of microprocessors and electronics to help automate the process, but the principles employed were exactly the same in that he identified and registered a measurable anatomical and/or behavioral characteristic that could be subsequently recalled in order to verify the identity of a given individual. In fact, Khasekem was way ahead of the majority of today's biometric practitioners in that he could select any number of biometric characteristics and merge them together as necessary to provide a suitably accurate identity model for each individual. It worked too - as the continual deployment of such methods acted as a powerful deterrent against false identity claims whilst providing an accurate log of who was doing what and where in relation to large civil projects and important affairs of state.

So the roots of biometric technology go back a long way - several thousands of years in fact. It is certainly not the new-fangled idea that many people believe it is today. We are simply rediscovering principles which, like so many other things, our ancient ancestors in the Nile valley had already refined and successfully implemented within that most elegant and remarkable civilisation. The debt we owe to ancient Egypt in many branches of science is incalculable and biometric verification represents just one tiny pebble on a huge beach of knowledge and understanding that is our precious legacy from that period.

## 1.1 Jumping ahead in time

The nineteenth century was also an interesting time with regard to the development of ideas synergistic with biometrics. At the beginning of the century a German named Franz Joseph Gall founded the discipline of phrenology whereby specific cranial shapes and features were thought to align with certain mental characteristics. A little later an Italian physician named Cesare Lombroso (1836-1909) further developed the concept of phrenology with specific regard to criminal behavior, trying to relate such behavior patterns with physical and biological characteristics. There were others who followed and curiously the subject of phrenology has continued in popularity long after it has been shown to have no real scientific grounding. It seems that people continue to be fascinated by the possibility of aligning character traits with physical characteristics. This brings us nicely to the subject of anthropometry, which deals with the measurement of different elements of the human body including weight, height, limb circumference and skin thickness.

Probably the first to have considered anthropometry as a distinct discipline was the popular Belgian mathematician and astronomer Adolphe Quetelet who published a treatise on the subject in 1871 entitled *'L'anthropometrie ou mesure des differentes facultes de l'homme'*. However, it was the Frenchman Alphonse Bertillon (1853-1914) who, while head of the identification service at the Paris police headquarters in 1880, really progressed the idea into what became known as judiciary anthropometry. Bertillon developed a system of identifying criminals by anatomical measurements which became quite widely used in France and further afield at the time. Clearly there was a general fascination with physiological or anatomical characteristics as a means of not only identifying known criminals, but even suggesting a propensity towards criminal behavior in the first place.

But what of fingerprints? Fingerprints and perhaps to a lesser extent hand geometry are probably the most obvious examples that spring to mind when people think of contemporary biometrics. Once again there is an interesting history involved here as we know that Babylonian kings used an imprint of the hand to prove the authenticity of certain engravings and works. They understood that no two hands were exactly alike and used this as a principal means of identity verification. However, it was in 1823 that the Czech Jan Evangelista Purkinje was studying sweat glands and realized when observing how the sweat glands opened out into the depressions in the grooves of the skin, that the precise patterns of these grooves and ridges seemed to be unique to the individual. It was at this point that the concept of fingerprints being unique first became lodged in scientific thinking and no doubt many explored this idea further with various levels of success.

The process of taking fingerprints in ink is known as dactyloscopy and the first known user of dactylograms, as these images are called, was an Argentinean police officer from Buenos Aires named Juan Vucetich. In fact, Juan Vucetich was so enthusiastic about the idea that he published a treatise on the subject of comparative dactyloscopy in 1888. Elsewhere, others were also intrigued by the concept of unique fingerprints.

In the 1890's Francis Galton, a cousin of Charles Darwin, was engaged in various research initiatives including that of hereditary genius, the study of twins and various psychological phenomena. He showed the applicability of statistics to psychological data and part of his work was around the classification of fingerprints. At around the same time a British Inspector General of the Indian police in Bengal named Edward Henry was also interested in the subject and the Galton-Henry system was finally put into operation by Scotland Yard in June 1900. The system was very successful and in 1901 Edward Henry became head of the Criminal Investigation Department at Scotland Yard and eventually Commissioner of the Metropolitan Police before retiring gracefully in 1918. The concept of fingerprinting as a means of classifying and identifying criminals was now firmly embedded and would become ubiquitous among law enforcement agencies the world over.

Figure 1.2 Fingerprints

Three main patterns predominate in fingerprints, the loop, the whorl and the arc. Curiously, the frequency of these patterns among individuals seems to vary according to ethnic origin. Europeans have relatively few arcs but plenty of loops. Pygmies and African bush men on the other hand have plenty of arcs, while Orientals seem to have a high frequency of whorls. Features within these patterns provide the means to match fingerprints for identity purposes. The number of matching features required to be considered as positive identification varies from country to country but is often between 10 and 16. Registering fingerprints has traditionally been undertaken by pressing the individual's fingers and thumbs onto an inked pad and then pressing them onto a card which would be stored within a card index system. Before the advent of computerized matching systems the matching process was undertaken manually and was a very labor-intensive task as the individual involved would need to carefully examine perhaps hundreds of potentially matching print sets. This required considerable expertise and diligence and some people became highly skilled in this area. Nowadays computers can scan databases of hundreds of thousands of fingerprint records in a very short space of time.

The algorithms used for matching vary from application to application and may be more or less successful at locating exact matches; however, many would maintain that a computer matching process is more dependable than a human one. If computers can be used to match patterns and images then surely they can also be used to match a live sample with a stored template in order to verify the identity of an individual? They can indeed and this is the basis upon which contemporary biometrics operate. But before we move on into this area, let's take a look at how we arrived at this position of computer power in the first place.

## 1.2 Parallel developments

Whilst the human race was developing interesting ways of identifying and verifying the identity of individuals, they were also fascinated by the concept of automatic calculation. People have always needed to count and some of our ancestors developed sophisticated numbering systems with which to count and record transactions. Our good friends the ancient Egyptians had a particularly elegant numbering system which allowed one to easily and quickly identify a very broad range of values. Through this system and the surviving records we are able to understand a great deal about their culture and lifestyle from thousands of years ago. It is not clear whether they had a mechanical calculator as such, perhaps they were so good at using the written system that they didn't need any mechanical aids.

Probably the first step towards calculating machinery came with the abacus, generally thought to have been introduced at around the third century A.D. in the Mediterranean area. This provided merchants with a fast and reliable means of calculation which was not difficult to learn or understand. In fact, so successful was the abacus that its use spread throughout the world and it is still used in some places today. Some time passed before other means of calculation were to be developed. In 1614 a Scottish mathematician and inventor named John Napier (1550-1617) took a significant step forward with his discovery of logarithms. A logarithm is the exponent of a base number indicating the power to which the number must be raised in order to produce another number. Napier realized that any number could be expressed in this manner and set about producing a complex series of logarithm tables which could be used by others. Logarithms simplified the calculation of large values once you had understood the concept and mastered the log and antilog tables. Later in the 1620's a gentleman by the name of William Oughtred who had been impressed and intrigued by Napier's logarithms took them a step further by incorporating them into a mechanical device known as the slide rule, which itself became widely used by mathematicians and scientists.

In 1624 a German mathematician named Wilhelm Schickard devised a mechanical calculating machine to help in the production of astronomical tables.

This device was probably the first calculator to use gears in its construction, although it has been somewhat overshadowed historically by a machine invented by the son of a French tax official. This young man was something of a child prodigy and went on to invent and develop many interesting concepts including the syringe, the hydraulic press and the mechanical calculator. His name was Blaise Pascal (1623-1662) and he was just 19 years of age when, inspired by the amount of dreary calculation required in his fathers job, he set about designing an automatic adding machine. Pascal's machine was a series of interlocking wheels and cogs housed in a wooden box which enabled the user to input a series of numbers to be added together. He revised the machine constantly, producing over 50 versions of it throughout a ten year period of development, although it remained practically restricted to additive calculations.

Whilst Pascal was engaged in his work on the calculator, a child was born into a well-to-do German family named Gottfried Wilhelm Leibniz (1646-1716). His father, who died when Gottfried was only six, was a professor of philosophy and most of the family were scholars of one sort or another. It was no surprise therefore that young Gottfried embarked eagerly onto a voyage of discovery and learning, teaching himself History, Latin, Greek and many other subjects. It was Leibniz who, independently of Isaac Newton, invented calculus and developed many concepts around Geology, Astronomy and Philosophy. He also perfected the mechanical calculator by taking Pascal's addition engine and further enhancing it in order to automate the repetitive additions involved in multiplication and division. This work was undertaken predominantly as a means of reducing the calculation burden associated with astronomy while Leibniz was studying with a Dutch astronomer named Christian Huygens (1629-1695) who among other things invented the pendulum-regulated clock in 1656. Leibniz believed that it was unworthy of highly educated men to have to waste hours in calculation which could perhaps be relegated to others if suitable machines were available for the task. He certainly proved the point with the development of his advanced mechanical calculator which was presented to the Royal Society in London where it was received with enthusiasm. Leibniz went on to become a diplomat and something of a philosopher, but his contribution to science was significant.

In the history of science and technology one often comes across individuals who were way ahead of their time. Sometimes they are able to bring their ideas to fruition and perfect them within their own lifetime, and sometimes available technology allows them only to sow the seed for some future generation to develop into reality. One such man was the Englishman Charles Babbage (1792-1871). Babbage was born into a wealthy Devonshire family and developed a passion for not only mathematics but accuracy and detail in all that he came across. He came to be known as something of an eccentric and would find various causes to champion while not being shy to publicly challenge opinions on scientific and other matters. His genius was never in doubt though and he became professor of mathematics at Cambridge University between 1828 and 1839, although he was rarely to be found lecturing there.

Babbage turned his attention to the accuracy of calculation with particular regard to astronomical and mathematical tables.  He became convinced that a machine could be designed to both eliminate calculation errors and produce printed output in the form of tables etc.  In 1822 he demonstrated his famous Difference Engine to the Royal Astronomical Society, which could compile tables of logarithms.  However, the Difference Engine was destined to never really be finished and Babbage eventually turned his attention to the design of an even more radical machine - the Analytical Engine.

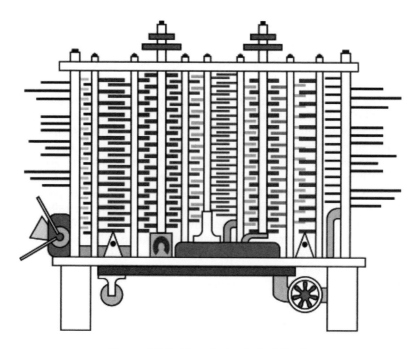

Figure 1.3 Babbage's Analytical Engine

Babbage had written to the Royal Society in an attempt to solicit financial aid for the Difference Engine and after much toing and froing was eventually granted a government award of £1,500 for the project.  This was soon consumed however and further grants were awarded to the tune of £17,000 - a considerable sum of money in those days.  Eventually, the British government became shy of donating further funds and the grants were stopped.  Undaunted, Babbage put aside his plans for the Difference Engine and started work on the design of an Analytical Engine.  This machine was to perform a broad range of calculation and was programmed with punched cards, a technique that had been developed earlier by Frenchman Joseph Marie Jacquard for looms in the textile industry.  The Analytical Engine had all the makings of a modern computer in that it was programmable, had a memory (the store) a processing unit (the mill) and a printed output.  Indeed, it could be said that Charles Babbage invented the computer a hundred years before its time.   The store within the Analytical Engine would hold 100 forty-digit numbers, any of which could be passed back and forth as they were needed for calculation by the mill.  This facilitated the solving of a wide range of mathematical problems.

One individual who immediately saw and understood the potential of Babbage's design was the Countess of Lovelace, the daughter of Lord Byron.  The Countess was herself a talented mathematician and was a great help to Babbage with her dauntless enthusiasm and gift for explaining the concept to others.  Indeed, Babbage said that she sometimes seemed to understand it better than he did and was certainly better at explaining it.  However, with all the enthusiasm in the world, the fact remained that contemporary technology was just not up to the task of building the Analytical Engine which relied on a great many moving parts and was to be driven by steam.  It was never completely built, but Babbage had started a train of thought that would never quite go away.

The next significant step towards what we now know as the computer came in 1890 when Herman Hollerith (1860-1929), an American son of German immigrants, successfully designed a punched card system with which to tabulate the results of the American population census.  Hollerith had been a mining engineer and had joined the American Census Bureau in 1880 to assist in the analysis of that year's census.  The task was only just completed in time for the 1890 census, which inspired Hollerith to develop an automated system using punched cards similar to that used by Jacquard's textile loom.  In 1896 Hollerith established the Tabulating Machine Company to develop his ideas further, and this company eventually became the International Business Machines corporation (IBM) in 1924.  IBM continued to develop and market machines in this context, but it was in the years leading up to and during the second world war that we really saw progress and development of the computer.

Just before the fall of Poland, the Polish secret service had managed to build a replica of the German cipher code device called Enigma and smuggle it to the British, together with a description of how it worked.  However, what was missing was the encryption 'key' and knowledge of how the telephone switchboard-like plugs should be set.  Nevertheless, this was an incredible piece of luck and the British intelligence quickly gathered together a group of mathematicians and researchers at Bletchley Park in order to try to break the code.  One of these individuals was a slightly eccentric young man with a stammer named Alan Mathison Turing (1912-1954).  No look at the origins of the computer would be complete without reference to Turing, whose mathematical genius and original thinking played a huge part in not only breaking the Enigma code but in pushing forward the boundaries of thought with regard to the development of computational machines.  Turing studied at Cambridge University and at the tender age of 24 wrote what would ultimately be recognized as a seminal paper on computer science, which dealt with mathematical logic and the description of problems which were theoretically impossible to solve.  As part of this work Turing introduced the concept of a powerful computing device which he referred to as a universal machine, whose characteristics closely shadowed those of the modern computer.

The men at Bletchley designed and built a number of computational machines, culminating in 1943 in a new design which was named Colossus. Colossus was in fact a series of machines which, unusually, used electronic valves (vacuum tubes) rather than electromechanical relays. Each machine used 2000 valves and was programmed via paper tape which was scanned by a series of photoelectric sensors, enabling up to 25,000 characters per second to be read. This enabled a large number of intercepted enemy messages to be fed into Colossus for decoding. Sadly, poor Alan Turing whose eccentricities became increasingly pronounced, eventually took his own life at the age of 41, but his contribution to both the war effort and computer science will be remembered for a very long time.

War has a habit of accelerating the progress of technology and on the other side of the Atlantic, the United States War Department's Ballistic Research Laboratory established a computing system at the University of Pennsylvania, which had a 'differential analyzer' to be used for gunners trajectory calculations. Two of the staff members at the university, John Mauchley and J. Presper Eckert wanted to design something even better. Mauchley's thinking had been stimulated by a visit to John Atanasoff in Iowa. Atanasoff and his associate Clifford Berry had been building a prototype computer which utilized vacuum tubes and obviously impressed Mauchley. Eckert subsequently encouraged Mauchley to pursue his ideas, which culminated in a five page document outlining a proposal for a high speed computing device. A few months later, after a certain amount of lobbying, the Army awarded a $400,000 contract to Pennsylvania University, Moore School to build the Electronic Numerical Integrator and Computer (ENIAC).

ENIAC was a highly complex design which stood 5 metres high and 24 metres long and contained 17,468 vacuum tubes. This high number of vacuum tubes not only generated prodigious amounts of heat, but also posed a reliability problem, even when they were run at a reduced voltage in order to prolong life. This was a complicated project and it was 1945 before ENIAC was finally completed, by which time the principal requirement for it had passed.

Fuelled by the experience with ENIAC Mauchley and Eckert started work on a successor which was to be known as the Electronic Discrete Variable Automatic Computer (EDVAC) and were assisted in the task by a well-known flamboyant and gifted mathematician by the name of John von Neumann. Von Neumann was to have a profound influence both on EDVAC and on the development of the computer in general, proposing an architecture which was to become standard thinking in terms of computer design. However, Mauchley and Eckert became disenchanted with the set-up, particularly with all the attention von Neumann was getting, and decided to branch out on their own and form a commercial company to market their ideas. This lead to the creation of the Universal Automatic Computer (UNIVAC) which eventually was to become very successful, but not until Mauchley and Eckert had run out of money and sold the company to Remington Rand.

While all this was going on, the US Navy, who also had requirements for automated calculation machines, had seconded an enthusiast named Howard Aiken to work with IBM on what was affectionately known as the Mark 1. The prototype was successful and was shipped to Harvard for further development. However, Aiken and IBM were subsequently to fall out over the acknowledgement of their respective contributions and went their own ways, with IBM accelerating their efforts to bring their own ideas to fruition independently. Once these seeds had been sown the future of the computer was assured and with the later advent of the transistor and integrated circuits a revolution in computer power and affordability would change our world forever.

## 1.3 Bringing it all together

So far we have explored two trains of thought, the development of ideas appertaining to personal identification and the development of ideas leading towards the computer and its associated technological developments. Bringing the two together provides us with the opportunity to produce devices capable of automated identity verification via biometrics. But before we go any further, let's examine what we mean by the term biometric. I usually describe a biometric as a measurable physiological and/or behavioral trait that can be captured and subsequently compared with another instance at the time of verification. This description includes the matching of fingerprints, voice patterns, hand geometry, iris and retina scans, vein patterns and other such methodologies. In a slightly different context it will include signature verification, keystroke patterns and other methodologies weighted towards individual behavior.

Pioneering biometric methodologies included voice verification, fingerprints and hand geometry. In order to get a feel for how these early ideas and devices developed into marketable products, let's take a look at the example of hand geometry. The original hand reader concept was in fact designed as a purely mechanical device in the late 1960s by the Miller brothers in New Jersey. It featured a platen with finger grooves upon which the user placed his hand while rods were driven along the grooves to meet the fingertips. The other end of the rods corresponded with a predefined pattern on a card which either matched or didn't match as the case may be. Refinements of this idea produced a more advanced electronic version utilising scanned photo cells and magnetic cards which was in fact produced and marketed as a product in the early 1970s by the Identimation Company. After a difficult time financially, the rights to the product passed to Identimat Inc, who developed the product further and found applications in diverse areas such as the nuclear industry and academia. This company was subsequently absorbed by a larger group who continued to develop and market variations on the original design until production finally ceased in 1987. However, the Executive Vice President of one of the group companies had been intrigued by the hand geometry idea and the mathematical challenge involved in measuring and comparing biometric parameters. Having left the group to pursue other interests, he eventually came around to experimenting with algorithms for hand geometry matching. These experiments showed promise and further work was undertaken with image detectors and other components necessary to develop a three-dimensional hand reader. Finally, in May 1985 David Sidlauskas formed Recognition Systems Inc to further develop and market his ideas and the ID3D-S hand geometry reader was born. An example of this reader was favourably tested by Sandia National Laboratories in late 1985 leading to sales in the government sector and other areas, providing the impetus for further development into the ID3D-U series of readers. These early devices relied on contemporary CCTV optics which tended to keep costs relatively high. In 1988 fate intervened when the supplier of the image arrays being used ceased production and an alternative was required. A suitable low-cost device was sourced from Texas Instruments which provided the opportunity to refine the optical design with shorter path lengths, reducing the overall size and complexity of the device. The resulting ID3D HandKey introduced in early 1991 went on to become a significant milestone in the fledgling biometric industry, providing a reliable biometric reader that was easy to use and versatile enough to be deployed in a wide variety of applications and environments. It was very successful and derivatives of the ID3D continue to be marketed by the company today.

Similarly interesting developments were taking place in areas such as voice verification and fingerprints and by the early 1990s the biometric industry was firmly established. Our two strands of thought, advanced identity verification and the development of computer technology had finally come together. It took a while, but we got there in the end.

# 2. Applications for biometrics

Before we delve too deeply into applications for biometrics, it would perhaps be useful to spend a little time looking at how personal identification systems have developed and what the traditional applications have been for related technologies such as cards and tokens.

One of the drivers for personal identification systems has been physical access control. One of the earliest and simplest techniques in this context was a numerical keypad which, when having the correct code number entered upon it, would provide an output, usually in the form of a relay, which could be used to activate an electronic lock, turnstile or other device to control access to a physical area. The keypad itself would typically be separated from the control box which, mounted in the secure area, would provide the operating logic, inputs and outputs and power for the internal electronics and sometimes for the locking device itself. This would sometimes be supplemented by a battery backup in order to protect against mains power failure. Early examples worked on the principle of a single common code, which meant that any individual who came to know this code, usually a simple four digit number, could gain access via this device. In practice, this meant periodically changing the code if you wished to maintain security, although one suspects that this precaution was not always undertaken as regularly as it should have been.

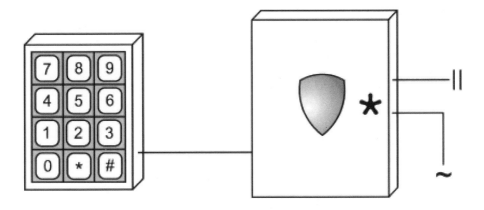

Figure 2.1 A typical keypad access control device

These days such a basic method of control seems almost crude and would certainly not be considered as offering particularly high security; however, a great many of these devices were manufactured and sold and provided an economical and reliable means of control.  One of the most popular was the original Cypher Lock from Continental Instruments Corporation, many of which are still in active service.  This provided a simple means of coding via a switchboard like panel in the control box and offered simple potentiometers to adjust the relay activation time and also a time penalty feature which deactivated the keypad for a period of time following an incorrect code entry.  This meant that the Cypher Lock was extremely easy to set up and use, characteristics which together with its rugged construction and low cost ensured its enduring popularity.

Eventually, keypad devices would become more sophisticated and offer full programmability for individual user codes together with a host of system functions.  There have even been fully-featured online computer-based systems using nothing but keypads.  Of course, if a user forgets the correct code he has something of a problem and will have to liaise with the security administrator in order to gain entry and be reminded of the code.  With a large workforce this would suggest that a certain amount of administration and support must be allowed for with any such implemented system.  Perhaps a better idea would be to imbed the code within a token such as a card, so that the user may simply carry the card with him at all times without having to remember a number.  It didn't take long for this to occur to vendors and before long the card access control industry was born.


## 2.1 Card technology

Cards used for personal identity have assumed a wide variety of shapes, sizes and utilized technology.  Some of them have not been cards at all, but tokens to fit on key fobs and other variations on a theme.  The most basic coded card technology was probably the punched hole card which simply had a series of holes punched within an area to form the code.  Obvious limitations of this idea were that the range of possible codes was a product of hole size and available real estate for the coding area which dictated a limited range of codes.  Furthermore, they were not particularly secure as duplicate cards could be made fairly easily by copying the pattern of punched holes.  However, they were cheap to manufacture and the associated card readers were relatively simple and reliable using either mechanical sensors or transmitted light to read the code.

A methodology not too dissimilar was that of Infra Red cards.  IR cards employed a mask between layers of the card which was coded to either allow or block the passage of infrared light.  This technology had certain advantages in that the code was now invisible to the user, making duplication extremely difficult unless you had access to sophisticated machinery and the cards themselves were quite robust.  There was a slight disadvantage in that the readers were relatively expensive compared with contemporary card access technologies, although the infrared approach did prove to be reliable with large numbers of readers and cards deployed across a broad variety of applications.

A somewhat less successful card technology was Barium Ferrite. In simple terms, a barium ferrite card may be thought of as a layer of magnetic material sandwiched between the plastic layers of the card. This material could then be polarized by a high intensity electromagnetic field in order to produce a set code pattern. The barium ferrite readers contained an array of coils in set locations which would detect the coded pattern. This required quite careful alignment of the card and reader, which could sometimes prove problematic in practice. In addition, there were all sorts of stories circulating about barium ferrite access control cards affecting other magnetic media, such as credit cards, when placed in close proximity, for example in a purse or wallet. No doubt some of these stories were exaggerated, but mud tends to stick and barium ferrite cards became increasingly less popular as other more reliable methods became available.

Figure 2.2 Access cards come in a variety of formats

Many people would associate the Magnetic Stripe card with access control and related applications, and certainly very large numbers of these cards have been used in this context. They have the advantage of being inexpensive, easy to code and easily read by inexpensive readers. Magnetic stripe enthusiasts will be happy to talk for hours about low and high coercivity and the ability for modified readers to work in harsh environments, and here lies a hint to the shortcomings of magnetic stripe technology for access control. Coercivity may be thought of as a measure of how easily the code on the magnetic stripe may be accidentally (or otherwise) erased. Initially, the standard was for low coercivity and it was soon discovered that the coding on low coercivity cards was not particularly robust and could be easily altered by the presence of magnetic fields. High coercivity cards offer an improvement in this respect and the majority of magnetic stripe cards you come into contact with today will be of this persuasion. The early magnetic stripe readers tended to suffer both wear problems and deployment limitations as their low cost construction was not really suitable for external use. In a magnetic stripe reader a reading head is employed which is not unlike the head in a domestic tape recorder and similarly reads the polarized encoding of particles on the magnetic tape. This involves physical contact and high usage will eventually result in wear to the reading head. If this reader is deployed externally where it may be subject to wind, rain, dust and corrosion (or deliberate sabotage) then its working life may be shortened accordingly. Ruggedized versions of magnetic stripe readers have been produced for external use, including insertion type readers where the head is more protected, however these are more expensive and one wonders why anyone would bother when other more robust solutions are available at comparable prices.

One of the most reliable and robust card technologies is undoubtedly Wiegand. Wiegand cards incorporate two rows of tiny wire particles representing binary zeros and ones. However, the wire itself is very special with a soft magnetic core contrasting against a hard magnetic shell. The physical placement and polarisation of these wire particles provides for a broad range of codes in a read-only format. Wiegand cards cannot be reprogrammed and are therefore very secure. Both cards and readers are very robust and can be utilized in harsh environments if necessary. The Wiegand reader is essentially non-contact in that the cards are swiped through a focused magnetic field and is typically hermetically sealed against dust and moisture, providing reliable reading in a variety of situations and environments.

Another technology that springs to mind when discussing cards is Bar Coding. There are various forms of bar codes, the most popular perhaps being the linear code as often seen attached to products for labelling purposes and the two-dimensional bar code, which is rather more sophisticated and can hold considerably more data within a given physical area. Bar codes do lend themselves to individual identity applications in that there are a large range of possible codes, even in linear bar codes, however, as linear codes are represented by a printed pattern they are easily copied and cannot be considered secure. This may be a little more difficult with two-dimensional codes, but not impossible. One way of getting around this problem is to obscure the code so that it is not visible to the human eye, but easily read by the infrared bar code scanner. This may perhaps be regarded as a step forward, except that bar code reading and writing equipment is readily available and therefore duplicates may be easily manufactured. However, one would probably not choose this specifically as an access control technology. It is more usual that an access control hardware manufacturer would add bar code reading capability as an extra function, enabling existing vending cards or similar to be used with its particular range of equipment. Two-dimensional bar codes are sometimes used purely to hold large amounts of encoded data on an identity card. For example, it would be perfectly possible to encode an identity badge photograph into an associated two dimensional bar code, enabling tampered cards (where the photo id has been changed) to be detected. Alternatively, we may choose to encode additional information into the bar code in order that it can be machine read where appropriate but not visible to the card holder under normal circumstances.

Proximity cards and tokens have been popular where a non-contact reading methodology is required. There are two potential advantages with proximity technology. One advantage is that as there is no physical contact between cards and reader, the reader itself can be made very durable for external use or even built in to another structure to make it relatively vandal resistant. For example, a reader may be hidden beneath a ceramic surface such as an office wall. The second primary advantage, particularly with long-range proximity cards and readers is that the user need not undertake a physical process to read the card. As long as he or she is in range of the reader, the card will be read, providing a 'hands-free' capability. The proximity token may even be attached to a vehicle in order to activate a car park barrier or otherwise track vehicles entering a particular area. There are also some disadvantages with this technology, not the least being cost as proximity cards and readers are considerably more expensive than the other popular card methodologies. In addition, physical placement of the reader can be important as in most cases the reader is emitting an rf (radio frequency) field into which the card is brought at the time of reading, both card and reader acting as an antenna. This field may sometimes be distorted by the close proximity of metallic objects, producing unwanted and sometimes variable effects. Proximity cards may be either active (with an integral battery providing power) or passive. Active cards offer enhanced performance and read range but have a finite life, after which they must be replaced, adding further to overall costs.

There have been other card technologies like optical cards for example, in addition to the popular types mentioned above, but let's move on to the more interesting area of smart cards, or as I prefer to call them, chip cards, which have been in development more or less since the early 1970s. As the name would suggest, chip cards incorporate a chip embedded into the plastic card. This chip may either be a memory chip or a more sophisticated processor chip, incorporating its own operating system and instruction set. Memory-only chip cards have become less expensive as larger numbers are deployed and therefore represent a viable and interesting alternative to the other technologies mentioned as they can hold a much larger amount of data in a relatively secure manner. However, the chip card readers are somewhat more sophisticated and expensive and may not always be suitable for harsh environments. Processor chip cards are particularly interesting and can offer a range of functionality including advanced data encryption techniques and the promise of a truly multifunctional card where appropriate. To many, this multifunctional approach is the way forward for chip cards and although progress has perhaps been a little slower than anticipated to date, there is no doubt that this idea is of considerable interest and offers some interesting possibilities for both organizational collaboration and real value to the user. One of these possibilities lies around incorporating a biometric template into the chip card for personal identification purposes and this is a theme that we shall return to elsewhere in this book.

## 2.2 The shortcomings of card technology

Interesting though the previously noted technologies are, there is one major and rather obvious shortcoming with the use of cards and tokens for personal identification purposes and that is the fact that when we read a card number at a point of transaction, what we are identifying is the card - not the person who is presenting the card. This means that if I have possession of your card, the system identifies me as you and logs all subsequent transactions against your name. Ah! you might say, but what about PINs, surely they get around this problem? Well, not really. You see, the problem with PINs (personal identification numbers) is that people are not always very good at either remembering them or keeping them secret. Would-be impostors know that PINs will often be written down in diaries or other obvious places and sometimes even on the card itself in order that the legitimate user doesn't forget the number and get denied access. Even if the would be impostor has not found reference to the actual PIN, he may take a chance on guessing it if he has possession of the card as it may be something obvious like 9999, 1234, 6699 or another easily remembered number if the user has had the opportunity to chose their own PIN. Another trick is to simply observe somebody entering their own PIN and remember it.

The manufacturers of access control and related systems have come up with all sorts of ideas to improve the situation, including randomly generated PINs and even scrambled key pads where the numbers appear on different keys with each use of the keypad (a process which usually just succeeds in slowing everyone down). No, we just have to acknowledge that the combination of card and PIN, whilst more secure than a card on its own, is still no proof of actual identity. It does serve to identify the card or token and tells us that the person presenting the card happens to know the associated PIN, but does not guarantee that this is indeed the person who the card was originally assigned to. It is surprising how readily friends or workplace colleagues will discuss their PIN numbers. I have on more than one occasion seen friends give their bank cards and PINs to others in order that they may pick up some cash for them when they are in town during the lunch break. It is hardly surprising that banks and credit card companies lose significant amounts of money on card fraud.

What is needed then is a method of accurately verifying the identity of an individual presenting an access or financial card at the point of transaction. We know by the card number who the individual should be, we just need a little extra confirmation of true identity. This is where biometrics come into the picture as they can effectively provide the missing piece of information. This is achieved by taking a sample of the particular biometric during enrolment (specific biometric methodologies will be discussed in the next chapter) and creating from this a biometric template which is a digital representation of the original sample. At the point of transaction a live sample is presented by the user and this is compared with the previously stored template. If the two match within previously defined limits, then the identity of the individual is verified and the transaction proceeds. If they don't match, the user will usually be given a second and maybe a third chance to present their biometric but will typically be denied the opportunity to provide multiple instances, as might be the case if someone was attempting to defeat the system. Now we have a much more reasonable expectation that the identity claimed, either by the presentation of a card or entry of a PIN, is indeed a true one. There is another dimension to this which we call biometric identification, whereby a biometric is used in isolation without a card or PIN number to perform a search of possible identities within a database of templates. However, this is another subject and will be discussed in more depth elsewhere in this book. For the moment, let's turn our attention to the popular applications of this technology.

## 2.3 Typical applications for biometrics

There are potentially a huge number of applications for biometric verification technology. Any situation where we have user interaction with a process and wish to verify the identity of the user is a potential candidate for biometrics. In this section we shall examine some of the more obvious applications where either trial systems or actual systems have been implemented using biometric technology. This is not intended as an exhaustive list, more a taste of what biometrics can offer in everyday situations. Other areas of potential application will be discussed elsewhere in this book.

### 2.3.1 Physical access control

Perhaps the most obvious application for the fledgling biometric industry was physical access control and many of the pioneer vendors aligned their products firmly with this market. Traditionally, access control systems fell into three groups: the stand-alone products intended for a single door or entry point; a dedicated controller capable of serving a group of readers - typically up to four; and fully-distributed systems utilising a series of controllers on a network and usually administered by a central PC application. Any of the card technologies mentioned previously could be applied to these basic configurations. Functionality would of course vary according to software / hardware sophistication and cost, with the better systems offering full environmental control via programmable digital inputs and outputs at each controller in addition to the expected access control functionality. Such a system might also be controlling CCTV cameras and interacting with intruder alarms and perimeter boundary systems.

Communications protocols were often either RS485 or RS422 with the controllers being addressable nodes on the network. Some of the more advanced systems offered a level of redundancy for network failures by having a distributed database whereby each node held all the information it needed about users and the control of all its inputs and outputs. A finite number of transactions could be stored locally in the event of temporary network failure, with these being uploaded to the host as soon as communication was restored. The upper echelons of access control systems usually featured a powerful reporting function whereby the system administrator could not only obtain real-time transaction information, but could query the database by any number of relevant parameters in order to produce detailed usage and event reports.

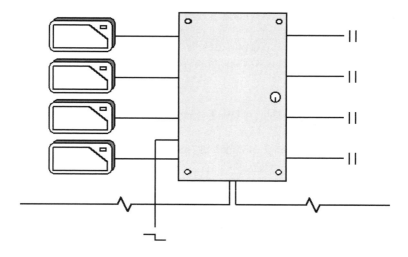

Figure 2.3 A typical distributed access control configuration

Other common functionality in multi-reader systems included the concept of time zones and access levels, time zones being a configurable list of time windows when transactions or events would be valid and access levels being combinations of readers which would be valid for a given individual at a certain time. There are of course many variations on these basic themes, especially with the PC-hosted distributed systems.

In view of the feature-rich functionality offered by many of the established access control systems, there would be little point in duplicating this simply to introduce biometrics and several biometric manufacturers chose to configure their products as effective card reader replacements for existing systems (with biometric templates being stored within the device) rather than reinvent the wheel. There were various ways that this could be achieved. In some instances the biometric device would be configured to give an industry standard output such as ABA Magnetic Stripe or Wiegand. In such cases the user would typically enter a PIN into the biometric device keypad which would call up the appropriate template for comparison and then upon a successful verification, this same PIN would be output as the card number portion of the data stream, together with other information such as the facility code (which identified a batch of cards for this particular site). The host access control system would then see this as simply another card transaction. Another approach would be to interrupt the data flow between card reader and controller by inserting the biometric reader at this point. In this case the user would swipe his card in the normal manner and the data stream output from the card reader would be held by the biometric device until a valid biometric verification took place, at which point it would be released unaltered to the host controller. The card number would act as the unique reference to call up the biometric template for comparison. Of course, the biometric reader would have to understand the format of the card data in order to extract the card number information.

Many biometric devices were and still are configured in the above-mentioned manner and marketed directly into the physical access control marketplace. Some devices, such as the ID3D hand geometry device, later versions of the EyeDentify retinal scanning device, the Fingerscan fingerprint device and others were also capable of being networked together to form an access control system in their own right, although the functionality on offer was not necessarily as sophisticated as with some of the more specialist systems from long-established card access control vendors. However, the important point was that adding biometric verification into the equation provided a valuable extra level of security. With a card-based system, as mentioned previously, all we are really doing is identifying the card. If this is lost or stolen, it may still be presented to the system by the wrong person, who may subsequently gain access into a private or prohibited area undetected. Of course, once we know it has been stolen we can invalidate it within the system, but this may be only after a considerable amount of time has lapsed since the misappropriation of the card. By contrast, you cannot lose or misplace your unique biometric traits and therefore a verified biometric transaction is much more reliable than a card transaction, with or without a PIN.

In spite of the obvious benefits offered by biometric verification to access control methodology, the market has been slow to embrace this technology. Part of this may be attributable to the higher costs of biometric readers in comparison to card readers, coupled to the perceived extra complexity of implementation and subsequent maintenance. However, a large part of it is undoubtedly due to resistance from users who have sometimes perceived the concept as being intrusive or simply unreliable. Early biometric vendors did not always help this situation as some of them made unrealistic claims as to the performance of their devices, which could often not be substantiated under real world conditions. Another important factor was the degree to which users needed to understand the device in order to be reliably verified and the implications of this among system administrators who would have to undertake a whole new enrolment process. Given that these same administrators were not always trained properly to start with, it is not really surprising that some early biometric access control installations were not viewed as successful. It is probably fair to say that vendors and system integrators have largely learned this lesson and that similar installations today can be expected to be much more reliable and successful, through a combination of more intelligent deployment and a structured approach to training and administration. However, it has taken a while to get to this point and poor early impressions are hard to erase from the public consciousness.

So is a biometric access control system really viable with contemporary technology? The answer is undoubtedly yes, and there are large numbers of such systems operating flawlessly in diverse applications around the globe. But biometrics are not a panacea for every access control problem and there are some situations where they would clearly be unsuitable due to environmental conditions or the occupational profile of the user base. The smart access control practitioner will probably ensure that he is well versed in biometric methodology and regard biometric verification as a most valuable tool within his solution portfolio. He may also like to develop the capability to integrate biometric verification into other processes and systems. Above all, he must really understand the user-related issues and the administration requirements for this type of system. These considerations will be covered elsewhere in this book. Then there is the question of which biometric methodology is best suited to physical access control applications. We may decide for example, that fingerprint devices are not going to be suitable for manual work areas due to potential contamination, or that voice verification is not going to be suitable for the front entrance of an office situated in a busy road, or that retinal or iris scanning is really an overkill solution for a medium security internal office application. As with all such situations, it is very much a question of horses for courses and choosing a methodology, and indeed a specific example of that methodology, that best fits the requirement. It is interesting perhaps to note that the leading hand geometry device has been one of the best sellers in the traditional access control market, presumably because of its ease of use, relative robustness and flexibility in how it is deployed.

In a broad context, physical access control includes access into and within office buildings via electronic door locking mechanisms, access to defined boundary areas via turnstiles and electronic gates, vehicular access into car parks and restricted areas via car park barriers, road blockers and motorised gates, access into public areas and other examples. There are also the more specialist situations such as controlled access into hazardous areas or areas where special skills are required, access into high security areas such as prisons and military establishments, secure access into high monetary value areas such as bank vaults and so on. Then there are some special implementations such as the security 'air lock' which may take the form of a full height enclosed portal area with a door on each side, necessitating an identity process whilst the user is enclosed in the portal and before the outer door is released. All of these situations offer potential for biometric verification technology to be effectively deployed, providing the user base and environment is suited to such a solution and where there is a sufficiently high security requirement to make confirmed personal identity an important issue. There is another dimension though, and that is where the convenience of not having to carry cards is actually embraced as being a valuable step forward in access control terms. There are both cost and administration implications in this respect. Naturally, we must ensure that in such a situation the chosen methodology is going to be as user-friendly and reliable as possible. There is some inherent configuration flexibility with most devices in this context and we shall explore that side of things a little later on when we discuss implementation issues.

## 2.3.2 Time and attendance monitoring

This in many ways is an ideal application area for biometrics. The concept of time and attendance recording is not new and employees have been 'clocking on' at factories and other places of work ever since there was a need to employ sizeable numbers of individuals in one place, and especially where shift work is involved. The impetus for this may have come partly from the concept of time and motion where manufacturing tasks were carefully analyzed in order to understand what human effort was involved and for how long, in order to reliably complete the task. This was in turn directly associated with materials and manpower cost, enabling an efficient working practice to be put in place. The idea is generally attributed to Frederick W Taylor, who during the 1880s made a careful study of the handling of raw materials in a Philadelphia steel plant, leading to conclusions which eventually lead to mass production techniques across several industries. This naturally meant employing larger numbers of workers, often in shift patterns to keep production moving and provide the optimum cost efficiencies. It was natural therefore to want to understand exactly who had been working on what shift and to ensure that individuals were correctly paid for the number of hours worked.

For many years the mechanism for recording this information was via individual paper cards and a 'clock' which noted the time in and out when the employee placed the card in the slot and pulled the handle. These time cards could then be collected at the end of the week and processed by the pay office. No doubt it didn't take the workforce long to realize that individuals could easily clock in and out for each other, whether for genuine reasons of emergency or simply as favours to be returned as appropriate. With a large workforce this was not easy to control, or in some cases even to detect and of course, over time it would affect the efficiency and productivity of the process in question. The advent of plastic cards as used for access control purposes, provided a theoretical opportunity to reduce this practice as the card could act as an individual identifier. This meant that the individual would have to loan his card to the accomplice in order to be illegally clocked in or out of the workplace. Of course this was easily overcome and people continued to abuse the system with gay abandon.

Over the years, computer-based time and attendance systems have become increasingly sophisticated and now do much more than just clock time. Employees who work on a flexitime basis for example can often check their flexitime balance at the time and attendance terminal together with other information. Time can usually be recorded against a number of different 'accounts' providing a mechanism for tracking costs against projects and there will often be a range of non-productive accounts to book time against, such as training, leave, sickness and so on. From the accountant's perspective, such systems can hold data about different rates of pay per job function, overtime rates and so on, automatically calculating the correct amount due and if need be feeding this information into a central accounting system. However, the more sophisticated these systems become, the more important it is to be able to verify that the information collected is correct and that includes being able to verify the identity of the person presenting their tokens at the time and attendance terminal. Without a biometric verification process, we are relying on cards and PINs to accomplish this, and as we all know, these can be defeated if the incentive to do so is strong enough.

Not surprisingly, one or two of the biometric vendors spotted this opportunity early on and started to provide some sort of functionality for it. Initially this tended to be rather limited as they were not necessarily expert in this field and it often consisted of being able to timestamp a transaction and flag it with an additional code to represent 'coming to work' or 'leaving for home'. There were certainly efforts to provide biometric readers as an option for established time and attendance software, but if biometric vendors didn't really understand the time and attendance market, then time and attendance vendors didn't really grasp the significance of biometrics. Indeed, what is surprising is that it seemed to take quite a while before the two disciplines came together in any sort of coherent manner that made sense to the user. Fortunately, the situation is somewhat better today and there are several options to choose from.

In many instances, an organization who is already using time and attendance to a significant degree would have invested much time and effort in fine-tuning the system to do just what they want it do and to provide exactly the right reports and interfaces to other systems, not to mention ensuring that the methodology and implementation is acceptable to unions where applicable. Having got this far, they are not likely to want to change their particular setup in a hurry and would be more interested in a biometric enhancement to the existing system rather than a start from scratch approach. Whilst biometric vendors would be quick to point out that their devices can interface to just about anything, it is not always as simple as that. The more capable time and attendance terminals tend to be rather more sophisticated than an average card reader, with considerably more user interaction. In addition, their designers would typically have paid more attention to aesthetics, ensuring that their devices blend into the workplace in an attractive and unobtrusive manner. It would not be appropriate therefore to simply 'bolt on' a biometric reader and call it a biometric time and attendance system (although some may argue this point). A much better approach would be to design the entire terminal as an entity, integrating the biometric reader with the time and attendance user interface and then ensuring that the terminal continues to interact with the host software as usual. This is certainly one approach. Certain biometric vendors have taken a slightly different approach whereby they have taken an existing biometric reader and developed it slightly differently in order to offer time monitoring facilities. Their software may not be as sophisticated as some of the more specialist systems, but may be quite adequate for a start-up time and attendance situation. Certainly, such products would be worthy of consideration if your organization was in this position. They may also be ideal for situations where the primary concern is not necessarily to calculate wages, but to monitor attendance for critical processes or potentially hazardous situations, in order to provide an audit trail.

If we really want to use biometrics as a verification entity for time and attendance systems, we should ideally design the system as a whole. This may mean taking an existing time and attendance database and host software, together with all the rules and report generation, and designing a new user interface that incorporates a biometric reader. The systems designer will have to think about the enrolment process (when biometric templates are created for each user), whether a global template matching threshold is going to be appropriate or whether this needs to be assigned on an individual basis, whether a token is going to be used to call the template for a one-to-one match, and many other items which were not previously an issue. In addition, he will need to consider where the templates will be stored, on the host, within the terminal, on the token or perhaps a combination of these. When properly considered and designed however, there is no doubt that biometric verification can add a powerful extra dimension to the time and attendance monitoring paradigm.

### 2.3.3 Prison visitor systems

One might consider that the use of biometrics within prisons would be an obvious application for the technology, with the promise of accurately verifying the identity of individual prisoners. Curiously, some of the earliest and most successful applications within prisons were not to do with identifying prisoners, but verifying the identity of prison visitors. In fact, the author can give a first-hand account of an example of this as he was involved with the design of one of the very first systems of this nature.

The problem as recounted to me on this occasion was that within a typical prison environment, prisoners and their visitors met in a large open-plan room, not unlike a restaurant with tables and chairs where people could sit and talk in a reasonably private fashion. On duty at the main door of this room would be a prison officer who would have the unenviable task of monitoring the situation and trying to ensure that the visitors, and only the visitors, would leave in a controlled manner at the end of the visiting session. Bear in mind that with more than one visitor per prisoner, there may be 50-60 people or more in such a session, providing something of a challenge for the prison officer in charge. What would then happen at the end of the session is that the correct number of prisoners would be counted out of the room and back to the cell block, while the correct number of visitors would be counted back out through the administration area and out of the prison. After a suitable amount of time had elapsed (enough for the visitors to be in their cars and away) quite often an individual would announce to one of the prison officers that he (or she) was in fact a visitor who had become confused during the exit procedure and come back to the cell block by mistake. Naturally, they could substantiate their identity claim with appropriate documentation, and after questioning would have to be released from the prison. Meanwhile, the real prisoner was happily on his (or her) way to their destination of choice. You might ask how this could possibly happen within a secure environment, but bear in mind that in the country in question prisoners are dressed casually (i.e. no uniforms) and two individuals of similar stature and similarly dressed are not always easy to tell apart, especially if they happen to be brothers or sisters. As far as the prison officer is concerned, he counted the correct number of prisoners out of the visiting area and they looked like the same ones he counted in, but of course with a little forethought and collusion it would not be difficult to distract him just enough to make a switch and this is exactly what was happening - on a fairly regular basis! Oh, and by the way, we were talking about serious offenders in this context, not petty criminals serving short sentences. You might surmise that this obviously places suspicion upon the visitor concerned and points towards a well-organized set-up. However, suspicion is one thing, proof is something else, especially if the inmate concerned had two or three visitors for that session.

So exactly what controls were in place to try and prevent this? Well, the established routine would be that visitors registered their intention to visit in advance and were duly allocated a date and time to visit the prison. The receiving officers therefore had a list of names of visitors and the inmates they were visiting. Upon arrival at the prison they would be 'checked in' to the facility and given a token, often a disk with a number on it, which they would be required to present to an officer on demand at any time during their visit and then surrender when leaving the facility. In some prisons an ultra violet ink marking system was used to mark the visitor's hand or wrist. It is not surprising therefore that somebody looking like the visitor and possessing either the token or an appropriate mark on their hand, would be assumed authentic and allowed to follow the exit procedure and eventually be 'checked out' of the facility. One might of course question the wisdom of having open-plan visiting areas and casual dress codes within serious offender prisons, but that is another story.

How could we solve this problem with biometrics, without causing too much disruption to existing procedures and in a manner that could be easily understood and accepted by all concerned? The first point was to preserve existing procedures wherever possible. This way, the prison officers were not subjected to a total retrain of the visiting procedures and bona fide visitors were not required to adopt a totally new and alien procedure in order to visit their friends and relatives within the facility. The pre-booking and registration at arrival were preserved exactly as they were, as was the list of visitors and inmates for each visiting session. The visitors were also given a numbered token, just as they had been previously, except that the token was now a Wiegand card which could be swiped through a Wiegand reader attached to a biometric device, in this case hand geometry, in order to call up a template from memory in readiness for individual identity verification. Now, when the visitors arrived at reception they were required to enrol their biometric into the hand reader and the resultant template was immediately downloaded to all other readers on the network. Prison officers would then take the card from the visitor, swipe it through the reader (which brought up their particular template for verification) and ask them to place their hand on the hand geometry reader. Their claimed identity would then be either verified or rejected as appropriate. This process would be undertaken at reception, at the entrance to the secure area of the prison and finally at the visiting room itself. After the visit, the process would be repeated at the visiting room, upon exiting the secure area and once again at the public reception area. This ensured that the individual's identity would be verified at multiple points during the visit with virtually no chance of identities being switched along the route. At the end of the visiting period and after all visitors had been accounted for and released from the facility, all biometric templates would be removed from the system in readiness for the next period. Needless to say this effectively solved the problem of visitor's and prisoner's identities being confused.

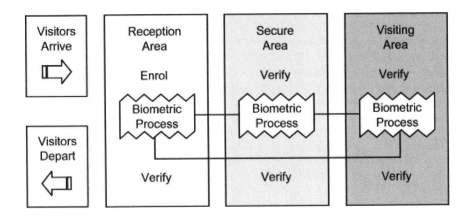

Figure 2.4 A typical prison visitor system methodology

The situation described above represents just one application for biometrics within prisons. There are potentially many others. For example, if the prisoners themselves were enrolled into a biometric verification system, their activities within the prison complex could be tracked. This might include the distribution of benefits or credits in relation to work undertaken, an area which I am led to believe can be the cause of many problems when certain inmates try to manipulate the system. Another application may be to remotely verify the identity of prisoners on payroll. Voice verification would seem to be a potentially interesting methodology in this respect, especially if we could get to the point where we were confident of its performance over a public network and its attendant variability. Then there is the area of physical access control for prison administration staff, where a biometric reader, or perhaps the combination of a biometric and token reader could provide secure authorised access for the individuals in question. There may also be potential for an interesting correlation between the graphic fingerprint records kept for prisoners and a fingerprint biometric system which can also produce images of the fingerprints used for verification purposes. There is no doubt about it, the prison environment offers much potential for the application of biometric verification technology. No doubt we shall see an increasing number of applications in this area as time moves on.

## 2.3.4 Benefit payment systems

In many ways the use of biometrics in relation to benefit payments may be considered as one of the most successful applications of the technology as it is an area where tangible and significant savings have been made as a result.

In the United States, reform of the welfare system has been a popular topic over the last few years with many states producing programmes to help navigate welfare recipients back to work and reduce the welfare-related burden to the state and ultimately the taxpayer. Naturally, this has also highlighted the question of welfare fraud, especially where individuals have been 'double dipping' by claiming welfare payments under more than one identity. Indeed, there is a well-documented example that was featured in the New York Times where a certain enterprising young lady was claiming benefit over a seven-year period of time using 15 different identity cards. During that period she also claimed for a total of 73 fictitious children including 11 sets of twins and netted around $450,000. If you extrapolate the possibility or indeed probability of this occurring across all the states, you can imagine the real size and cost ramifications of the problem. Of course, the United States does not have a monopoly on welfare fraud - it happens to varying degrees anywhere where there is a welfare system in place. However, America has been quick to realize the potential of biometrics in this context and put in place both evaluation and actual systems to combat this particularly nasty social problem.

One interesting effect of implementing biometric identity verification systems that immediately became apparent in the US was that people mysteriously disappeared from the welfare role when such systems were introduced. Not one or two people, but tens of thousands of people at a time. Obviously the deterrent effect was extremely powerful and this alone would generate huge cost savings. One of the first states to implement a system and closely monitor its effects on numbers of claimants was California who introduced their LA Affirm system back in 1994. They concluded that of the disappearing claimants, some of them were perhaps genuine and were simply reacting against the introduction of a system they did not approve of. Of these individuals, some would undoubtedly return as claimants, perhaps after two or three months absence. Others were undoubtedly fraudulent claimants with multiple identities and hopefully these would disappear from the role on a more permanent basis. Other states who experimented with biometric verification within welfare systems reported similar findings. The potential for cost savings was simply enormous and more than warranted the cost of evaluating and perhaps implementing this technology.

Naturally, there is more to a successful system than simply bolting on some sort of biometric. One needs to think carefully about existing procedures and how these might be enhanced with the introduction of a biometric. It may be that existing procedures could be usefully revised in order to take full advantage of the improved confidence in identity verification offered by biometrics. Perhaps the relevant investigative department for example could benefit by focusing their efforts towards cases where identity was clearly in question. There may be ways of searching a database of templates to look for examples which are close enough to warrant further investigation, apart from the obvious incidence of mismatch at verification time. In addition, one would need to think carefully about the enrolment procedure and ensure that personnel are properly trained in all aspects of this and that the logistics of enrolling large numbers of individuals makes sense. Similarly, there would be a staff communication and training requirement with respect to everyday use of the system, especially in the important area of individual identity verification under real world conditions. Lastly, there is of course the public communication and training exercise which would need to be handled carefully so as not to generate unnecessary problems which might lead to a political backlash. This element would of course be easier to handle in some countries than in others, but would probably represent an important consideration in most. Once all of the practical and operational requirements had been carefully considered, one could turn one's attention to the technicalities of the systems design and architecture necessary to meet them - but that is another story.

Whilst we are discussing benefit payment systems and how biometrics might usefully enhance them, it may be interesting to consider the potential for collaboration, particularly within the United States and perhaps at some stage within the European Community and other areas. If relevant information could be shared without compromising existing data protection rules and regulations, one could imagine the potential for even greater savings coupled perhaps to a more effective and therefore efficient overall administration. No doubt there would be strong views both for and against such an initiative, but it will be interesting to see how far this idea might develop over, say, the next decade. Indeed, it will be interesting to watch the progress of biometric verification technology and its adoption within benefit payment systems world-wide over this same period. Of course, benefit payments may be related to a number of things including medical aid, housing benefit, food and energy subsidies and of course unemployment benefit. There is certainly some interesting potential here.

### 2.3.5 Border control systems

There are many who would argue that the travel and tourism industry is the world's largest industry (worth about 3.5 trillion dollars annually) and one of the world's largest employers, especially when you consider all the supporting services that go to make up the international travel and tourism infrastructure. Within this all-pervading industry there are many operational issues, but one of the more worrying is that of finite capacity at the world's busiest airports coupled to the difficulty of creating new airports at optimum sites due to public resistance and other political and/or environmental concerns. This inevitably leads to increasing congestion at existing airports which in turn leads to increasing queues at immigration control points and reduces the quality of the overall end-to-end experience for the traveller. If you overlay this against a steady increase in international air travel over the last decade which looks set to continue into the future, particularly for the more popular destinations, then you can understand how this presents something of a dilemma to all those involved. Now consider the same situation from an immigration department's point of view. Typically, they are under pressure to control their budgets, and yet are expected to maintain effective controls against improper or illegal immigration. Consider the plight of a lone immigration control officer on an early morning shift when two or three large aircraft have just landed and queues are starting to build. After a couple of hundred people have passed through, his or her ability to easily detect the use of fraudulent documents or visas may be impaired somewhat, especially under pressure of getting people through the process. This implies no slur on the individuals concerned, overall they do a great job under difficult circumstances, but they have an unenviable task. The increase in traffic described earlier doesn't exactly help their cause either. Against this background, it would be nice if technology could offer even a partial solution to the problem. Perhaps biometric identity verification could help?

This was certainly the thinking some years ago within the World Travel and Tourism Council headquartered at Brussels. Biometrics had come to the attention of several of their members and much thought was being expended into how this technology might potentially help to speed up the immigration process by automating certain aspects of it. It was thought that if an individual's identity could automatically be verified, particularly when returning to their own country of origin, then perhaps they could be allowed to bypass the usual manual procedure and thus avoid queuing at the immigration control points. With more than 400 million people travelling annually, this idea would indeed be worthy of consideration. Some sort of automated biometric identity verification would seem to be the answer, but how to organize both the operational aspects and the logistics of enrolment would no doubt present a challenge.

One of the more interesting aspects of this was template storage. Some biometric devices, for example the hand geometry reader used partly in border control trials, required a relatively small amount of storage for the template - typically around nine bytes. This provided the possibility of the user carrying their own template with them on a low cost token such as a magnetic stripe card. Other devices, including fingerprint readers also utilized in border control trials, required up to around 1k of storage, requiring more sophisticated token technology if the user were to carry their own template. The alternative was of course to store the templates in a central database and recall them from memory when the user presented his token at the kiosk. This was the methodology used in the relatively high-profile INSPASS border control trials undertaken at Newark, JFK and Toronto airports. Frequent travellers were invited to join the INSPASS system and upon acceptance would be enrolled into the database at special facilities within the airport complex. This would involve giving typically three samples of their biometric which would be averaged in order to produce a representative template which could be used for subsequent verification purposes. They were also provided with an INSPASS plastic card to be used at the special fast lane kiosks provided at the airports. In some cases, the user could choose between fingerprint or hand geometry technology. In this instance, it would probably be fair to say that hand geometry proved overall to offer the best balance of usability and accuracy. The idea was that the traveller could insert their card into the kiosk receptacle (which would call up the appropriate template according to the card number) and place their hand on the hand reader for identity verification, upon which the necessary immigration form would be output from the kiosk and they were free to leave the airport. The scheme was well supported by interested travellers with several thousand voluntarily enrolling into it and trying the facilities for themselves. This generated many tens of thousands of transactions, providing a useful benchmark view for the utilisation of biometrics within a reasonably large-scale voluntary use application. A not dissimilar scheme was the IBM-promoted Fastgate system as initiated at Bermuda airport, again focusing on hand geometry as an easy to use biometric methodology.

However, the trials referred to above may represent just a small slice of the potential for biometric technology within the travel and tourism sector. Consider for a moment the various loyalty schemes being operated by airlines and indeed airline alliances, many of which provide the traveller with a plastic card in recognition of their status as a frequent flyer with that particular carrier. Now imagine that this card is in fact a chip card which incorporates, among other things, at least one biometric template, collected at a convenient time and location to the user.

Figure 2.5 Possible travel card

Imagine further that the card is supported by a major credit card organization for travel-related transactions. Now consider all of the processes you may undertake in the course of organising and undertaking your trip. Telephoning the reservation service of your preferred carrier (or booking on line) and understanding any credits you may have in the form of air miles etc. Organising and booking your hotel accommodation. Arranging for car hire at your destination. Checking in at the airport. Going through customs and immigration procedures. Checking at the boarding gate. Purchasing inflight goods and services. Going through the arrival and immigration procedures at your destination. Collecting and paying for your hired car. Checking in at the hotel. And so on. After enjoying your business or social visit, you will then go through most of these processes again in reverse before arriving safely back home. Imagine if you could facilitate all of these functions and procedures with just one entity - your own personalised travel card.

With the cost of associated components such as chip card and biometric readers becoming much more realistic, plus increased support for such devices within mainstream computing platforms, the above scenario is starting to look realistic. If a traveller had the fictitious card referred to above, you could perhaps imagine him or her inserting it into a slot in their PC, placing their finger onto the fingerprint reader incorporated into the PC keyboard and booking their ticket on line, at which point the chip card transaction details would automatically be updated. Alternatively, they may walk into a travel agent, present their card and book their flight, hotel accommodation, car hire and other sundries, secure in the knowledge that they will receive any privileged pricing arrangements granted by their frequent flyer status as indicated within the card. Now imagine them arriving at the airport check-in reception and using this same card to identify themselves, confirm their booking and produce the boarding pass. This may be undertaken via a kiosk or via the check-in clerk. If the latter, the check-in clerk will be able to see at a glance this passenger's status, preferences and recent history and react accordingly. Perhaps at the departure gate they will take advantage of a fast lane automated procedure where they present their card and boarding pass and provide a biometric sample to confirm identity before boarding. This information may perhaps be transmitted by satellite to the destination immigration authorities, enabling much of the routine processing to be undertaken in advance. When our privileged traveller arrives at the other end, he or she simply presents their card once more at a special fast lane kiosk, provides a biometric sample and is free to pass out of the airport and on their way. Imagine that this same card can be used to purchase goods on the aircraft, or withdraw cash from ATM machines in the destination country. Now we are truly providing an enhanced end-to-end experience for the traveller, easing their flow through the necessary processes, acknowledging their individual status and generally making life less complicated for them. In addition, we would also be enhancing security as automated biometric identity verification tends to be more reliable and less emotive than other methods. This in turn would free up immigration personnel time, allowing them to concentrate their resource on the exceptional cases. Pie in the sky? Maybe not. As previously mentioned, there have already been applications of biometric technology for border control purposes (not just at airports either) which have proven the technology beyond doubt. One could imagine an enthusiastic airline, or maybe an alliance of interested parties, looking at this from a commercial perspective as a means to win and retain customers and in so doing enabling the border control functionality element which has been of interest to many administrations for some years now. Certainly there would be many issues to unravel and gain agreement on, but something along these lines may well become feasible in due course and it will be interesting to monitor developments over the next few years in this context.

## *2.3.6 PC/Network access control*

This is the application that many saw as the large-scale enabler for biometric technology. Indeed, many new entrants to the biometric market have targeted this area as their only real application, so strongly do they believe in it. So why have we not seen a massive and immediate take-up in the use of biometric PC access control? It is not a particularly new idea and has been possible for the best part of a decade in one form or another, but within the last 24 months we have seen costs tumble and several exciting new devices appear, which may swing the balance in favour of practical implementation at a realistic cost.

Not so long ago, if you had configured a PC or workstation for biometric user log on, you would probably have spent several hundred dollars or more in the process and also expended a fair amount of time in configuring the whole shooting match and getting it to work. Today you can purchase a suitable fingerprint biometric reader together with all the necessary software tools for less than a hundred dollars. This will connect up to your PC easily and be running in a matter of minutes. Such is progress.

Figure 2.6 PC biometric access control

In fact there are a wide variety of such devices available, mainly centerd around fingerprint technology, sometimes integrated with a chip card reader. Whilst other biometric techniques have also been used for PC access control, including iris scanning, fingerprint technology does offer a cost effective and easily understood solution and has tended to predominate for this particular application.

In a typical scenario, the fingerprint reader will connect physically to the PC via either a parallel or serial port. No doubt we shall begin to see more devices offering USB connectivity, but currently the aforementioned methods seem to prevail. Most PC's or workstations in an office environment have at least one spare serial port, making this a convenient choice, although parallel port connection may not be so convenient if you are using the only available port for a printer or document scanner connection, necessitating some sort of junction box or switching device. Certain devices designed for parallel port connection do indeed come supplied with a rudimentary adapter which your LAN administrator may or may not believe is up to the task on an ongoing basis. In any event, having physically connected the device, we shall need to load the accompanying software in order for the system as a whole to operate.

This is where it gets interesting. There are several approaches that the biometric systems designer may have taken to PC access control. At a basic level, a choice may have been taken to simply inhibit the boot procedure until the biometric sample is verified, thus blocking access to everything. A more usual approach is to integrate seamlessly with the operating system's own security log on procedures. You will thus see many devices designed for use with Microsoft Windows 95 and Windows 98, where the identity verification process is integrated into the operation of the log on password dialogue. For local networks utilising Windows NT server and perhaps Windows NT at the desktop there are various enhancements that may be incorporated into a centrally administered security model, based upon biometric user identity verification. But what of other operating systems such as Linux or BeOs? Or other networking systems such as Novell? No doubt we shall see increasing support in this area also.

However, we are still talking about the operating system start-up routine. Surely there is more to PC access control than this? After all, I might find a way to boot to a previous version of DOS and access confidential files from there, or even copy them to a floppy drive for subsequent use on another PC. Fortunately, some of the biometric access control applications are rather more sophisticated and offer a range of protection possibilities right down to folder or application execution levels. Such a system may be configured to offer a secure computing environment while remaining intuitive in use for the busy professional who is probably more interested in the contents of his or her files than precisely how they are secured. This is where the business case for such systems can become quite valid. If we can offer an intuitive, easy to use security model that requires little or no learning curve and yet offers the undoubted benefits of biometric user verification, at low per seat cost, then we have a proposition which must at least be of interest to LAN administrators and corporate users. When you consider how easy it is to build, say, a fingerprint sensor into another device such as a keyboard, mouse or notebook computer surface, then you might imagine that we shall be seeing much more of biometric PC access control.

There is another interesting dimension to this in the form of secure transactions, either across or between networks or across the Internet. This raises some other issues such as the use of biometrics with Public Key Encryption services. This is an area of interest to many and we can expect to see some interesting developments in this context. There are some synergistic areas of interest here such as the use of chip cards and telecommunications services which perhaps sit quite comfortably with biometrics.

Then there is the interesting area of client-server database access. Some corporate operational databases can become quite complex and unwieldy, necessitating full-time administration and posing some interesting security problems. It is rarely a matter of access or no access, but a question of access to which physical entities (down to table and field level) and which processes (such as queries, stored procedures and so on). Most popular database vendors do indeed offer comprehensive security tools in order to precisely configure access rights across even the most complex of databases. This can get messy and probably registers highly on the DBA's worst nightmare scale, especially with a constantly evolving employee or user base. Whilst biometrics will not solve the complexity of configuration   issue, they might offer several extra degrees of security-related comfort when dealing with access to sensitive data. In this respect, it will be encouraging to see the major database vendors looking closely at biometric verification technology.

In conclusion, whilst we have seen a number of devices and software programs targeting the PC access control scenario, the idea is still in its infancy in many respects. We need to see a more sophisticated approach to exactly what is being protected and how, coupled with a seamless hardware integration model. With the pace of progress in the PC industry, I have no doubt that these will come along quite quickly - perhaps by the time you read this book!

## 2.3.7 ATM-related applications

This represents an interesting area that has been under discussion for several years. What is the benefit of biometrics in this scenario, to whom and at what cost? One could easily envisage that adding biometric identity verification to the ATM transaction process would cut down on fraudulent use of bank and credit cards at ATM terminals and would therefore provide worthwhile savings. The leading banks however may look at this a little differently. If they were to take the percentage of bank and credit card fraud perpetrated at ATM machines (this represents just a part of total card fraud) and place a value upon it, that figure would look pretty substantial to you and me, especially if we considered that it is us who is ultimately paying for it. Against this though, the banks would need to consider the cost of rolling out biometric functionality to thousands of existing ATM machines, plus the increased cost of new ones. In addition, there would need to be a well co-ordinated communication campaign to advise their customers of the new functionality and how to use it. Then there would need to be some thought about the enrolment procedure, whether customers could undertake this themselves actually at the ATM terminal, whether they would need assistance, in which case staff would need to be on hand at convenient times, or whether a completely separate process would need to be put in place to gradually enrol all of their customers. All of this costs money and the bank would need to consider this cost carefully against the returns of reduced ATM-related fraud.

Quite apart from the technical and logistical considerations, there is the area of user acceptance. This could become a thorny issue if handled incorrectly and much depends on how the idea would be proposed and managed from a customer service perspective. There are many positive aspects to such an idea, in that you might offer enhanced services to the customer via the ATM if their identity can be verified in this manner, such as increased withdrawal limits, the ability to access more detailed information appertaining to their personal accounts and other options. From a customer point of view there might also be an element of increased security, providing something of a comfort zone in knowing that if you do inadvertently misplace your card, it is less likely that a stranger could access your account with it. Against these positive points, there are some potential negatives which would need to be addressed. Firstly, uninformed customers will quite naturally want to know what is happening to their unique biometric data and whether there is any possibility of someone being able to replicate the biometric trait and effectively steal their identity. This is a point to be taken very seriously as it reflects a genuine concern among many as to the use of biometrics. Then there is the 'big brother' issue where some people will take the view that this is another nail in the coffin towards total control over the individual by large corporations and state departments. Again, these concerns should be taken very seriously. On top of these issues sits the slightly more basic one of using technology. Many people are very apprehensive about using something which appears as very high tech or complicated. Remember, it is not only computer engineers and technology enthusiasts that use ATM machines, but a broad cross section of society including the elderly and people whose daily lives feature little or no 'technology'. Whilst it is true that people will eventually adapt to almost anything provided that they perceive a benefit to themselves, getting over the initial technophobe hurdle is not easy for some individuals. How often have you heard people say "that device simply never works for me" or "I can't be bothered with all this technology rubbish" and similar remarks? True, many of them could be gently educated and shown how to use the system to their advantage - the point is, all of this takes time and effort, which relates directly to cost. And even after all of your best efforts in this direction, there will still be some users who simply can't get along with the technology.

So far we have outlined two factors which suggest that implementing biometric verification functionality across a large network of ATM machines is not a concept to be taken lightly and would certainly incur substantial direct and indirect costs. We haven't even considered the nitty gritty systems design yet, a subject which has many angles. Consider template storage for example. Perhaps it would be nice if the customer carried his or her own template on a chip card. This would ensure that they have direct control over the biometric data at all times - or would it? Unless you undertake template matching directly on the chip card, you will need to extract the template for matching purposes and have it resident in the ATM processing cycle for this period. Customers will need to be assured that there is no possibility of this data being misused. Would banks actually wish to maintain a database of biometric data for customers, perhaps as a security backup? There are all sorts of questions to be considered here. Then there is the question of which biometric technology would be most suitable. Contact methodologies such as fingerprints or hand geometry would require a capture surface which could conceivably become dirty or damaged, thus affecting the reliability of scans, and some people raise health concerns over using methodologies that require physical contact, although they are already using keypads and touch screens which also require physical contact. Contact-free methodologies such as iris scanning or face recognition may seem attractive in this context, although there are also environmental issues to take into account here including lighting conditions and the variable stature and attitude of individuals.

All in all, the use of biometrics in ATM terminals is an interesting concept and one which will surely become reality one day, although the implementation of such an idea is currently not perhaps as straightforward as it may at first appear. In spite of this there have been various trials around the world, most of which have reported positive feedback from participating users and have no doubt provided valuable experience for the organizations concerned. Perhaps it would be nice if some of these organizations got together to share their ideas and try to create a common approach. After all, as a user, you may not be too enthusiastic about being expected to use different biometric methodologies in different machines in different locations in order to access different functionality. Maybe we still have a little way to go with this one.

## 2.3.8 Clubs

Here is surely an ideal application for contemporary biometrics. A situation where you have a reasonably contained user base accessing a small number of facilities (maybe just one) and where there are many opportunities for providing related benefits. There are many types of exclusive clubs, from golf and sports, through gambling to special interests where it is important to ensure that only bona fide paid up members enjoy the facilities on offer. Sometimes there are limited opportunities for joining such establishments due to the number of individuals that can reasonably be catered for, and it becomes particularly pertinent to ensure that there are no 'gate crashers' or intruders. In many such situations there may be levels of membership and associated privileges that require a certain amount of administration and in the case of gambling clubs there may also be extended credit parameters that need to be managed. It is natural therefore to consider some sort of computerised membership management system, usually coupled with some sort of membership card. Why not extend this a little to incorporate biometric identity verification?

Let's explore this a little. Suppose that I apply to join an exclusive downtown gambling and social club. After being satisfied with my credentials, the administration decides to grant me provisional membership and supplies me with a membership card accordingly. But what does this card mean? Is it just a piece of plastic with a number on it, or can it be used in a proactive manner to control my use of the facilities according to membership status? For example, maybe there is a gymnasium attached to the club for member use, but only if they have paid a higher level of subscription. Perhaps I need to produce my membership card at the cashier in order to be issued with chips and maybe there are credit limits in place for different categories of membership. Maybe my membership covers admission to special events at the club premises and maybe it doesn't. Sometimes guest facilities are available for certain categories of membership and sometimes otherwise. If the card is the only indication of my membership status, what happens if this card is lost or stolen and subsequently produced at the club by an impostor?

Apart from the issues mentioned above, we have to acknowledge that many such clubs like to portray an upmarket, luxurious ambience where it may be inappropriate to have overt manual security processes at every turn. This would clearly be rather off-putting to the targeted membership and not in keeping with a place of retreat and relaxation. The intelligent use of biometrics however may even lend an air of exclusive high technology to the overall picture, whilst notably enhancing security for both members and club management. In this respect, there may be many opportunities for such a system.

A suitable application for clubs might start with a comprehensive database of users, providing all the pertinent information that the management requires, including date of joining, subscription type, payment record and so on. Naturally, it would include the ability to quickly generate reports according to a number of pertinent parameters and should be intuitive and easy to use for club personnel, whose experience of computers may be variable. Perhaps it would be nice to add a photo field to this database in order to provide a visual record of members, this would also facilitate the creation of photo ID badges rather than just a plain membership card. Photographs might conveniently be captured via a digital camera and easily uploaded onto the host PC, from where they can subsequently be added into the database. If we are using coded cards such as magnetic stripe, optical or even basic chip-cards, then the provision of a suitable reader at strategic points such as the main entrance, cashier booth, restaurant and so on could, upon a card transaction, quickly bring up membership details on a discreetly sited terminal. If we now add a biometric, either to the token or within the membership database, we can also verify the identity of the individual concerned and be sure that they are indeed the same person who was originally granted membership.

Configuring a system in this manner can, according to the software employed, provide us with a detailed and accurate audit trail of transactions, making it easy to determine precisely the level of attendance and usage of facilities by each individual member. From this information, associated costs may be calculated accordingly and now that each 'transaction' has been biometrically verified, there is no doubt about the correctness of such charges. This approach may also be useful in instances where named guests may enjoy a limited number of complimentary visits to the club before they are required to apply for membership. This is an area which has been abused in the past leading to misunderstandings and other problems; which the simple adoption of a biometric and tracked transactions can overcome. The guest may indeed be automatically approached with the offer of membership after the authorised number of complimentary visits have been undertaken, adding further to the value of such software.

Figure 2.7 A typical user database within a biometric application

The physical design of some of the contemporary biometric devices lend themselves well to this sort of application, being neat, attractive and reasonably robust. Together with equally attractive and intuitive software, a well-designed and implemented system could provide real benefits in a variety of club situations whilst blending in with an up market ambience. In addition, one could envisage the payback being fairly significant in terms of greater accuracy in charging, member profiling and general administration, not to mention the enhanced security and reduced opportunity for fraudulent activities. Yet another dimension to this could be in the area of membership loyalty schemes where regular attendance and usage of facilities qualifies the member for additional discounts or promotional offers. We might even equip a strategically-sited terminal or kiosk with a biometric reader, enabling the club member to check his or her own account status on line at any given point in time, displaying personalised messages accordingly. Maybe our club offers office facilities such as telephone, fax, Internet access, copying facilities, conferencing and so on, all of which may be accessed securely via our membership card and biometric. With a little imagination, we might enhance the overall membership experience with the use of such technology while streamlining our administration and providing a higher level of security into the bargain. All in all, a proposition worthy of serious investigation.

### 2.3.9 National identity cards

There are a variety of national ID cards and passports in use throughout the world, with relatively little commonality in their design. This makes it relatively easy to forge such a document, at least well enough to pass unnoticed in everyday usage. Imagine the situation where there are a queue of people waiting to pass through a checking point or service of some description and there is only a limited amount of time whereby an official can scrutinize a document. If there is something obviously wrong it may get detected, but minor inconsistencies could go unnoticed. Whilst the introduction of a carefully conceived biometric is not an absolute guarantee against this, it would make it that much more difficult to duplicate such a document or to modify an existing one in order to steal the identity.

Naturally some thought would need to go into the medium concerned, whether it be a chip card, optical card, 2D barcode or a more conventional passport-type document, and how the biometric template would be encoded into it in a secure manner. If the template is small enough in size, it may even be encoded into the OCR segment of a conventional passport, although a robust chip card might offer a more versatile solution. It may even be interesting to consider a dual technology approach such as basic chip card with a 2D barcode on the reverse. This could facilitate much flexibility and perhaps provide something of a multi-functional usage, which in itself would strengthen the business case for such a card.

Figure 2.8 Possible national identity card

In this case for example we might have the individual's photograph visible on the front face of the card and also encoded together with other information such as date and place of birth and issuing office into a 2D barcode on the reverse. The chip on the card may contain two biometric templates (perhaps face and fingerprint) for use in identity verification situations, together with a suitable encryption methodology. There may also be other information such as blood group, any medical anomalies, national insurance number and so on which may be accessed by third party systems where appropriate. Obviously the above is just a sketched-out idea of what might be utilized to good effect, but with a little careful thought a national identity document designed and configured something along these lines could be used for all sorts of purposes where the individual needs to be positively recognized. Such a document may be utilized for cross-border travel purposes just as the passport is today, it may be used for benefit claimants within welfare systems, as an emergency medical card for those involved in serious accidents, as personal identity verification for financial transactions and many other purposes where confirming an individual's identity is important. In addition, it could be made relatively secure, certainly more so than the majority of current national identity documents.

Some would argue that such an idea would involve additional administration as the biometric templates would ideally need to be registered under controlled and observed conditions. This is true, but given the ease with which passports may be currently obtained maybe this is no bad thing. Do you know how many forged and fraudulently obtained passports are currently in circulation? No? Well, you are in good company as neither do most of the world's immigration and issuing authorities. One thing is for sure though, the number is not a small one. Even a methodology as outlined above might still be fooled sometimes by a determined individual, but it would be much harder to do so, especially by the opportunist middlemen to whom this is such a profitable business. But exactly how would you register the biometric templates in this instance? Perhaps it could be organized via a network of public authority offices such as police stations or local administrations, whereby the applicant could specify his or her preferred local office at which he or she would present themselves together with the appropriate documentation such as birth certificate, proof of address, employment or whatever the issuing authority requires. If the card is subsequently lost or misplaced, perhaps a charge would be levied for a second issue (which would be tagged as such within the central database) but at least we can be reasonably assured that the chances of the lost card being successfully used by another are negligible, especially if a dual biometric is used.

We have concentrated on the national identity card scenario in the above example, but a similar approach might be used for drivers licences. In fact a useful synergy here would be the use of the national ID card in order to apply for the provisional driver's licence, at which point the individual's identity would be verified and captured. When they come to take the driving test, their identity would be verified by the instructor before entering the vehicle. This would guard against the extremely prevalent practice of the wrong individual turning up on the test day and taking the test on behalf of a friend who is not confident of passing. How many licences have been issued in this way? Once again, your guess is as good as anybody's, but it is certainly a problem and one that could have serious consequences if an untrained and incompetent individual is involved in an accident. The two cards could also be cross-correlated in some way as an additional security measure. They could even be the same physical card with different sections enabled as appropriate.

Of course, there will always be an element of society who will shout 'big brother' and object to any such scheme. But if you are a bona fide tax-paying and responsible citizen perhaps you would warmly welcome such moves as an extra assurance against someone stealing your identity, as well as the other obvious benefits referred to. Naturally you would require strong assurances from the issuing administration that the methodology is secure and that no information is misused by the authorities (although some would argue that this is hypothetical as they already hold substantial amounts of data about you anyway), but this could be easily arranged and demonstrated to an independent watchdog. Some administrations have already been experimenting with biometric technology along these lines and it will be interesting to observe if and how this idea develops over the next decade.

## 2.3.10 Other applications

In this chapter we have taken a brief look at some of the obvious applications for biometric verification technology. Hopefully this has given the reader a taste for how the technology may benefit existing everyday processes across a variety of situations. Of course there are dozens if not hundreds of other potential applications which we have not touched upon, some of which will be specific to organizations and authorities seeking to improve the reliability of identity verification or perhaps just automate the process. There may also be some strong marketing lead initiatives where manufacturers or service providers can provide additional user benefits via the adoption of the technology (in a reliable and intuitive manner). Will we see biometric car entry systems? Biometrics integrated into mobile phones? Biometrics for parental control over in house entertainment systems and the Internet? Biometric-enabled ticketless travel? Biometric voting systems? Biometric vending machines in the workplace? Biometric environmental controls that automatically adjust to user preferences? The list goes on and on and is limited by imagination as much as anything. One thing is certain however, biometric verification technology has come along in leaps and bounds over the last few years to the point at which it is affordable, reliable and increasingly understood as a concept by the general public. If we couple this to increased performance in many cases and the ready availability of a range of software tools, things are certainly looking a lot more positive for the biometrics industry than they were just a few years earlier. There is still something of a question around user acceptance in some quarters (a point which will be covered elsewhere in this book) but this may be matched to some extent by a greater understanding among systems integrators and user administrations of the issues involved and how to manage them. Exciting times undoubtedly lie ahead.

# 3. Biometric methodologies

In this chapter we shall explore some of the popular biometric methodologies and consider how they work and what applications they may be best suited for.

The question "which biometric is best?" is one of the most often asked when people are looking at this technology. But in truth there is no 'best' biometric, it all depends on what we are trying to achieve, with whom and under what conditions. A methodology which works well within a contained and constant office environment may be less suited to a busy public airport, or a factory shop floor for example. We need to carefully consider the application, understand the situation from the user's perspective and be crystal clear about the benefits of introducing the technology into a given process. We may then be in a position to undertake some trials and evaluate a short list of devices and software. So let's look at some of the more popular examples of biometric technology.

## 3.1 Fingerprints

Fingerprints are perhaps what the majority of people immediately associate with biometrics. No doubt this is partly because in many minds biometrics are synonymous with security and identification, and fingerprints are of course the primary means of positive identification among law enforcement agencies the world over. In fact, the design of many fingerprint systems reflects the way that fingerprints have been matched manually over the years by seeking to identify minutiae features and their relative position within the print. Trained fingerprint experts have traditionally employed a very precise methodology for categorising fingerprints into primary types such as whorls, loops and arches and then identifying individual minutiae features such as ridges, forks, islands and crossovers, noting their relative position. One can imagine that with large collections of fingerprints stored on cards, this was a time-consuming process requiring significant resource and expertise. These days, automatic fingerprint identification (AFIS) computer matching systems drastically reduce the time needed to scan even very large databases of fingerprints and produce potential matches. In this application (which is subtly different from biometric identity verification) the system is searching for a matching print and may in fact produce a list of many potential matches, each with an accompanying score representing the degree of similarity with the supplied print.

Interesting though AFIS systems are, we are really concerned with the real-time verification of a live biometric sample against a stored template, typically on a one-to-one basis whereby the template for the claimed identity is called from the system via an input PIN or card swipe and then compared with the live sample (although one-to-many searches are also possible in some instances, whereby the live sample is compared with a number of templates within the database).

As previously mentioned, many fingerprint biometric systems work in a similar manner to the law enforcement-related AFIS systems in that they seek to identify minutiae features and their relative position. However, before they can do this they must have both a good quality reference template for the individual in question and also a good quality live scan.

Figure 3.1 Minutiae features within a fingerprint

This is not quite as straightforward as you might imagine as there are a number of variables which may conspire, singly or in unison, against the probability of capturing a good quality fingerprint image. These include the precise position and attitude of the fingertip as it is placed upon the scanning surface, the prevailing  environmental conditions including temperature and humidity, the degree of dryness or otherwise of the skin, the cleanliness of the scanning surface, the presence of foreign bodies, damage to the individual fingerprint, calibration and reliable operation of the scanning function and several others. You may wonder how we ever manage to get a reasonable quality of image for our purposes, but generally speaking the image scanning and capture process has been refined to the point where it works quite well. However, a certain amount of image processing is usually necessary in order to identify the bona fide matching minutiae features without getting confused by spurious image information. The first step is usually the 'raw' grey scale image from the scan.

Figure 3.2 Grey scale fingerprint image

This grey scale image will be processed down into a high contrast binary image by taking the average pixel grey level and processing every pixel above this level as a binary one and all other pixels as a binary zero. This will produce the necessary binary image which may be further processed in order to compensate for luminance deficiencies until we end up with a nice clean, high contrast image of the fingerprint in question. The resultant binary image may still be further processed in order to provide a more skeletal representation, making it easier to determine the specific features of the print. Depending on the system in question, this may reduce the ridge lines of the fingerprint down to one pixel in width in order to more clearly identify specific features. In some systems, there may be additional processing to compensate for the effect of slight rotation of the finger on the scanning surface compared to the original reference template. We then have the question of how much of the print do we use for our matching purposes? If we try to use too great an area, there is a chance that the live sample will be significantly different due to cut-off effects produced by inconsistency of placement of the finger upon the scanner. For this reason, many systems will use a smaller portion of the scanned image for matching purposes. Indeed, in some cases the image may be broken up into more than one region where identifying minutiae features are present. One benefit of reducing the comparison area is that there is less chance of false minutiae information, as may be produced by abrasions for example, confusing the matching process and creating errors. Once all of the mechanical issues inherent in capturing a suitable fingerprint image have been attended to, we can then get on with the matching process to see how well the live sample correlates to the reference template. This is a function of the matching algorithm particular to a given device and in most cases will be referenced to an adjustable threshold setting which will influence the accuracy of the resulting match/no match decision. Performance issues will be covered in greater depth within the next chapter.

Figure 3.3 The processed binary fingerprint image

The result from the matching process will be passed to the controlling software for interpretation as appropriate. What happens now will depend upon the software and application in question, which brings us nicely to the question of which applications are fingerprint-based systems most suited to.

Fingerprints have in fact been used in a fairly broad range of biometric applications, with varying degrees of success according to just how well the systems have been designed to meet the particular requirement. However, there are clearly some situations where the methodology would not be well suited; for example, applications where the biometric reader would be deployed in a harsh environment and subject to higher than usual levels of contamination or abrasion. Similarly, an application where users are likely to have dirty hands due to the nature of their work would not be ideally suited to fingerprints, neither would extremely cold or wet external situations. Perhaps the best application areas for fingerprint biometrics are where the readers can be deployed in controlled interior situations and integrated seamlessly into a familiar process. For example, PC or network access control utilising fingerprint biometrics is a popular application where you have (usually) a relatively clean, controlled environment and a user who is used to interfacing with technology and will probably adjust well to using the fingerprint device. Furthermore, the fingerprint reader will typically be small and unobtrusive enabling it to blend well into the office desktop environment - it may even be integrated into the computer keyboard, a mouse, or other familiar device. Time and attendance monitoring terminals may represent another application where a fingerprint scanner could successfully integrate into the existing process while adding a valuable extra level of identity authentication. One can also envisage an increasing use of fingerprint biometrics integrated into chip card applications. Already, there are several attractive combination readers featuring chip cards and fingerprint biometrics which may be easily integrated into suitable applications. The ability to integrate biometrics via custom application development and the provision of readers on an OEM basis is another area that is well served by the variety of fingerprint readers available with SDK's (software development kits).

The performance of fingerprint devices tends to be good once the user has become familiar with the concept and understands how to give a good live sample. Historically, certain examples were considered to offer good false accept performance (where the chances of accepting an impostor were low) but rather poor false reject performance (where a valid user may be incorrectly rejected). To be fair, some of this would invariably be down to either poor quality enrolled templates or unfamiliarity on the part of the user leading to inconsistency in use. Both of these factors can be managed with good quality communication and training of both administrators and users (more of that later), but nevertheless, some people struggled with some of the earlier fingerprint devices. More recently, the realized performance from fingerprint readers has almost certainly increased as more experience has been gained in real world large-scale applications and both software and hardware have been refined.

In conclusion, fingerprint biometrics offer a good starting point for consideration as a methodology to enhance personal identity verification within a given process. There is a wide choice of available products at different price points and most vendors offer an SDK of some description for the adventurous.

## 3.2 Hand geometry

The biometrics industry in general owes something of a debt to hand geometry as it was one of the first biometrics to prove practical in use across a variety of real world applications. As we are all aware, it is one thing to develop and evaluate a device under laboratory conditions with enthusiastic personnel, and quite another for it to work flawlessly in a real application where the users may not be quite so understanding of, or sympathetic towards the technology. The leading hand geometry device enjoyed early success in the biometrics industry by virtue of the fact that it was easy to use, performed well and was easily applied to a variety of applications in physical access control, time monitoring and other areas. It was also easy to configure and administer, making it an attractive option for systems integrators, particularly in the conventional security electronics sector. This success tended to raise awareness of biometrics in general and pave the way for other devices and methodologies to explore the rich variety of potential applications that exist for biometrics as a fast-developing technology.

Hand geometry systems work by taking a three dimensional view of the hand in order to determine the geometry and metrics around finger length, height and other details. There exists a wealth of information within the geometry of an individual hand and in fact, the leading hand geometry device measures around 90 such parameters. This information is processed via a proprietary algorithm and a representative template created accordingly for the individual concerned. This template is represented as a digital 'string' of information and it is not possible to externally recreate the hand image from this information. In common with many other devices, multiple samples (usually three) are taken and averaged in order to create the biometric template. Interestingly, the leading hand geometry device features a template size of around only nine bytes, providing for flexibility in storage and transmission.

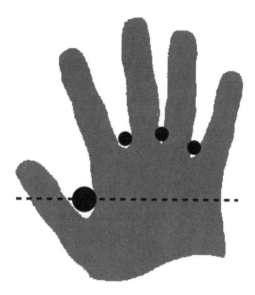

Figure 3.4 Hand geometry

It is predominantly the front part of the hand, as illustrated above which is used for the hand geometry measurements. The hand is placed on a reflective platen surface and the image is captured via a CCD (charge coupled device) sensor and a series of mirrors in order to capture the three-dimensional information. An infrared led (light emitting diode) array is employed in order to provide a constant light source. Naturally, it is important that the hand be placed upon the platen surface in a consistent manner and to help facilitate this a series of guiding pegs are fitted to the platen. The user simply slides his or her fingers up against the pegs with the palm downwards and flattened against the platen surface. This is quite an easy and intuitive task for most users, a factor that has helped hand geometry readers to be readily accepted in a variety of applications. Having a relatively large physical area to work with also ensures that minor variations in placement during subsequent verification transactions does not have perhaps the same consequences as might be the case with some fingerprint devices which are dealing with a much smaller physical area for capture and comparison purposes. All of this points towards operational flexibility and reliability and indeed, hand geometry as a methodology is strong in this respect. Performance is also quite good with the leading device featuring low equal error rates and a sliding threshold with which to bias the reader towards lower instances of either false accepts or false rejects according to the requirements of the application.

Where would you use hand geometry? Perhaps the primary applications to date have been in physical access control and time and attendance monitoring, but there have also been diverse applications such as voting systems, meal allowance verification and many others. Generally speaking, hand geometry is an easy biometric methodology to deploy, is likely to elicit few user-related objections and will usually perform well in most situations. Against this is the fact that the readers are a little bulky and are not easy to blend seamlessly into other equipment. If they are situated in a high-use environment, the platen surfaces will require periodic cleaning, both from an operational and especially an aesthetic point of view. Operationally, there are some sectors of the population, for example young children (under the age of twelve perhaps) and those with physical disability such as advanced arthritis, who will not be able to easily use these readers and this factor should be taken into account when planning a system, especially if a broad public user base is anticipated. The leading hand geometry device does offer a partial solution to this by effectively bypassing the verification process for nominated individuals, provided they enter the correct PIN number (or have possession of a valid token) but this is not ideal. Due to its physical bulk, the hand geometry reader is perhaps not well suited to applications such as PC or network access control and consequently there has been little effort to develop the methodology in this direction, either by manufacturers or third parties. Similarly, it is hard to envisage the use of hand geometry in association with telecommunications devices, where fingerprints and voice patterns might provide useful benefits, or seamlessly integrated into everyday processes where lower cost methodologies might be more attractive. However, there are still many applications where hand geometry biometrics can prove invaluable, as the relatively large number of installed devices around the world testifies.

In conclusion, hand geometry provides for a good general purpose biometric, with acceptable performance characteristics and relative ease of deployment coupled to a low learning curve for users. The leading product offers good flexibility in its configuration, at least within the manufacturer's framework of intended application, catering for stand-alone or networked use. As previously mentioned, there will be some applications to which the physical size and construction of the readers will not be suited, but these may be few and mostly self-evident within the early stages of systems design.

## 3.3 Iris scanning

Iris scanning is one of the particularly interesting biometrics. It is tempting to think of the iris as a straightforward mechanism for controlling the amount of light passing through the 'lens' of the eye and focused on the retina, but the iris is in fact an interesting and complex structure which serves us well as an individual identifying feature. Irises were first thought to be unique when ophthalmologists noticed that iris patterns were not only very individual but didn't seem to change with age. Further study of clinical photographs spanning several decades served to confirm this and the idea of the iris being at least as unique as a fingerprint was established. It was additionally discovered that not only was the iris pattern unique to the individual, but that left and right irises themselves were unique within the same individual. Furthermore, this is true of family siblings and even identical twins, where other genetic details such as facial appearance are so similar. The texture of the iris is made up of a complex fibrous and elastic structure sometimes referred to as the trabecular meshwork, the fine detail of which is established prior to birth and remains intact throughout the life of the individual. This provides us with a unique personal identification feature which is not easily tampered with and offers scope for evaluation via a non-contact process.

Of course, uniqueness is one thing, but capturing this uniqueness for the purposes of automated identity verification is quite another. There are some theoretical benefits in that the iris tends to be of a somewhat regular polar geometry making it easy to develop a co-ordinate system for feature recognition, but then there is also the fact that the iris surface tends to be mobile as the pupil expands and contracts, a point which needs to be taken into consideration. In addition, the visible portion of the iris will tend to differ according to ethnic origin and genetic inheritance and in some individuals with particularly dark eyes, there is the question of how easily the boundaries between pupil and iris may be identified.

Having decided upon an image capture methodology utilising available CCD camera technology, the first thing is to identify and locate the presence of an iris within the video image. This can be thought of in terms of the application of a circular edge detector to define the distinct boundary between the iris and the white tissue of the eye (sclera) followed by further refinement in order to distinguish the boundary between the iris and pupil. It is then necessary to describe circular contours of increasing radius in order to create zones of analysis which maintain reference to the same portions of the iris, irrespective of pupil resizing activity. Parts of the iris occluded by the eyelids or eyelashes, or corrupted by specular reflections from the cornea or from eyeglasses, are detected and masked out so that they do not influence the encoding of the iris code. It must also be acknowledged that the pupil is rarely absolutely central to the iris and might be shifted by up to

15%. Because of the constant movement inherent in the pupil and iris relationship (a factor which additionally provides evidence of a live sample as opposed to a static recreated image) multiple image frames are captured in rapid succession until the presence of a suitable and bona fide image is confirmed. The user can observe the process via a reflected image of the eye present in the capture device, which also serves as an aid for the user to focus and stabilise the image ready for processing.

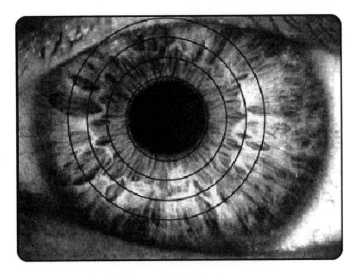

Figure 3.5 Iris texture

Having produced our zones of analysis we must now examine the texture of the iris for distinguishing features within these zones. This is achieved by the application of 2-D Gabor filters which provide information about orientation and spatial frequency of minutiae within the image sectors. From this information a 256 byte iris code is produced as a representation of the features of the individual iris. Naturally, some irises contain a richer count of distinguishing features than others, but much consideration has been given to the commensurability of the resultant iris codes in order to facilitate ease and speed of comparison. It is a credit to the algorithms used in iris scanning (created by Dr. John Daugman) that the entire process of image capture, zoning, analysis and iris code creation is typically undertaken in less than one second. The efficiency of the iris codes also facilitates the searching of large databases at up to 40,000 templates per second on a 486 PC in order to locate an individual. In the matching process, high-confidence decisions can be made, even with slight mismatches between templates, due to the general robustness of the iris codes and the amount of information contained therein.

Potential applications for iris scanning biometrics are widespread and installations have been undertaken in the financial sector for ATMs, for more general access control in several sectors and various high-security applications.

The inherent high accuracy of iris scanning lends itself to applications where perhaps a higher degree of certainty around individual identity verification is required.   In current implementations of the technology there usually exists a certain amount of user interaction in order to properly locate the image for comparison due to variances in individual stature etc., but it is essentially a non-contact approach and therefore relatively non-intrusive.   One could perhaps foresee certain applications where the verification or identification process (iris scanning is one of the few biometric methodologies that work well in identification mode) could be undertaken with no particular interaction with the user, and it will be interesting to see how things develop in this context.   Questions are often raised about spectacle wearers or those who favour contact lenses and how this affects the performance of iris scanning.   In fact, the iris-scanning process has been found to work well with both spectacle and contact lens wearers.   In the majority of cases, spectacle wearers may leave their spectacles in place without affecting performance.

In conclusion, iris scanning represents a high accuracy biometric for appropriate applications.   One needs to consider the user interface and mechanical requirements, which may not be suitable for some applications.   In addition, the installed cost may be currently a little higher than with some methodologies; however, this is all relative to the application under consideration and the associated perceived benefits of introducing a biometric into the process.

## 3.4 Retina scanning

Retinal scanning devices were available commercially before iris scanning was developed and have been utilized in various military and other high-security applications for some time. The leading vendor organization was founded in the late 1970s and has produced an ever evolving line of retinal scanning products, providing it with unique experience and insight into this technology. Whilst the technique has often been applauded for its relatively high accuracy in terms of false acceptance, it must be said that the user interface has not always appealed to users outside of the typical high security environment. This is largely because users were required to look into either a binocular or monocular receptacle and focus their vision on a central point, an action which in early implementations of the technology required physical contact with the reader and with which some users were not comfortable. Whilst the process has been subsequently refined so as not to require actual physical contact, it might be argued that it is still not as friendly or intuitive a process as is the case with some of the other biometric methodologies. For example, spectacle wearers must take off their spectacles before using the device, a requirement that could be a little inconvenient in some situations. This slight awkwardness of operation is unfortunate as the technology tends to work well and much thought has gone into the development of the leading product. In addition, retinal scanning is a biometric technique which lends itself well to operation in identification as well as verification modes. This is partly because the biometric being used is relatively stable as well as being considered unique, making for reliable and efficient matches.

The principle behind retinal scanning is that the blood vessels at the retina provide a unique pattern which may be used as a tamper-proof personal identifier. The relative uniqueness of retinal vascular patterns was discovered in 1935 when doctors studying eye diseases found that the patterns were both intricate and stable and subsequently published a paper on the potential use of retinal photographs for identity purposes. Additional research was undertaken in following years, leading to the conclusion that the retinal vascular pattern was as unique a personal identifier as might be found, even among identical twins. Furthermore, this characteristic is not subject to wear in the way that a fingerprint might be for example and is relatively impervious to fluctuations of individual health and other external influences, making it a good choice for a biometric. A side effect of this is that a good quality retinal scan template will not need to be periodically updated, as is desirable with some other biometrics, as the trait is inherently stable to begin with.

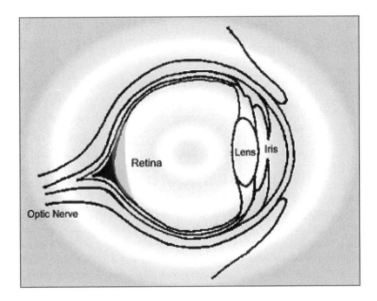

Figure 3.6  Principal components of the eye

To read this characteristic, a low intensity light source is utilized in order to scan the vascular pattern at the retina. This involves a 360° circular scan of the area taking over 400 readings in order to establish the pattern of the blood vessels. This is then reduced to 192 reference points before being distilled into a digitised (96 byte) template and stored in memory for subsequent verification purposes. Naturally, a certain amount of precision is required in order to locate the eye in a suitable position for scanning, hence the need for a receptacle as described, the use of which enables the user to focus on a central point in order to align the eye ready for verification. Phase compensation within the software allows for minor variations in head placement. The verification process itself takes around 1.5 seconds, which is a little longer than with some other techniques, however the difference may be regarded as academic in most situations. An adjustable threshold biases the device between the likelihood of false accepts or false rejects as with most other biometric systems, although with retinal scanning the scales seem to be tipped firmly towards an especially low likelihood of false accepts. This makes the technique an attractive proposition for very high security applications where occasional false rejects are preferable to an impostor being able to defeat the system.

In conclusion, retinal scanning is hardly the most user-friendly biometric technique, but it does promise high levels of accuracy where this is the primary requirement. It can also operate satisfactorily in identification mode, although the individual transaction time will depend somewhat on the size of the database being searched. The leading product is well conceived from a systems perspective and should be easily implemented for most applications.

## 3.5 Facial recognition

Of all the biometric techniques, facial recognition is perhaps the most fascinating in concept, especially to the layman who may tend to underestimate what is involved in reliably identifying individuals by their facial characteristics under real world operational conditions.

When considering facial recognition systems we might usefully subdivide into two primary groups. Firstly, there is what we might refer to as the 'controlled scene' group whereby the subject being tested is located in a known environment with a minimal amount of scene variation. For example, in a typical access control situation the subject will ordinarily be facing the camera at a fairly constant distance, producing a square on image of generally similar proportions. Secondly, there is what we might refer to as the 'random scene' group whereby the subject to be tested might appear anywhere within the camera scene, at various distances from the camera and in various degrees of axis from the straight ahead position. This situation might be encountered for example with a system attempting to identify the presence of an individual within a group or crowd. These two groups represent quite different propositions to the systems designer. In addition to these primary groups, there is the question of whether we require verification (a one-to-one match) or identification (a one-to-many match) functionality.

Let's consider a straightforward verification requirement within a controlled scene environment. The individual subjects to be tested will have been previously enrolled into the system and their facial images captured according to a predefined and repeatable process. When using the system, they will effectively be claiming an identity by calling up their stored image from the database via either an input PIN (personal identification number) or perhaps a card swipe or similar token-based action. The system now has to match the stored image from the database with the live sample being captured by the camera. Firstly, for the live sample it must confirm that a facial image is present within the scene and locate it in space accordingly. In most cases this will be relatively straightforward as the system may detect the edges of the head against the background scene and the subject will after all be relatively static. However, if the scene is subject to strong and random lighting changes, this may not be quite so easy as the tonal variations within the grey scale image seen by the camera may tend to fluctuate wildly, making it difficult to locate the edge reliably. Having captured the image, the system may typically work on the principle of locating and matching features within a grid. For example, the relative and actual position of the eyes, nose, mouth and ears within the grid. This may be achieved by grouping clusters of pixels together in order to determine the grey scale attributes of a given area. This may indeed be part of an initial refinement process which produces a binary image map for comparison with the stored template. With a one-to-one matching process, we can then sum the number of matching features and reference this to a system threshold setting in order to arrive at a simple match or no match conclusion for our identity verification process. If we are operating in identification mode, we must of course scan the database of templates in order to find the one which most closely matches the live sample, according to system threshold parameters, or indeed conclude that no stored sample matches to the required degree of precision. In any event, we have the basis for a user-friendly, non-contact biometric identity verification process which may be usefully deployed in a number of applications.

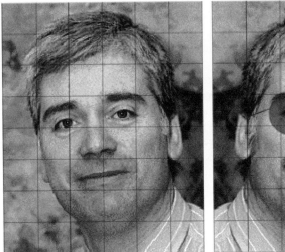

Figure 3.7 Facial recognition - is this the same person?

Now let us consider a random scene situation where we wish to identify an individual from within a group. Firstly, we must identify and locate within the scene anything that appears to be a human face, of which there may be many examples. Bear in mind that individual faces at varying distances from the camera will be represented as varying pixel cluster sizes within the overall scene. Also consider that faces may be square-on to the camera, in either left or right profile, facing away from the camera or anywhere in between, and will additionally be mobile while they are within the overall scene. This provides us with something of a challenge and some systems will stipulate that the facial image must be no more than a given number of degrees off axis from the straight ahead position if it is to be reliably detected. Having located the facial image within the scene we can then attempt to match it against either a single sample if we are looking for a specific individual, or against a database of individuals with whom we are interested, in either case attempting to match within predefined criteria. In the situation thus described, our database templates will need to contain adequate information about the individual if we are to reliably match them either in semi-profile or straight ahead aspects and at varying resolutions in relation to the scene. This is a factor that must be considered carefully by the system designer. It could be that we do not have adequate template information for certain individuals that we are particularly interested in, and they may be unlikely to volunteer for enrolment into our system. We should also understand that given individuals may appear within the scene for hugely varying amounts of time, providing us with equally varying opportunity to capture good quality facial images. In short, there are many variables which may make it realistic or otherwise to expect to reliably detect the presence of a particular individual in such a situation.

Of course, the random scene functionality, for which numerous and sometimes questionable claims have been made by vendors in recent times, is naturally attractive to many law enforcement and general security practitioners, offering the promise of positively identifying Knuckles McNasty as he wanders around the crowded avenue, attends football matches or arrives at the airport terminal. In practice, it may not be quite so easy, as real life randomness is often a little too random for automated systems to keep pace with, especially if Knuckles McNasty is on the case and has a vested interest in remaining incognito. We should remember that the human brain after many thousands of years of development has become pretty good at quickly recognising familiar individuals from within sometimes quite complex scenes. Computers still have a way to go before they can match this level of functionality and sophistication. However, within the facial recognition fraternity, much research continues to be undertaken, including the use of neural networks and other techniques in order to provide ever better tools - but we must be realistic as to the application of this technology in everyday environments, especially with respect to the random scene situation. In addition, one would like to see a little more emphasis on performance measurements for facial recognition biometrics.

In conclusion, facial recognition is a very interesting biometric technique which will no doubt continue to be developed in coming years as it does indeed offer potential for certain applications that could not be easily matched by other means. Its application does perhaps require a little more thought than with other biometrics and would probably be well suited to bespoke situations which can be carefully designed to accommodate the special requirements of this technique.

## 3.6 Voice verification

Voice verification was one of the early biometric examples in terms of commercially available products and could perhaps be considered a fairly natural technique as after all we use our voices in everyday conversation to expedite a number of transactions. It should therefore constitute an acceptable biometric from the user's perspective, provided we can get the interface right. Furthermore, one can imagine a broad range of applications where voice verification might prove to be a suitable technique.

The principle behind voice verification is that the physical construction of an individual's vocal chords, vocal tract, palate, teeth, sinuses and tissue within the mouth will affect the dynamics of speech. For example, if we ask two individuals of the same sex, of similar physical stature, born and raised in the same town and with the same regional accent to annunciate the same word or phrase into a microphone and then analyze the resulting waveforms of the recorded samples, we will find quite noticeable and repeatable differences, even though to our ears the two sound superficially alike. The same is true among brothers and sisters. We may think they sound alike, but there will always be some subtle difference that can be measured if captured correctly. Note that this is not just a question of the 'sound' of a spoken word or phrase, but the inherent dynamics of its annunciation. A good mimic may be able to produce a fairly convincing 'sound' of the phrase, but will not be able to easily replicate the overall dynamics of the original speaker. An obvious question is whether a tape recording of a spoken password could fool such a system. A very high quality recording played back through similarly high quality reproducing equipment might indeed fool some systems under carefully controlled laboratory conditions. However, to attain this level of quality we would require the use of professional studio quality equipment, hardly the sort of everyday kit one carries around in a business environment. Furthermore, one would appear a little conspicuous in this activity.

Early implementations of voice verification tended to take the form of a wall-mounted stand-alone device which users would be required to speak into in order to annunciate their password or phrase and be verified. There were some issues with this approach though. Firstly, at what height do you fix the device to the wall in order to cater for a mixed user base of varying physical stature? If you fix it in a comfortable position for a 6' 3" tall individual, it will be a struggle for a 5' 3" individual to operate successfully. They will be off-axis to the microphone and almost certainly suffer from a higher than normal rate of false rejections. Similarly, if you fix it at the right height for a 5' 3" individual, the 6' 3" person will have to stoop in order to use the device and will have difficulty being consistent. You might obviate this problem by employing a microphone element with a broad polar response pattern, but then you will also pick up a lot of unwanted background noise. Secondly, we have the problem of variable and sometimes unpredictable acoustics. For example, users may be enrolled into the system in a quiet office environment, under supervision and with plenty of time to create a good quality voice print. When they come to use the system at a remote reader, the local acoustics will be different - sometimes alarmingly so, and often significantly different from one reader to the next, causing each reader to 'hear' something a little different from the enrolled voice print. Furthermore, this local acoustic may change dynamically with the presence of fewer or more people in the vicinity, other items such as furniture being moved into the area, local doors or windows being open or shut and a variety of other factors. You could apply simple bandwidth filtering of the incoming signal to exclude some of the extraneous information, but extreme cases may still be problematic. One must therefore accept that environmental conditions will need to be taken into account with this type of free-standing voice verification device.

Another approach is of course to use a proximity transducer, such as a telephone handset for example. In this case the impact of the environmental acoustic is lessened as the user is much closer to the device and in a more consistent relational attitude to the microphone element. The quality and consistency of the microphone in mass-produced telephone handsets may be a little less than desired for our purposes, but we compensate for that in other ways. In fact, contemporary voice verification systems using this methodology can be very good at distinguishing between unwanted noise caused by either the environment or the communications path and the wanted signal, often employing a sophisticated pre processing stage to filter out extraneous noise before moving on to feature analysis and matching. Another advantage of using a standard telephone handset is of course that people are familiar with its use and do not need any special training, other than to follow the verification procedure.

There are several voice verification systems available. Some of them utilize their own proprietary matching algorithm, while some may licence the verification engine from a third party and build their own system around it. The important thing from the user perspective is how well the system operates in their specific application. Voice verification applications have largely fallen into two groups. That of conventional, physical access control, and the broader area of remote identity verification as may be utilized for prison inmates, on line transaction processing, automated call center applications and other similar areas. One could also foresee voice verification technology playing an important role from the marketing perspective in some industries. For example, with automated call centers there would be many potential benefits in having a high level of confidence as to the caller's identity in order to direct them smoothly through a given process, including access to confidential information, or to quickly call up individual details and transaction history for the operator in a manned situation. Then there are a raft of straightforward security access applications where voice verification might prove a valuable aid.

In conclusion, voice verification is surely a biometric methodology with considerable potential and it will be most interesting to follow developments in this area over the next few years.

## 3.7 Signature verification

Signature verification is a little unusual within this group in so far that it is a behavioral biometric rather than an anatomical biometric such as a fingerprint or iris pattern. However, one advantage with signature verification from a user's perspective is that it is perceived as a natural and familiar action. After all, we have been signing our name as a form of identity verification for years - thousands of years in fact, from the great civilisations of ancient Egypt, China and Mesopotamia through to the current day.

Some people were pretty good at signing their signature. In China, a calligrapher by the name of Wang Xizhi (AD 306-365) produced such beautiful writing that examples of his signature would be paid for in gold. Chinese calligraphy was indeed nothing less than an art form, which duly found its way around the world. In seventh century Japan for example, Chinese words called 'kangi' in Japanese were incorporated into the writings of Buddhist monks, who were themselves expert calligraphers. This newly evolved script which they named 'hiragana' was extremely beautiful and graceful in its appearance and perhaps the finest example of the written word that we shall witness. But what has all this got to do with 21st century biometrics? Well, simply that the mechanics of how we write is something very personal and often quite distinctive. Consider for a moment the famous manuscript of Beethoven's third symphony, the Eroica. Beethoven's hand inscribes the title page and dedicates it to Napoleon. When he finds that Napoleon has the audacity to proclaim himself emperor, he picks up his pen and angrily scratches out Napoleon's name, with such a force that it tears through the paper itself. Both the original inscription and the subsequent 'alteration' were actions very personal to Beethoven. Nobody else would have done it in quite the same way. OK, Beethoven was quite an exceptional human being, but us lesser mortals also have a distinctive way of writing and signing our name. Graphologists (those who study handwriting) would suggest that not only can they identify a person from examples of handwriting, but that they can also determine character traits, although there is no scientific support for this last factor. In any event, our signature and the way we sign it is considered as a unique enough identity verification methodology for a variety of personal transactions.

Biometric signature verification seeks to analyze not only the appearance of our signature, but the dynamics inherent in writing it. How hard do we press down on the writing surface? How quickly do we execute the first pen stroke? How does the writing speed vary from the beginning to the end of the signing process? How long does it take on average to write a given signature? How and when do we cross the letter 'T'? There are a number of such parameters inherent within the dynamic process of signing our signature. In addition, there exist several appearance-related factors such as the overall scale and proportions of different elements of the signature. A given signature verification system will typically utilize a combination of these and other features in order to verify the identity of the signatory against the stored template information for that person.

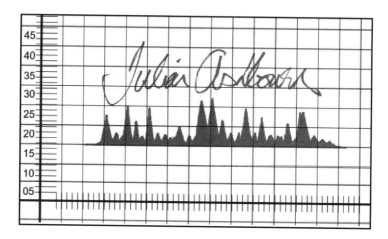

Figure 3.8 Capturing signature dynamics

Most biometric systems require multiple samples of the biometric in order to create a template and the same is especially true of signature verification, where it is important to gain a truly representative signature at the time of enrolment. The enrolment process and environment in which it is undertaken should therefore be carefully considered in this context. A properly instructed enrolee in a relaxed environment will no doubt produce a good quality template and therefore reliable subsequent verification transactions. An improperly instructed enrolee in a pressured environment might perhaps supply erratic signatures which are not truly representative, leading to problems at verification time. Some signature verification systems may provide an ongoing learning facility whereby each successful verification sample is taken and averaged with the existing template in order to provide an increasingly refined and representative template for that particular individual. This process, while not unique to signature verification, is perhaps especially pertinent in this case, particularly if the initial template was sub-optimal.

Applications for signature verification might include any where the signature is currently used as an identifier. Financial transactions such as cheque or credit card signing come to mind, as well as signatures on legal or otherwise important documents. Specialist applications involving the issuance and subsequent access of engineering drawings might be an interesting area, as might be the sign off of project or budget plans by an authorised manager, possibly remotely over a network. Then there is the area of signatures on audited accounts, signatures of those claiming state benefits, signatures on medical prescriptions and a whole raft of other areas where the appliance of biometric technology may provide additional and useful benefits. It is a curiosity that, in spite of the ease of use, numerous potential applications and general user-friendliness of signature verification, as a biometric methodology it has not to date enjoyed the scale of success of some of the other techniques such as hand geometry or fingerprints. Perhaps this reflects the relative maturity of the technology, or maybe the ease with which it is typically implemented? Maybe users would like to see the seamless integration of signature verification technology into existing processes in a way that makes it invisible to them as a separate technology? An example of this is the use of the signature to access functions within hand-held computing devices such as the popular Palm Pilot. This makes sense as there is already a writing tablet and stylus methodology inherent in the device itself and the addition of signature verification may be perceived as a relatively small step.

In conclusion, there have been some good products in this area and some relatively successful trials of the overall technique, but perhaps signature verification needs to be implemented in a way that catches our imagination a little more strongly.

## 3.8 Other biometric techniques

The above examples of biometric methodologies represent the currently popular techniques. However, there are several others, some of which have come and gone, some of which are under active development and some of which may not progress beyond the theoretical. Vein pattern scanning is an interesting idea whereby the veins in the back of the hand and wrist are scanned while the user grips a bar within the reading device. As a biometric technique it has the advantage of being relatively tamper-proof and not easily damaged by minor surface abrasions in the way that fingerprints could be for example. However, it hasn't to date really been able to compete with the more popular methods. The use of individual scent is a somewhat more controversial idea, although there are many questions that remain unanswered with this technique, especially around relative uniqueness and the ease or otherwise of capturing an individual's scent pattern. Perhaps we shall see someone develop this idea further, but at the present time it is not really a practical methodology. Various alternative parts of the anatomy have also been considered for a biometric including ear lobes and other areas, although it is perhaps hard to understand why these should be used instead of the more established techniques. Another interesting idea that was the focus of much research was that of keystroke dynamics, whereby the highly individual way that a user interacts with a computer keyboard was considered as a potentially unique identifier. This concept seemed to stall at a certain point and never really made it as a mainstream biometric, but who knows? Someone may pick it up again at some point in the future. Then there are the ideas that represent a little lateral thinking, such as the biometric watch for example. The idea being that the watch would be capable of interacting with other devices and providing an authentication signal, provided it is on the wrist of the correct person. This has the attraction of being something of a personal consumer item whilst additionally placing the management of the biometric in the hands of the user, if the enrolment process were to be intuitive and straightforward enough for the average user to understand and complete. This is a very interesting concept, whether the device be a watch or some other personal item capable of holding a biometric template, because we are effectively empowering the user with not only the management of his or her template, but also the occasions for use. This might represent an interesting area for further research.

There are other ideas of course, together with countless variations on the themes of the established methodologies. No doubt in time we shall see some more radical thinking in both methodologies, device design and applications, but for now, the techniques referred to above represent the popular implementations of biometric verification and identification and hopefully serve to give the reader a basic understanding of the principal exponents of this technology. The next few years may adjust our thinking somewhat in this context, especially if more large-scale public implementations of biometric technology are undertaken and there is commonality of approach as to the methodology used. However, that is quite another story.

# 4. Identification, verification and templates

In this chapter we shall examine the distinction between identification and verification, the management of biometric templates and the impact this has on systems design, and we shall also take a look at the question of established performance criteria and how this relates to actual system performance. These are all issues which are important to understand if we are contemplating the use of biometrics. Furthermore, they are factors which should be considered in advance of any detailed planning with respect to biometric systems design.

## 4.1 Identification and verification - the distinction

People sometimes misuse the term 'identification' with respect to biometric systems. The way in which the majority of biometric systems work is in verification mode. The two operations are in fact significantly different and it is worth taking some time to explore this. Let's start off with verification as this is the more widely-used operating methodology.

With biometric verification systems the enrolled user has a template residing on the system which is firmly associated with that user, usually referenced by a user number, which may in fact be the record number within the database. When a transaction is undertaken the user firstly calls up this particular template from the system database by inputting this specific user number. This may be achieved via a familiar numerical keypad, or via the reading of a token such as a card or proximity key fob. The correct template is called and held in memory ready for comparison with the live sample about to be provided by the user. The user then provides his or her sample biometric and the comparison takes place, resulting in a binary true or false condition as to the identity of that user. The user is in effect claiming an identity by inputting the reference number and the system is subsequently verifying that the claim is genuine or otherwise, according to the matching criteria setup within the system. From a technical perspective the system has a relatively straightforward task to perform. We are supplying it with two sets of information (the two template representations) and asking it to compare the two according to a predefined matching threshold. In simplistic terms we are saying, 'look at these two sets of information and if you find 'x' or greater matching points return a 'true' condition, or if you find less than 'x' matching points return a 'false' condition'. With a robust algorithm and good quality templates this process works well and is accurate enough to substantiate the identity claim, or otherwise, in the vast majority of cases.

A system operating in identification mode (an area in which only a handful of systems are currently competent) is attempting something quite different. In this case, a database of templates associated with users is present in the same manner as before. However, the user does not claim one of these identities by calling up a specific template from memory, but instead simply provides his or her biometric sample and expects to be recognized by the system as an authorised user. From a technical operation perspective this is a different kettle of fish altogether as the system has a heck of a lot more work to do. Firstly, it has to recognize that it has received a suitable quality template submittal and then run off to search through the entire database of templates in order to find the matching one and return a specific user reference accordingly. We are in effect saying, 'here is a template, please tell me who it is'. But this is not as straightforward as it sounds. Firstly, what if none of the templates within the database match the submitted sample particularly well? Do you return the user ID of one which is 'sort of' like the submitted sample, or do you reject the transaction altogether? OK, for this condition we can configure a minimum matching criterion and ask the system to reject any claims which fall below this point. But what if there are several templates within the database which qualify as a potential match? Does the system make an arbitrary decision and say 'I think it's this one'? A bit like sticking a pin in a list of names from a telephone directory - or do we require a greater rationalisation process? Let's think about this a little more. Supposing you had a database of just five user templates and the users concerned represented a mix of sexes and genetic origin, providing distinctly different templates. In this situation, the system would not have too difficult a task as none of the stored templates are particularly alike and it could probably reliably identify each of these five users time and time again. Now supposing you take on extra staff and you now have ten users. The number of the same sex will certainly be increased and there will be a greater chance of similarity between the templates. Sarah and Helen may actually appear as rather similar to the system and it may have to think carefully in order to distinguish between them, but it can probably do so easily enough with a database of ten users. Now let's suppose that your organization merges with another and you now have fifty users enrolled into the system. Furthermore, there are two sets of brothers within this mix, one pair of which are twins. Now our system is really having to do some work. When Gary provides his biometric, the system may discover that actually seven templates meet the potential matching criteria. Perhaps two of these return a significantly lower matching 'score' and can therefore be eliminated from the process. Maybe one of the remaining five is a little questionable so we shall drop that one also, but it still leaves four. Now imagine your database grows to one hundred users. Now imagine it has grown to five thousand users. Now consider that you have a database of twenty-five thousand users - not inconceivable among large organizations. As you will appreciate, we are asking quite a lot of a system if we expect it to reliably return the correct identity of an individual from within a database of twenty-five thousand templates.

The key to whether a system can perform well in this mode of operation lies in the confidence level of the matching process. This in turn requires a sufficient level of uniqueness among the generated templates. Certain systems such as iris scanning and retina scanning can work well in identification mode, although we may still like to consider the implications of large databases. Certain fingerprint systems also offer an identification mode of operation, although they usually point out that this may be more or less reliable with databases beyond a certain size. From a user's perspective we might usefully ask the question of why we wish to operate in one mode or the other. Naturally, verification mode is a much simpler prospect, within which we can engineer a certain amount of flexibility for users according to the level of security required. In addition, system performance will typically be good as we are undertaking a straightforward one-to-one comparison which does not require too much 'horsepower' from the system. Alternatively, identification mode is certainly a realistic prospect with some methodologies, but not with all, and we should understand that searching through large databases takes a little longer than comparing two templates. In reality, this will depend upon the methodology chosen, the system architecture and the specification of the core system components, but it is conceivable that performance may be impacted to some degree.

In conclusion, whether you choose a verification or identification system will depend upon the application under consideration and how well you believe biometric technology can deliver the expected benefits. It is recommended that the prospective user undertakes some sort of trial or pilot system in this context.

## 4.2 Template management

We have already discussed templates in so far as their relevance to the overall concept of biometrics and the matching process is concerned, however, there are other factors which should be taken into consideration when considering the implementation of a biometric system.

The biometric template is the digital representation of the sampled characteristic from the user and different methodologies and systems create templates of varying size. For example, the leading hand geometry device boasts a raw template size of only 9 bytes whilst a typical fingerprint device may create a template of several hundred bytes or more and some biometric devices create raw templates exceeding 1k bytes in size, or perhaps larger if other data is included. The size of the template has implications for how it is stored and retrieved and also for overall systems architecture in terms of numbers of users per point of transaction. If a device is storing templates internally (as many do) then the designer would have made some decisions concerning memory capacity and usage. For example, within a given specification the designer may have allowed for a certain number of transactions to be stored in memory and also a certain number of templates. Typically, you will find many devices which have an internal capacity of around 1000-1500 templates, whilst some exceed this number, depending on template size and available memory. Obviously the devices creating smaller templates have something of an advantage in this respect. But what if you have a user base of 20,000 and your chosen device can only store 1000 templates? Then we have to consider other ways of providing the appropriate template for comparison. Some of the options are as follows:

1. The template is stored internally within a single device.

2. Multiple devices on a closed loop network may share templates between them within a distributed database architecture.

3. The template may be stored on a central database and downloaded to the biometric device at the time of transaction.

4. The template may be stored on portable media such as a card or token and loaded into the device by the user at the time of transaction.

Let's examine these options in more detail. Firstly, in number one above the situation is as previously described with an independently deployed biometric device holding a number of templates within its internal memory. This may be fine if the numbers of users involved fall well within the capacity of the device, and also if there is a practical way of backing up and restoring the database in the case of device failure. If you have laboriously enrolled 750 users into your single device and then one week later it decides to roll over and die, you will not be very pleased. Such a device should therefore feature a communications port and a backup utility for both the template and systems data.

In option number two above, a network of units may be able in some cases to share a distributed database with individual templates residing mainly within the devices where they are most used. For example, if your chosen device can store 1000 templates and you have a local network of ten such devices, then you may be able to store 10,000 templates provided the network allows you to access templates across devices. In this scenario, if user number 3579 inputs his PIN at reader number 3, the device will first scan its own database for the template and if it cannot be found will send a message out across the network asking if another reader has this template. If the answer is yes, it will be transferred back to reader number 3 in order for the comparison with the live sample to take place. This is quite feasible if the network has been designed in this manner, in which case one of the readers may be designated as the network master and will act as a central point of interface for data backups etc. alternatively, the network master may be a PC attached to the network for management and control purposes. There may be some slight performance implications here if most of the users use most of the readers most of the time as there will obviously be a fair amount of network traffic resulting from template management, although on a properly designed proprietary network one would expect this to be minimal.

In option number three above, the templates are stored on a central database and only downloaded to the reader when a request for verification is made. This has the promise of accommodating very large databases irrespective of the chosen biometric device, but also introduces some additional issues of its own according to the systems architecture. Firstly, we are introducing some additional processes to the verification transaction. When the user claims an identity by inputting the template reference number, the system must make a request to the remote database. The database in turn must acknowledge the request and run off to find the requested template before sending it back across the network to the reader in question, hopefully with some data encryption and transmission error checking involved at the appropriate points. The transaction may now go ahead and if successful the template, which may now be modified slightly, can be returned to the database, again with the appropriate encryption and error checking. This may be fine on a small high-performance local network with infrequent traffic, but what about a large enterprise-wide network which is also used for other purposes and features a large number of biometric readers with a usage pattern that peaks at certain times of the day? If one of these peaks coincides with a peak of activity from an unrelated process which shares the network, then the user may experience some delay in receiving their template. An understandable reaction in such a scenario is to assume the request didn't get through and key in your user number again, and again, thus compounding the problem. If several users are doing this simultaneously and other non-related network traffic continues to rise, you can imagine the result. In addition to this usage-related situation, there is the stability and integrity of the network itself to take into consideration, especially if we are dealing with a complex enterprise-wide system perhaps spread over several buildings with all the attendant routers and hubs, not to mention the spaghetti joining it all together. Of course a competent systems installer will know better than to tie the data cables to the main 415v building supply for support, won't he? And all those nasty switching devices and relays that control the various building services will all be properly suppressed, won't they? And the various generations of additional circuitry will all comply with the strictest architectural specifications, won't they? And we need not even mention that all data cables will be of the highest quality and terminated to perfection. Anyone who has had the dubious pleasure of supporting a large network within a multi-site situation will understand that actual network performance can be affected by a thousand and one things, many of which are outside of the immediate control of the network administration team. If we extrapolate this situation to that of an equally large multi-tenanted site, perhaps in a public area, then the situation becomes even more interesting. We haven't even considered yet the processors themselves, the database software and any interfaces which need to be provided. Add all of this together and one can appreciate that any such system needs to be carefully considered and designed with copious amounts of system redundancy built in. That's not to say that such a system needn't be perfectly reliable and functional, but that it does require some quality planning. We must also ensure that we calculate correctly for the number of potential users (which may be high in a public system) and understand the worst case scenarios and how these will affect the operation of the system as a whole. No doubt we shall also pay attention to data backup and recovery scenarios both for templates, transactions and system-related data. In such a system an organization might be wise to have the IT department manage the project together with the biometric vendor.

In option number four above, the template is stored on portable media and becomes the responsibility of the user. This portable media may be a humble magnetic stripe card, a contact chip card or perhaps a non-contact rf device. In this scenario the user carries their template around with them and loads it into the biometric device for comparison. This has the advantage that we don't need to rely absolutely on the network for the provision and integrity of the template (although in some cases we may still wish to have the central database as a fallback) and also that we will not experience any network-induced delays for the verification transaction. Of course, we have incurred a certain amount of cost in the provision and management of the tokens and we shall need to have a suitable process in place for when a user inevitably loses or misplaces their token, but to place this in perspective, we seem to manage this issue tolerably well with large access control systems. Another element of this approach is that, depending on system design, the user can take comfort in that they have possession of their template and it is not stored on some distant database or flying around a network. There is a psychological factor here which may be of greater pertinence in some situations than others, but it is an interesting one nonetheless. If we do use a portable token for template storage, we must consider how this will work with devices which update the template at each successful transaction. Assuming that we wish to retain this functionality, we may like to ensure that the original template is not deleted until the revised one is confirmed as being safely back on the token. There are various ways of achieving this but the template size and available storage space on our preferred token may need to be carefully considered.

The four options above represent typical ways of managing template data. A bespoke system may take some other approach, possibly utilising a combination of the above in order to provide a robust and reliable system, depending upon the precise application. Hopefully this section has raised the issue of template management and made the point that it is a factor which should be taken into consideration with any proposed biometric application of a sizeable nature, especially those within the public domain.

## 4.3 Performance criteria

This is a subject upon which those closely involved with the biometrics industry can ponder for hours, often with no further resolution. The snag is, as with many things, laboratory measurements and theory do not necessarily translate into real life experience. This is not so much a flaw in accepted biometric performance criteria, but a realisation of the many variables that together make up the perceived performance of a given device or system, some of which are outside of the scope of the system designer. In light of this situation, when a vendor makes performance claims for his particular device, which on paper may look quite impressive, one is tempted to ask, by what means did they arrive at these figures? Was it as a result of a thorough and detailed testing program? Or was it perhaps based on some initial tests accompanied by some extrapolated mathematics in order to arrive at likely figures? Or perhaps there were no tests at all, just calculations based upon the perceived uniqueness of template data?  If tests were conducted, what was the profile of the user base?  How many individuals were involved?  1000?  100?  10?  Did they represent a typical cross section of genetic make-up?   Under what conditions and time scales were these tests undertaken?   In what environment?  This is the sort of detail missing from quoted specifications, and until we come up with a universally agreed and accepted methodology for quantifying and describing biometric device performance in a manner which reflects real life operational conditions, we shall always find it difficult to compare like with like or relate the quoted specifications with our proposed implementation.

However, we have to start somewhere and the commonly quoted parameters of false rejects (type 1 errors) and false accepts (type 2 errors) are perhaps as good a place as any.  False rejects refer to the likelihood (in transaction percentage terms) of an authorised user being wrongly rejected by the system.  False accepts refer to the likelihood of an impostor being wrongly accepted by the system.   The majority of biometric devices incorporate a sliding threshold adjustment which may be thought of as a tightening or relaxing of the template matching criteria.  Thus, we can make the system easier to use by relaxing the threshold adjustment, at the expense of an increased likelihood of false accepts, or we can tighten the threshold to reduce the likelihood of false accepts at the expense of an increased likelihood of false rejects.  For a given device, a curve may therefore be plotted to show the effect of the threshold adjustment. In an ideal world, the curve may look something like Figure 4.1.

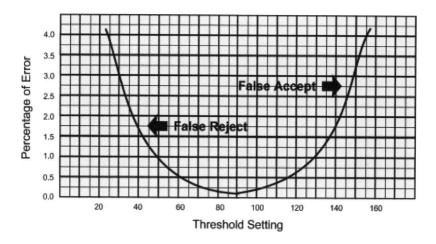

Figure 4.1 An ideal performance curve

In this example, the two curves showing instances of false accepts and false rejects meet at a point of zero error at an arbitrary threshold setting of 90 on this particular scale.  Adjusting the threshold setting may bias the device in either direction, although in this case there would be little point in a lower threshold setting (biased towards increased false rejects) as we are already suggesting that there will be no false accepts.  We might decide to increase the threshold setting and the likelihood of false accepts if we found it made the system easier to use, although again, we are suggesting that there would be no false rejects at a setting of 90.

Naturally, in the real world things are not so clear cut and typically devices will not meet this ideal curve. A more representative picture may be that of Figure 4.2 whereby the two curves intersect at a point above zero error.

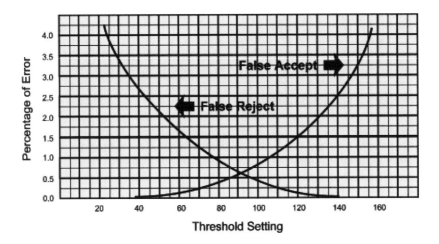

Figure 4.2 A more typical performance curve

In this example, we can see that while we cannot achieve a position of zero false accepts and zero false rejects, by adjusting the threshold setting we can at least bias the device performance in one direction or the other. For example, if we are adamant that we do not want any false accepts under any conditions we might set the threshold to 40. On the graph above, this would result in a likely false reject figure of 2.75%. On the other hand, we may decide that we definitely do not want to reject a valid user and will be prepared to tolerate a small likelihood of false accepts as a consequence. Setting our threshold to 140 on the above scale would achieve this but would result in a likely false accept figure of 2.5%. As you will appreciate, the setting of any such threshold parameter will always represent something of a compromise (unless somebody designs a perfect biometric device) and this will depend very much on the application in question.

In Figure 4.2 the two curves are shown as approximately equal for the sake of clarity. In reality this is very rarely the case, with most devices being stronger in one direction than the other. For example, a device which claims extraordinarily good false accept performance may be notably weaker when it comes to false rejects. This can be a little confusing for the potential user when reading the specifications, especially if different vendors express the figures to a different level of granularity. It is sometimes more meaningful therefore to compare the figure at the point where the two curves meet. This is expressed as the 'equal error rate' and will perhaps provide you with a more easily understood and comparable metric with which to compare published performance criteria, provided that the manufacturers in question do indeed publish this figure. You will note that our theoretical device in Figure 4.2 has an equal error rate of around 0.6%. This may appear favourable compared with a device that stipulates an equal error rate of 1.5%; however, these figures only tell part of the story as we shall see later on. Certain manufacturers and others in the industry are starting to question whether the traditional false reject and false accept figures are adequate expressions of performance; however, until there is some universally accepted alternative, they are the closest we have to a comparable metric of performance across devices.

There are other parameters which are of interest to the systems designer and these revolve around the timings of enrolment and subsequent transactions. This may at first seem somewhat academic, but if you are dealing with large numbers of users these are very real issues that need to be considered. If you plan on enrolling 20,000 users into your system, the difference between a 12 second enrolment window and a 3 minute enrolment window becomes significant. Similarly, the average successful transaction time will help you determine the logistics of handling 20,000 or more transactions at peak time within a given environment. Actual transaction times also influence the user's perspective of the system as a whole and how easy it is to interface with it. In both enrolment and subsequent use, proper guidance and training is important and the systems designer must take this into account when planning the implementation of a given system. The timings referred to above are important in this context and will influence the content of such a training program. Do you think this has anything to do with performance? Read on.

## 4.4 Additional performance criteria

As mentioned earlier, the regularly quoted device performance metrics only tell part of the story. A complete transaction (successful or otherwise) requires two primary players, the biometric device and the user, with perhaps the user interface acting as the referee. The biometric device has some performance characteristics which are relatively constant, provided it is fed with appropriate information. The user on the other hand has a broader variety of performance characteristics, some of which are not constant at all and many of which may be influenced heavily by external forces and conditions. This situation can sometimes make a mockery of the device manufacturer's published performance figures.

Let me introduce you to two individuals who are about to be enrolled into a fingerprint biometric system used for controlled access into a computer laboratory. Heather is a newly graduated student of computer science in her first commercial role as an analyst and developer. She is interested in technology and happy to accept and absorb the working environment around her. Frank was trained originally in mainframe programming and has since taken over the hardware and network support role for the laboratory as his programming skills are not quite so relevant to the organization now. He was against the implementation of a biometric access control device and was happier with the previous arrangement whereby he had the keys to the labs and effectively controlled access himself. He is also rather sceptical that a fingerprint device will be able to reliably distinguish between individuals and perform the role that was previously part of his responsibility. During the training and familiarisation process Frank expressed some doubts and concerns about the operation of the reader. In being advised on how to correctly place his finger for enrolment, he commented that the device was not up to the task if you had to have 'special procedures' for using it. Enrolling Frank was difficult and had to be undertaken twice due to inconsistencies in finger placement. Heather enrolled with no difficulty. A few practice runs confirmed that Frank was still inconsistent in how he approached and used the enrolment reader, leading to a number of errors caused by a combination of poor finger placement and not allowing the reader sufficient time to undertake the comparison. Heather was a little more measured in her approach and seemed to have no problems at all. The procedure for using the device was carefully explained once more and both users agreed that they understood and were comfortable with the concept. When the system went live and they came to use the actual reader by the laboratory door, Heather was delighted to find that she was accepted straight away by the system and thrilled to see the technology really working as planned. On seeing this, Frank tried hard to use the reader and was duly accepted on the second attempt. However on subsequent attempts he experienced increasing rejections and was becoming very frustrated by the whole thing. Typically, he would enter his PIN to call up his stored template and press his finger against the reader scanning surface. If there was no immediate reaction, he would start to move his finger around on the surface or sometimes remove it altogether and replace it impatiently back on the reader, an action usually accompanied by a verbal tirade against biometrics in general and this device in particular.

Now, let us consider the performance characteristics published by the manufacturer of this device. The manufacturer quoted a typical false rejection figure of 0.5%. With the threshold adjusted to bias the device towards ease of use (and lower likelihood of false rejects) this figure looked reasonable in Heather's case as, so far, she had not been rejected by the system at all. Frank's experience though was that he was lucky if he was accepted in one in five attempts - a false reject rate of around 80%. Re-enrolling and retraining Frank brought this down to a figure representing a false reject rate of around 20% in his case, with an acknowledgement that he would have to make a conscious effort to be both patient and consistent in the way he used the device. Note the difference between 0.5% and 20%, although we would expect Frank's false rejection rate to improve further with time. Is this an extreme story? Not at all. Different individuals have a different perception of technology and react differently when asked to interface to it. Experience to date shows that the majority of people will have no particular problem, provided that they are properly instructed in the use of the device and that they are comfortable with the overall concept. However, there will always be some individuals who struggle. Sometimes this will be due to infrequent use, sometimes because they just can't seem to grasp the procedure, sometimes because they are hostile towards the whole concept and sometimes because they have actual physical difficulty in using the device. These things must be taken into account when planning a system.

In the example given above, we have assumed that both Heather and Frank were given proper and adequate training by someone who really understood the system. Indeed, in Frank's case he was given additional guidance due to the problems he was experiencing. This is how it should be. But what would the situation be if this training was not available to the same degree? Suppose for a moment that the individual conducting the enrolment process was not very familiar with the process themselves and didn't really understand the concept anyway, resulting in a batch of variable quality reference templates. Further suppose that after the enrolment process this individual was no longer available for consultation, what effect would this have had on Frank's false reject performance? Of course, you wouldn't conduct an implementation in this way yourself - but some people have done. Also in this example, Heather and Frank were pretty reasonable folk really. They could understand technical concepts and were generally ready to listen to guidance and instruction in order to make the system work for them. Are all people like this? Not really; it's quite surprising how emotive the situation can become when someone is determined not to use such a system, or if they believe it is an infringement upon their personal rights by the management, in which case a little proactive 'marketing' might need to be undertaken.

From this we can deduce two things. Firstly, that human beings are complex devices with a multitude of variables that affect the way they behave and react to everyday situations. You can predict a certain amount, but you must always be ready for a few surprises. There are many psychological factors at play here, and they must be given the space to be understood and incorporated into the general scheme of things. Secondly, that training is of paramount importance and can have a significant effect on the subsequent realized performance of the system. The larger the user base, the more important this becomes and it must be planned and budgeted for as part of an implemented system.

We have loosely touched upon one or two of the people-related issues, but there are more. Let's visit Heather again. In our example system she was in a small contained environment, among friends and not under any pressure while using the system. She could take her time to use the biometric device studiously and ensure that her transaction was a successful one. Now let's take Heather and drop her into the middle of a busy international airport where she is required to use an automated border control system. There is a small but highly vocal queue of people behind her impatient to use the system, which incidentally has been performing badly all day due to network problems. This is the first time that Heather has used the live system and she is trying to remember the procedure as it was explained to her, whilst also looking around the booth for guidance. She is hot and perspiring a little due to being overdressed and is struggling with some awkward luggage items. She is also a little self-conscious as she is away from her home environment and on her own among strangers. Do you think that Heather will use the system as calmly and precisely as she does the one back in the office? I doubt it. Suppose that there is now a slight but unfamiliar delay in processing (due to the network problems). Heather does not understand what is going on and so, suspecting that maybe she has made an error, she registers her biometric again. The system gets itself in a loop and eventually cancels the whole transaction. The queue is becoming impatient. Heather is getting nervous. What affect is all this having on the real performance figures for this system? Are they as quoted by the vendor?

The reader must forgive me for laboring the point, but it is an important one. The degree to which a user understands and therefore correctly operates a system, coupled to environmental conditions and personal attitude, is as much a performance factor as any criteria published by the device manufacturer. Looking at published specifications in isolation is a bit like looking at the specification of a popular automobile. It may look good, but nothing actually happens until someone hops in and turns the key, after which it pretty much depends on the road ahead and the abilities of the driver.

## 4.5 Total system performance

So far, we have looked at device specifications and also acknowledged that the users themselves play a part in the realized performance of a biometric system. However, we are still not quite there with our understanding of performance issues as there are other factors to consider, especially with regard to the larger systems. Actual realized performance depends upon the users, the environment and the whole physical architecture of the implemented system. This is what I shall refer to as total system performance (TSP).

The concept of TSP is especially important when planning a system. We have the manufacturer's specifications for the chosen biometric device, but this device will not necessarily be deployed in isolation. More probably, it will be connected to a host PC, perhaps via a closed loop proprietary network, or maybe via an existing network. If the device depends upon communication with the host before it can make a verification decision, then obviously the performance of the host and the software running on it play a part in TSP. In such a situation, we should consider what is required of the host in terms of processing power and memory. Does the software require a particular operating system version in order to give of its best? Do we assume a particular version of system DLL's residing on the host? Should the CPU be of a specific type? Are there any additional requirements based upon our expected number of users? Has the vendor tested various scenarios in this context and can they advise you on these points? It is worth asking a few pertinent questions. Of course, there may be a few grey areas where it would be unrealistic to expect the vendor to have all the answers. For example, the vendor may know their own software inside out, but if you are integrating biometric functionality into an existing system and process, then that particular system is also going to play a part in TSP.

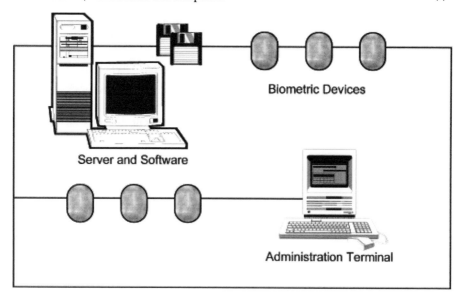

Figure 4.3 What does the total system look like?

The illustration above serves to remind us that there is usually a network involved somewhere, and that this also needs to be taken into account. If you plan on using an existing network, do you already have a good idea of the performance characteristics of this network? What about capacity planning? Does your LAN administrator have a good idea of available bandwidth and peak time traffic? This may seem like splitting hairs, and indeed it might be if we were only concerned with relatively small systems, but for larger systems or systems expected to be hosted on an existing infrastructure these may be pertinent points. Naturally all of this depends on what part the network plays in your overall systems design. If the verification process and subsequent output (for example in an access control situation) takes place entirely at the biometric device and the network is only used for communicating the result back to the host, then you will probably not be so concerned with the absolute performance of it (as long as it is reliable). If on the other hand, you need to pass template information back and forth across the network, then you will not want any additional delays to result in frustration at the user interface. Let's return for a moment to the software. If the verification engine is residing on a host somewhere on the network, has the vendor established the relative performance of this with the number of users you are anticipating? What happens with concurrent verification requests? Indeed, have you considered the likelihood of concurrent verification requests? Do you have any flexibility in this respect, perhaps around distributed processing? There may be a number of questions that you should consider in this context. In addition and as previously indicated, if you are integrating biometric functionality into an existing application of your own, there will be some interesting interfaces and relationships to understand, all of which may have some impact on overall performance.

We have very briefly considered the issue of what I refer to as 'total system performance', really just to make the point that it is a concept that should be understood and considered. It is curious that this hasn't always been the case and in some implementations of biometric technology overall performance has suffered as a result of ill-considered systems design. In conclusion, the actual realized performance of a biometric system depends on a number of related factors, each of which requires careful consideration. It is not just a matter of choosing a device, plugging it in and expecting to automatically and immediately obtain the performance levels quoted by the device manufacturer. We must additionally consider the profile of our users and how they are likely to use the system within our particular environment. We must also consider the overall systems architecture and how we might best implement the system in a way that makes sense for the number of users and the precise application requirements. This is all part of the performance paradigm.

# 5. Implementing biometrics

In the first chapter, I made reference to the ancient Egyptians and their use of biometric principles thousands of years ago. When people think of ancient Egypt they naturally think of the pyramids, astronomy and perhaps their endearing mythology. However, the ancient Egyptians were clearly very well organized and proficient in the more mundane day-to-day requirements of life. They were master shipbuilders, architects, farmers, manufacturers, scribes, administrators and if you think about it, by definition they must also have been pretty good project managers. Some of the staggering achievements of the ancient civilisations still baffle us today, in spite of our technically advanced society.

I mention this here because the practical implementation of a typical biometric project requires careful project management if it is going to be successful. This is especially true of the larger projects which may involve a mixture of hardware and software, some current, some legacy, from a variety of sources, to be implemented sometimes across multiple environments. In addition, there are a raft of user-related issues which need to be carefully considered and managed. It is easy to get carried away with discussions around the front end devices and theoretical performance coupled with a view of the potential benefits for your organization, but at the end of the day someone has to take responsibility for tying the whole thing together and getting it up and running. Past experience suggests that we could definitely do with a little ancient Egyptian project management guidance in this respect! On some occasions we have witnessed a 'too many cooks' situation, which together with a rather weak concept of ownership, has certainly led to sub-optimal end results, if not complete failures. It is usually easy with hindsight to identify where things have gone wrong in these situations and how perhaps they should have been managed, but it would be so much nicer to pre-empt any such difficulties within a carefully constructed plan and a sound understanding of the issues involved. Of course, this applies to any process-related project supported by technology, but it is especially the case with biometrics.

In this chapter we shall therefore examine some of the issues inherent in implementing a biometric system. Whilst this will not represent a blow-by-blow account of how to run a biometric project, it may perhaps highlight some of the areas worthy of special consideration by those contemplating such an initiative and provide a preliminary framework on which to build a suitably comprehensive plan.

## 5.1 Understanding the requirement

It sounds obvious, doesn't it? But sometimes there is a tendency to get carried away with the technology and what it *can* do, perhaps forgetting in the process what we actually *need* it to do. The first step therefore is to think clearly about why we think the adoption of biometric technology might be useful to us, and exactly how. This would often take the form of identifying an existing process and then considering how biometrics may be integrated in order to complement or enhance this process.

For example, let's consider a typical physical access control scenario. Assume that we already have a comprehensive access control system which includes all the functionality we really need for our organization plus a raft of management reports which have been carefully customised and refined over time. Furthermore, our facilities staff who manage this system are very familiar with it and have a good support and maintenance contract in place with the supplier, who has proved to be trustworthy and reliable. We would not particularly want to discard this system in order to implement a biometric solution as it serves our purposes well in all other respects. It would be far more appropriate, if possible, to simply integrate biometric identity verification into the existing system. Our requirement in this case is therefore quite straightforward. We are looking for a biometric methodology that can interface with our existing system while appearing invisible to the core system processing. In other words, our existing system neither knows nor cares whether a biometric has been involved in the user identity verification process, it just needs to receive the result, to which it will respond in the manner to which it has been programmed. In this hypothetical example, we would be looking for a biometric device which could emulate our existing token readers either in a stand-alone format, or in conjunction with the presentation of a token (access card). We might be impressed with some of the systems scenarios presented as possibilities by the vendors, but we shouldn't lose sight of our original objectives and reasons for looking at the technology in the first place. In this instance, the primary reason would have no doubt been that we were not sufficiently confident that the tokens being presented were being so by the bona fide individuals who were the original recipients. Perhaps we had a number of generic or 'visitor' tokens in circulation and/or our token management procedures had been slipping.

A slightly different case might be in the context of a call center whereby we would like to offer automated facilities to our customers provided we can have a high confidence level in the true identity of the caller. This may be in order to allow the caller to access private and personal information in regard to a customer loyalty scheme for example. In this instance, we would naturally need to identify exactly what information we have in mind, how this is stored and how we would utilize the verification result and user identity to retrieve and present this information. Once again, the bulk of the process lies externally to the biometric identity verification element and we must consider how to integrate the two. We would probably be looking for a verification engine and procedural process that can interface seamlessly with our existing technology and be manipulated in a familiar manner, perhaps via a scripting language for example. No doubt various vendors could describe some alternative or additional functionality that their particular product can provide - but this is not the point, we are looking for some specific functionality which, if it is not available off the shelf, we may have to provide on a bespoke basis.

The point I am making here is that the biometric functionality should be under consideration as an enhancement of the business process - not the other way around. We must be clear about our requirements and understand to what degree contemporary technology can provide what we are looking for. If we allow ourselves to be swayed by the various possibilities on offer, we are in danger of losing sight of the potential benefits of the technology to our particular situation. That is not to say that we should be blind to new ideas that may not have previously occurred to us, but that we must at all times keep things in perspective and directly related to our base requirements. In almost all cases, these requirements will be process driven. In other words, we have identified a business or organizational process which we believe would benefit from the enhanced personal identity verification offered by biometrics. The challenge is to integrate the biometric technology into that process in the most efficient manner. There will be few systems that revolve around biometrics for the sake of biometrics. This is an important point that has sometimes become unfocused when people have allowed themselves to get carried away with the technical detail and theoretical possibilities on offer. Is the requirement to implement a biometric system, or is it to enhance and refine a necessary process within your organization? If it is the latter, then biometric technology is a powerful tool to have in your collection, but it is not an end in itself. My own recommendation is that potential users should thrash out and document the requirement before they start looking at specific devices. They should then write this requirement in big letters on a whiteboard in the project office where it will be seen every day by those involved. Beneath this might usefully be a list of project objectives and relative milestones. It goes without saying that we should have a properly constructed project plan against which to baseline our objectives and measure progress towards them accordingly.

There is of course a possible variation on the above philosophy and that is where the advent of biometric technology suggests a brand new process or function that simply wasn't possible beforehand, thus opening up a new avenue of opportunity. However, the same principles apply in that we must carefully think through the opportunity and perceived benefits and then ascertain exactly how the technology might deliver the requirement we have identified. We should be testing the business case for implementing the system we have in mind in exactly the same manner that we would do if we were considering any other enhancement to our operational systems or processes.

In conclusion, it is important that we regard biometric technology as an available methodology to support pertinent personal identity processes. It should not end up as the proverbial solution looking for a problem. One way of ensuring that we keep our thinking clear and start off on the right foot, is to absolutely understand and clarify the requirement up front and then not be swayed from it.

## 5.2 Understanding the users

This is an area worth spending a little time on. You see, people are rather complex mechanisms and don't necessarily think alike or react in the same way to a given situation. They come in all shapes and sizes - doctors, footballers, politicians, artists, construction workers, musicians, butchers, bakers, candlestick makers and a whole lot more besides. They also have different shades of intellect and aptitudes in certain areas. Some have a distinct technical bias, some are artistic, some have natural linguistic abilities and so on. It is difficult to legislate for such a complex and varied species, whose understanding, views and logic will alter from one individual to the next. Similarly, their attitude and approach towards a process which they are required to follow in an everyday transactional situation can be equally varied. In the context of using biometric devices, the perception and attitude of the individual is also likely to be influenced by the situation within which the technology is being deployed. For example, a prisoner or prison visitor who is required to use the system within a prison environment might have a slightly different view to that of a retail customer who receives a direct marketing/loyalty related benefit from using the technology. This latter user may again have a different view from a benefit claimant who uses the technology in order to receive a given benefit. Then there are physical and logical access control users, time and attendance recording users, voting systems users, ATM machine users and a host of others who will all make some personal association between the technology and the situation within which it is implemented.

Earlier in the book, we discussed how the user could have a dramatic influence on realized system performance according to a number of parameters which might shape their attitude towards the process overall and the way in which they interact with the device under real-time operational conditions. A certain amount of this variability may be anticipated and managed in advance if we take a little time to really understand our user base and what their perception of the process we are introducing is. Perhaps the first step here is to understand the current process and how users interact with it. For example, let's consider a time and attendance recording system where users carry a card token which they swipe at strategically-placed terminals throughout the facility when they are entering or leaving their workplace. Let's further suppose that the existing terminals require a certain amount of user interaction in order to choose options such as arriving, leaving, project code and other organization-specific details. In such a situation, if we believe that incorporating biometric verification is going to provide benefits, it is probably because we want a higher confidence level as to the true identity of the individual entering information into the terminal. In other words, we have a sneaking suspicion that Walter Smith is occasionally swiping a card through for Chuck Higgins while Chuck is really down at the Last Chance Saloon Bar working diligently on a couple of beers instead of on his job back at the office. No doubt Chuck returns the compliment from time to time. Now, you and I may see the introduction of biometrics in this situation as a useful methodology to help towards increasing efficiency in the workplace. Chuck and Walter may need a little persuading, however, before they come around to our way of thinking. OK! This is an extreme case - but you get the drift? It could be that not all of the workforce will immediately share the enthusiasm of the manager who is seeking to introduce biometric identity verification into the organization. If we know this in advance, we can take steps to ensure that good communication allows such views to be taken into consideration and answers any genuine concerns that may exist. If we haven't even thought about this side of things, we may be in for an interesting time when we come to implement the system. But how do we discover what the underlying perception among the workforce really is? The short answer is by being close to them and testing the water for views accordingly. Most organizations will have a hierarchical structure which allows for information to be cascaded in both directions where appropriate and this shouldn't be too difficult to achieve. Section managers or team leaders will probably have a reasonable understanding of the personnel working in their particular area and the best way of communicating with them in relation to proposed new processes.

But what if we are dealing with the general public? In such a case, similar principles apply, but the mechanism for collecting views and disseminating information will clearly be a little different. It would in most cases be useful to undertake some sort of consumer research, perhaps via a survey of a targeted section of expected users. You may like to set up a demonstration facility where interested individuals could come and see the technology in action and express their views accordingly - if logged methodically such views might prove enlightening and very useful to the overall project. In any user survey it will of course be important to place things into context by outlining the expected benefits of the proposed system and exactly how it would work in practice. We might also offer some multiple choice questions in order to gauge user reaction to the different biometric methodologies under consideration and also state our proposals for how templates might be managed. We may well be surprised in the amount of interest expressed in the technology. Having collected a useful amount of user feedback data, we then have to be clear on how we are going to use it. A structured and objective approach will be necessary if we are to extract meaningful information without bias. Furthermore, we should consider carefully what this information is telling us, even if it is not what was expected or what we particularly wanted to hear.

But why go to all this trouble? Why not just implement the system and handle any issues as they arise? Well, it is important to obtain user 'buy in' when implementing any new system or process, but especially so with biometrics as it is an area which requires direct user interaction with the system in a very personal manner. In this context, the more you know about your users the better, as this knowledge will help shape your thinking around a number of systems design and overall project-related factors, from choosing the most appropriate biometric methodology to tailoring the environment for best results. You might argue that in a situation where users are required to use the system anyway (as with a benefit claimant system for example) that this side of things is unimportant. I would counter-argue that it is still important as it provides you with an insight into how people are going to react and also delivers a strong psychological message around the importance you place on identity verification. In addition, it will help you to think clearly about the optimal systems and process design for your particular situation and user base.

In conclusion, if we are considering the implementation of any biometric system or process, one of the first key tasks should be an analysis of the prospective user base coupled to some sort of initiative to capture their thinking and response to such a proposal. Using our automobile analogy, designing a biometric system without understanding the users is a little like designing a car without knowing what sort of terrain it will be driven on - it's possible, but you would probably do it better if you had this information.

## 5.3 Understanding the environment

If understanding the users is important, so is understanding the environment in which the proposed system is to be used. This will certainly affect the way you deploy the user-interfacing components, and may indeed affect your choice of biometric methodology. There are perhaps two strands to consider in this respect. Firstly, there is the effect that the environment may have on the technical components and infrastructure and their ability to function reliably. Secondly, there is the effect that the environment has on the users, both from a practical and psychological perspective.

Let's consider for a moment the biometric reader devices themselves and how they may be affected by the environment. If we were thinking of deploying a free-standing voice verification device, we would probably think twice before installing it outside in the elements where it might be subject to extremes of heat, humidity, rain, frost and so on, not to mention the variable levels of ambient noise from traffic and other everyday factors. We might also not be too keen on installing it in a corner location within a stone-built church where the acoustics are likely to be a tad reflective. What about fingerprint readers? Fine for PC access control within a clean and controlled office environment, but would we deploy them on the shop floor of a busy steel works or engine shop where the optical surfaces could become contaminated within minutes? Possibly not. These are obvious examples of how we need to consider our application in the context of its operational environment. There are more subtle situations to consider. For example, if we were designing a system where relatively large numbers of users were expected to pass through turnstiles, having had their identity verified, then we would need to consider a methodology which was both fast and easy to use with the minimum of user-related process. Perhaps a swipe card and either fingerprint or hand geometry reader might be suitable in this case, as we could use the card swipe to either load or call the biometric template with the user simply placing his finger or hand on the device for a fast yes/no result. This could be accompanied by an obvious visual indicator prompting the user to proceed or wait accordingly.

In short, we need to consider the environment where our system is going to be deployed and what effect it may have on the biometric devices and how people interact with them. We should be aiming to make the process as invisible as possible in order that users are not inconvenienced by unnecessary queues caused by either bad planning or system malfunction. Needless to say, our choice of biometric methodology is important in this context and should reflect the activities of the users in this situation. If they are in a public place such as an airport or railway station, we shall need to make things as fast and easy for them as possible. If they are in a more relaxed situation, perhaps in an office environment, then we may have a little more flexibility in our choice of devices and how we deploy them. The interaction between the devices and host processing system is also important, especially if we are dealing with a large number of users through multiple verification points, creating high levels of concurrent usage. Depending on how we have designed our system, where the templates are stored and where the matching process takes place, this could be significant. If we have chosen to store all the templates on a central database, and the matching process is also undertaken on a central host machine, then there will be a fair amount of traffic on the network at peak times as packets of information fly back and forth to communicate between the user and the host. If this is using an existing network, it is likely that it will also be a peak time for other on-site activities, leading to a degradation of network performance in general. Such a situation, if leading to a perceived delay at the verification point, would not endear itself to your users, especially if there is a queue forming behind them.

Another factor to bear in mind is the electrical environment. How clean and stable is the power supply in your proposed environment? Were you anticipating that you were simply going to plug your host server into the nearest electrical outlet? And what about the equipment at each verification point? Do you have a dedicated spur for this which has been tested accordingly. Strange things have been known to happen to data processing equipment when hooked up to questionable sources of power. Sometimes this manifests itself in an obvious manner when sudden surges or excessively noisy 'spikes' can zap electrical components in your system and bring it to a standstill. Other times the effects are more subtle and could lead to random data corruption or the occasional software crash. Of course, every systems or LAN manager thinks that it will never happen to them and in any case, components are pretty resilient these days, aren't they? Furthermore, in any public building great pains will obviously have been taken to ensure the regulation and stability of its power supply, won't they? Have a look out the window, you may see a few pigs flying by. Even if the original design of the electrical infrastructure was satisfactory when the building was built, it is likely that all manner of alterations and modifications may have been undertaken since then by a variety of contractors in order to accommodate additional equipment on site. These contractors may have had different views around best practice and the interpretation of electrical standards. When considering the environment from this perspective the best advice one can give is to take every precaution to protect your system's infrastructure from the vagaries of the immediate environment. Use regulated power supplies and surge protection, pay particular attention to the quality and routing of all cables and ensure that the critical components of your system are also physically secure. This is naturally important with any system, but particularly so if it is one with which the public are expected to interact.

The other strand of thought with regards to the environment, is the practical and psychological effect it can have on the users. If you are considering the implementation of a small system within your own organization where users are positively required to use it, you may not consider this aspect particularly important, although even in that situation, a little forethought can pay dividends. If you are implementing a system in a public place where its use is optional (although you would like to encourage people to use the system) then this factor becomes very important indeed. Leading retailers and supermarkets have expended much effort in understanding the environment and providing the best experience for their customers. They have learned that the overall ambience plus perceived ease of the shopping experience makes a big difference in enticing people into their stores. Similar principles apply if you wish to attract people to your system and the benefits you are portraying for it. You can easily frighten them away if it appears as too technical or complicated or if the operational procedure is anything less than crystal clear. In a more subtle sense, the very appearance of the verification points is also important. If it looks like things have been cobbled together in a low budget haphazard way and squeezed into a most inappropriate location, then people will not take it seriously. Similarly, if the whole operation has an air of ultra high security, then it will probably not appear as attractive to most people. It would surely be better to make the verification points attractive and bold so that people naturally migrate towards them. There is much that could be achieved in this context by giving the whole project an identity, with a suitable and immediately identifiable logo and color scheme which is reflected in promotional material and on site, enabling users and prospective users to quickly understand what is happening and where. In the opinion of the author, many public trials of biometrics undertaken in the last decade have missed this point completely. Sometimes it has even been hard to locate the trial verification points, and even harder to find anyone who can advise on the correct procedures or answer questions on the project overall. As for an attractive and welcoming environment - this seems sometimes to have been the very last point on the agenda. This is a shame, as it misses a valuable opportunity to explore some of the more subtle elements of user psychology around the subject of biometric identity verification and its implementation in public places.

Providing the right environment together with the most comfortable and intuitive operational procedures is as much a part of systems design as configuring the communications protocols between devices or designing the user interface. In addition it can also, as previously mentioned, have a significant effect on realized systems performance. The acknowledgement of these points and how to incorporate them into your project can help you design and implement a better system, which in turn will have a better chance of user acceptance and success.

## 5.4 Putting the system together

Having carefully considered the original requirement and objectives, the profile of the users and the environment in which the system is to be deployed, we can then turn our attention to how our system is going to be physically configured and deployed on site.

Perhaps the first thing is to understand the systems architecture and ensure that this is optimal for the particular requirement we have in mind. If the system components are to be provided in their entirety by a third party, then we need to question them carefully about this as their standard recommended setup may not be suitable in our particular case. Many such questions will be centerd around the template management methodology, the number and location of verification points, the systems administration functionality and of course the technical environment within which we are working. Our choice of front end capture device will also be important in this context. For example, if the template matching function can be undertaken within the device itself and we are additionally loading the user's template from a token such as a chip card, then we will be concerned mostly with the reliable collection of the transaction data and administration functions at the designated physical locations. Alternatively, if we are seeking to download a template from a central database for comparison, or if the matching process is undertaken via a separate processing unit, then we shall be far more concerned with network performance and security issues.

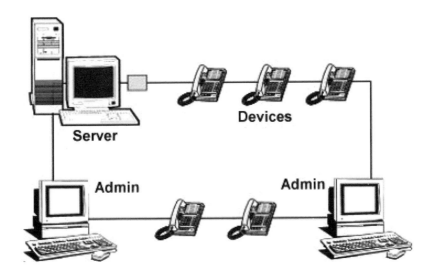

Figure 5.1 A possible systems architecture

If we were to assume an architecture as depicted in Figure 5.1 with a central server undertaking the matching process and holding the template database, then obviously the performance of this server must be well up to the task, with some spare capacity in hand in terms of processing horsepower and data storage. In addition, we must consider its resilience. In such an architecture, if this server goes down, then so does our system as no template retrieval or matching process can be undertaken.  In such a case we would almost certainly be thinking of a parallel secondary server (probably in a different physical location) which can automatically switch into circuit if the primary server fails for any reason.  With the example given in Figure 5.1 we would also be paying particular attention to the network and the resilience of the whole, including any hubs and routers as well of course as bandwidth availability.  This latter point may be complicated if we plan to use an existing network for our system.  The administration stations, which may incorporate the user enrolment functionality as well as more general reporting tasks will also have to be suitably configured for purpose and of robust quality.  The popular habit of pressing into service any old PC that happens to be lying around on site is not likely to yield optimum results in this case.

Of course, we may have a much simpler architectural requirement whereby the bulk of the processing is undertaken at the verification point within the devices themselves and we need additional computing power simply for administration and user enrolment purposes.

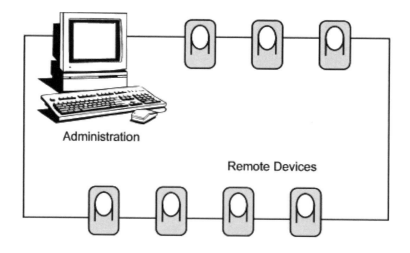

Figure 5.2 A simple systems architecture

The above diagram depicts just such a system whereby the verification process is handled by the devices themselves without reference to a central database.  In this case we may be slightly less concerned about overall network performance, but we will still be concerned with the resilience of the network and also that of the administration PC, which will be holding our transaction history. We shall certainly wish to implement some rigorous data backup procedures on this PC and may decide to mirror either the hard drive, or perhaps the whole computer.

We have briefly covered the topic of systems architecture to illustrate the point that this is a subject which should be considered in some depth as a prelude to the more detailed systems design. This will particularly be the case if we are considering a system in the public domain which will be catering for a large number of users with minimal administration support and where reliability will be a key issue. If we are contemplating the use of an existing network, it follows that we should start with a good understanding of the network architecture, together with related performance and capacity measures. We may then decide whether the existing network needs to be enhanced before we implement our biometric system.

Let us now turn our attention to some of the more obvious system components, starting with the verification device itself. We have probably thought long and hard about the choice of verification device and finally chosen the one which we believe best meets our particular objectives for this system. However, it may or may not be suitable for our purposes straight out of the box. We may wish to integrate a card reader or other components to obtain the functionality we need. In fact, the verification device may be thought of as a collection of entities including the biometric capture device, the user interface, the power supply, any additional local interfaces such as relay outputs or annunciators, any synergistic devices such as card readers or keypads and of course any controlled devices such as a turnstile. These entities may be integrated into a physical whole, perhaps within a suitable structure, in order to provide an attractive and logical interface to the user.

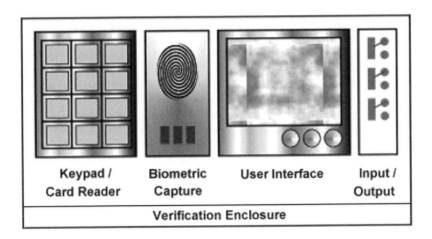

Figure 5.3 Principal components of the verification device

It is important that this collection of entities looks and functions as a whole from the user's perspective and that they are assembled in an ergonomic manner which makes their use intuitive and obvious. It is also important that each of the components is robust enough to take the level of use that we envisage for this system. This is especially important where keypads and card readers are concerned and it is worth using the best components available in this context. The cosmetic design of the individual components may or may not be an area that you have direct influence over. If you do, it is worth paying attention to consistency of finish in order that the whole looks as homogenous as possible. If you do not, you may still be able to construct the enclosure in a way that presents a unified appearance. Another area to pay attention to is the power supply. This should be a regulated and smoothed supply, preferably with battery backup where applicable. The enclosure should be attractively presented and of sound ergonomic design allowing easy use and maintenance of the component parts, which should ideally be replaceable in the field without having to bring the system down. It would be useful from an engineering perspective to include a panel where the commissioning engineer can note the reader or node address and other relevant details. Having designed the whole, it is worth documenting its construction in some detail. You never know when you may need to build additional units and if it will be the same team building them.

At the other end so to speak, the administration PCs and database server (where applicable) should be purpose designed and documented accordingly. Let's start with the server. Discussion with the device vendor, coupled to a little experimentation and calculation should determine the processing power and memory requirements in this respect. Having arrived at the optimum figures for both, it is perhaps a good idea to increase these by 25%. Wherever possible, stick to standard components from the leading manufacturers as these will be easier to replace should it become necessary. With regard to hard disk requirements, we should bear in mind that this component is going to get a real bashing in any system design that involves retrieving templates and writing transactions in real time to the database. The rule of thumb is simple, choose the best quality component available and for safety reasons mirror this within the server. Whilst ultimate disk access speed isn't critical, it may be considered an important factor within a large system featuring multiple readers and large numbers of concurrent users. The network interface should also be considered carefully. Steer away from budget network cards and hubs and install only proven components from the leading manufacturers, ensuring that you have replacements for each component on site. The server itself should naturally be sited in a physically secure and clean environment which is temperature controlled if possible. The server enclosure should additionally feature adequate cooling with spare fans kept on site. Access to the server is an issue that you should consider carefully. If this relies on the operating system security model, then ensure that the passwords are noted securely within the maintenance office and that engineering staff are properly trained from the security perspective. Of course, you may be using a biometric for secure access to the server, in which case ensure that at least two engineers are registered on the system at any point in time, plus one senior administration person. If a second standby server is incorporated into the overall system, then this should be sited in a different physical location with all the same security rules applying. Your LAN administrators will be able to advise on keeping the two in sync as appropriate.

The administration PCs may be simpler in specification from an outright performance perspective, but should be specified and constructed with the same care and attention to detail.  Once again, it would do no harm to keep a few spare components on site, even if you are outsourcing the support and maintenance of the system, you may like to ask for this within the contract.  The finer details of the network, including protocols, wiring standards and ancillary components we shall leave outside the scope of this book, but suffice it to say that you should have full written details of this, together with as-installed diagrams, signed off by the commissioning engineer.  This should be accompanied by a complete systems inventory detailing every component and its precise specification and configuration. This information should be held in duplicate both on and off site for future reference.  It is surprising how many systems are installed without this discipline which is, in the opinion of the author, a fundamental requirement for any operational system.  If a supplier is unwilling or unable to comply with this requirement, then deal with someone else who is.  If you have a serious on-site problem further down the line, or you fall out with your original supplier, you will need this information.

The actual systems design in terms of topography will be closely linked to on-site conditions.  Naturally we shall want to configure our various building blocks in the most efficient manner to provide the best and most reliable overall performance. We have already discussed in an earlier section some of the options for template management and the effect on overall performance.  Depending on the front-end biometric device you have chosen, you may have no opportunity to vary this parameter.  Generally speaking, the more processing that can be undertaken locally at the verification point the better. Therefore if the template can either be stored or otherwise provided locally (from the user via a chip card for example) and the biometric device can perform the matching locally, then we have the makings of an efficient system from the network perspective as all we are communicating is the transaction result and we can balance our overall systems design accordingly.

It may be that the biometric device can perform the matching function locally but we wish to store the user templates on a central database.  In this case we shall have a three leg discussion across the network as first we send a request to the server to send us the template for the user claiming an identity at the verification point.  Secondly, the server sends the requested template back along the line and thirdly, after the matching process has been undertaken, the result is sent back to the server to be written into the transaction database.

In situations where we are undertaking the comparison at the server end, things are slightly different as this time we are sending the user reference and the live biometric data across the network on the first leg and receiving the result back from the server on the second.  In theory this may be a little faster as the reference templates stay on the server where they can be accessed quickly by an efficient database engine and compared using the higher performance of the server, but in reality much depends on the components involved.  The final systems topography and operating methodology you choose will no doubt be a product of the components chosen and the prevailing on site conditions, including number of users anticipated and single transaction speeds required. In most cases, you will have some variables to juggle with in order to provide the best compromise. One aspect that should not be compromised however is the quality of the individual components chosen. The weakest link will be the breaking point under strain.

We have now discussed some of the points to consider when designing your biometric system. Naturally, there is far more detail to attend to than has been covered here, but hopefully we have set the scene and given a few pointers in this respect. You may consider it strange that we have covered some of this ground at all in a book which is primarily about biometrics. But the biometric device itself represents only one component within an overall system and we must consider the system as a whole if we are to understand how the overall design will deliver the benefits we are seeking. This leads us neatly towards installation.

## 5.5 Installation issues

It is not my intention here to go into enormous detail about installation and indeed, I pondered over whether this point should be covered at all in the book. Looking back on biometric systems which I have seen implemented, together with reasons for their relative success or failure, convinces me, however, that the topic should be raised, if only to lodge the phrase 'installation issues' firmly in the consciousness of the reader.

When an organization considers a major new operational IT system it will typically pay a good deal of attention to its design and deployment, usually involving senior IT specialists from within its ranks to manage the project through to implementation and beyond. With biometric systems this hasn't always been the case, with projects often led by the security department and sometimes running to unrealistically limited budgets. This in turn, coupled with the relative infancy of the biometric industry, has often led to installations being undertaken by smaller private companies from the physical security sector whose grasp of the broader IT networking scenario and associated best practice might be less than optimal. This is not necessarily their fault, as they may be undisputed experts at putting in a security fence or installing an alarm, but slightly out of their depth with the finer points of a complex networked biometric system. At the other end of the scale you have the situation where the leading global consultancies are paid vast sums of money to manage the project in its entirety, including the installation which may or may not be sub-contracted out to a third party. However, this scenario would probably only be applicable to the larger system, or where there is little in-house expertise. There is fortunately a middle ground where we can find professional companies who are experienced with biometrics and IT systems and capable of intelligent systems design and competent on-site installation by experienced engineers. Needless to say, it is well worth seeking these companies out. My own preference would be for a small dedicated in-house team to manage the project with assistance from a specialist company with a proven track record in biometrics. The in-house team would no doubt include the project sponsor from the appropriate business area, and would certainly include a senior IT project manager and network specialist who can liaise with the third party as appropriate to ensure that the chosen solution is architecturally sensible within your environment and installed according to accepted practice. This may add a little to the overall project cost in terms of utilising expensive internal resources, but it will be well worth it in the long run.

Having made the above point, let's highlight some of the areas which, while seemingly obvious, have nevertheless contributed to significant failures in the past. My favourite among these is probably cabling. For any situation where we are connecting electronic components together, whether it be a serial printer direct to a computer, or multiple devices on a network, there is an optimal specification of cabling according to methodology, distance covered and so forth. Unfortunately, the optimal type of cable is not always used. When, on a Friday afternoon, Charlie Brown calls over to his mate Ernie and asks for a certain length of two twisted pair screened cable of a particular reference type, if Ernie replies that he doesn't have any but has found some four core just long enough to go from A to B, it will often get installed. Is this an exaggeration? The author has previously discovered major systems in prestigious buildings, installed by the top industry names with just this sort of error. One case springs to mind where the flagship offices of a major multinational had been experiencing data corruption on a primary operational system. Key components had been exchanged, terminals re-sited, and much expensive maintenance had been undertaken over a two-year period by a very well-known IT support organization, all to no avail. When stripping the system down to its fundamental components, I was immediately struck by the sloppy wiring and variance in cable types (none of which were correct) between components. After stripping out the old cabling and re-wiring with the correct specification of cables, the system ran perfectly. It is not just a matter of the correct cable type either, but the way in which they are terminated and routed. Poor termination can cause all sorts of problems on a network. Some devices employ straightforward physical connections such as screw type terminal blocks, while others utilize special plug and socket arrangements. In the former case, a certain amount of patience and attention to detail is required in order to make a secure connection, whilst in the latter case sometimes specialist tools are required, which if not available may lead to certain compromises being made. A good engineer would be expected to carry a comprehensive and good quality toolkit plus a selection of termination accessories for all the popular methodologies. You may like to examine the tool kit of the next engineer that arrives on your site.

The routing of cables can sometimes be an issue as well. Every electrical engineer would have been taught how not to run data cables in parallel with the primary AC building feed, how to avoid placing unnecessary stress on cables during installation, how to ensure that the elements do not take their toll prematurely and so on. To be fair, the theory isn't always easy to follow in practice due to on-site complications, but sometimes the manner in which cables are routed still leaves something to be desired. I am reminded of an engineer who tied a bunch of (sub-standard quality) data cables directly to a 415VAC cable as it snaked its way through the basement of a building because it saved installing proper conduit or cable trays. Then there are those who like to use data cables as draw-strings, or run them naked in service ducts between buildings and so on. What's the answer? Ask your installation company for a set of cable topography plans, including specifications of cable and conduit, and ask to inspect the installation at the time of system commissioning before handover. Don't be afraid to crawl around in service ducts yourself with a torch if need be.

Another favourite area is that of power supplies. This is particularly relevant to system peripherals such as biometric devices, card readers and so on. Sometimes manufacturers will supply a rudimentary power supply of some description (often of the 'wall wart' type) with the device. These are often unbranded and made in various parts of the world in order to drive down costs. They are also often quite variable in their quality of manufacture. It is entertaining sometimes to measure the output of such power supplies, under load and otherwise, to see if they come anywhere near the stated level. Many biometric devices and synergistic peripherals may be fairly tolerant of having a shade extra voltage or current coming in, as long as it is stable. What they do not like is insufficient voltage or current, or huge spikes and wallowing dips in the supply, symptoms which some low cost power supplies delight in providing. To put it bluntly, there is no place for such components within a good quality installation. There are plenty of companies who make good quality, properly regulated and protected power supplies designed for 24 hour on-site operation. Certainly they cost a little more, but a few tens of dollars is probably not going to push your organization into bankruptcy and the amount of headaches that can be saved by using good quality power supplies, makes them well worth the extra expense.

It may seem a little pedantic to draw attention to the areas outlined above, but it is surprising just how much they can affect the performance of an installed system. Many times equipment has been returned to the manufacturer in perfect working order because it has been perceived as faulty on site, when in reality it has been the quality of installation and installation consumables which has caused the problem. As you can appreciate, it doesn't take too many such occurrences to outweigh the slight extra cost of good quality installation materials and practice. If you were buying a brand new Ferrari, you probably wouldn't ask the factory to supply it to you with second-hand tyres, heating oil in the engine and the battery from a moped - well you might, but the realized performance and reliability may not be what you expected. The same is true of biometric systems. Ensure that installation consumables and system peripherals are of good quality and properly installed and the system will have a sporting chance of performing as expected. If your installation engineers are allowed to skimp on this, then watch out for trouble.

There are additional environmental issues in this respect, especially around the siting of system components. If you are employing a database server for example, this should be in a clean (from both a physical and electrical perspective) and secure environment and not stuck on the floor under somebody's desk in a shared office. It is also a good idea not to site peripherals and terminals adjacent to heavy electrical machinery or have them sharing the same power outlet. This reminds me of a security control room that I visited on one occasion where a security officer had brought in a multi-way mains plug so that he could connect his electric kettle and brew up a nice cup of tea in the mornings. Unfortunately, it was not a good fit and usually required a certain amount of waggling around and sometimes even a good kick in order to make contact for the all important tea ceremony. The main access and environmental control system computer, together with the network master interface was also connected to this mains plug arrangement, and it was strange that every morning people would complain of erratic performance of this system.... Yes, of course the components should have been connected to dedicated spurs, preferably on a separate fused circuit, but this obviously didn't occur to the installation engineers.

The siting of biometric readers or terminals may also be important in your particular system. If you have to site readers in an semi-external environment, ensure that they are not only protected from the elements, but that the enclosures are thermostatically controlled for temperature. Naturally, you will not want to site them in an abrasive environment whereby the control surfaces will become damaged, or where they will become quickly contaminated, as this would have a negative affect on user perception. You should also allow sufficient physical space around them in order that users are comfortable with the overall operational environment, and remember to think about access for maintenance purposes.

In conclusion, we have touched upon some of the more obvious issues around systems installation which, whilst applying to IT systems in general, are no less important for biometric systems. Having spent a good deal of time and effort on designing your biometric system and attendant processes, it is well worth paying a little extra attention to detail with regards to its installation. Do not assume that you can outsource and forget this element of the project - it is of primary importance to the initial success and ongoing reliability of the system as a whole.

## 5.6 Training the users

This is another crucially important area which can significantly affect the initially realized performance of your biometric system, as well as the user's perception and acceptance of it.

If you are introducing biometric identity verification as an enhancement of an existing process, then the way in which this process is changing, the reason why it is changing and what the users have to do differently are all subjects that need to be communicated properly and in a timely manner to the prospective users. If the whole concept is new and untried, then this communication is very important indeed. We need to ensure that all users are comfortable with the processes that they will be required to follow, and that they have had the opportunity to ask whatever questions occur to them in this context, however naïve or unrealistic they may appear to be. This is important, as naturally some individuals may initially view biometrics as an invasion of privacy, especially if they believe that actual images of their biometric parameter are being stored on a database somewhere. Probably a good way of handling this initially is via a series of workshops where the overall system proposal may be presented and be questioned or even challenged accordingly by prospective users. At this point, the fundamental questions around how the proposed biometric device is actually working, template management and storage and other issues may be addressed. In addition, the organization can explain its rationale for going in this direction, what the expected benefits are and to whom.

Having undertaken a successful marketing and communications program in order to pave the way for the introduction of the system, we may now turn our attention to user training. Depending on the expected number of users this may need to be undertaken in phases. Within a single and contained medium-sized organization of perhaps 100 - 200 individuals, this will not be too difficult a task as we can partition them into manageable small groups and probably complete the exercise in one or two weeks. A large organization with several thousand individuals working from multiple locations will obviously have a more complex task to perform, complicated by the fact that the first people to be trained may forget some of what they have learned if they do not quickly have the opportunity to practice it on a live system. This may be addressed by having a working sub-system, perhaps in a non-critical area, with a simple manual override in place. If we are introducing a public system such as may be the case with a benefits agency or commercial organization, then this becomes something of a military campaign as we shall have much co-ordination and planning to undertake. In fact, the larger the number of prospective users and the more likely they are to be within the public domain, the more complex these tasks become with the more overlap between the communication, training and implementation phases.

Another important aspect to this is the co-ordination between the technical systems design and implementation team, the process engineers and the communication and training teams. It is no good having the system implemented if users don't know how to use it. Similarly, it would be pointless to train users on a system which is nowhere near implementation. Where this can become a little complicated is in the context of a major system spread across several locations with large numbers of prospective users. In such a case we will almost certainly be considering some sort of phased implementation as this will be much easier to manage than an overnight 'big bang' approach. Furthermore, it facilitates testing and refinement as the system gradually progresses towards full usage.

This may be an aspect of biometric systems implementation that you had not previously considered in any sort of depth. But with any significant system this is an element which should be incorporated and budgeted for at the outset. It is clear from the diagram in Figure 5.4 that there should be an involvement from elements of the organization other than the technical implementation or project management team if we are to achieve a high quality, reliable implementation of a biometric based system.

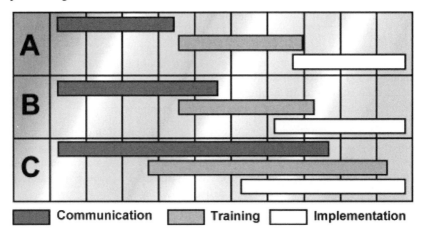

Figure 5.4 Scheduling the introduction of the system

In the diagram above, A depicts a small to medium organization contained on one site, B represents a larger organization distributed across multiple sites and C portrays a system in the public domain distributed across multiple sites. As the complexity of the installation increases, there is an increasing overlap of the communication, training and implementation requirements over time, with significantly more effort required for the communication and training-related tasks. This will particularly be the case where the implementation is phased. Clearly this is an aspect which requires careful consideration and planning.

Let us now consider the actual training requirement. If we wish to realize something approaching the performance that our chosen device is theoretically capable of, then the quality of the reference template and the quality of the live sample against which it is matched are very important indeed. Our users therefore need to be properly enrolled into the system and also capable of offering good quality live samples for subsequent comparison. It is unlikely that they will be able to meet these demands if they know nothing about the biometric verification process and how it works. The first thing then is to provide some fundamental training that covers this ground, before moving on to actual utilisation of the biometric device, allowing them to practise outside of the live environment.

The chosen biometric methodology will naturally have some impact on this. If we were using fingerprint readers for example, then the users would need to understand how to place their fingers properly on the scanning surface in order to give good quality samples in a consistent manner. With hand geometry, the task is made a little easier by the provision of guide pins around which the fingers are located, provided that individual users have average adult-size hands. With iris scanning, the users must focus the image of their eye by aligning with the camera device. With retinal scanning the users are required to focus on a given point, and so on. Voice verification will perhaps be a little more challenging in some instances as users will need to understand the correct operation of the transducer device as well as make a conscious effort towards consistency of enunciation. In each of these cases the individuals conducting the training must of course have a thorough grasp of the situation themselves and should have taken some time to become thoroughly familiar with the device in question and its operation. The device manufacturer should be able to help in this respect by providing training for the trainers, together with all the appropriate documentation.

We have been discussing the biometric device itself and the necessity of getting the users familiar with both the concept and the reality of its operation, but there is of course another element to consider and that is the operational process itself. This could vary significantly from one application to another depending on the degree to which the user is required to interact with software or some other form of user interface. Take voice verification for example. In theory this should be quite straightforward as the user can react to voice prompts programmed into the system as appropriate. In practice it may depend on the strength of the programmed error-catching routines coupled to the way that the biometric element interacts with the core process. In a straightforward physical access control system, a simple LCD or equivalent display may be sufficient to communicate operational status to the user with plain language prompts for each stage of the process, plus the final verification result and any other instructions. With a system controlling access to a computer, network or even specific functionality within computer programs, this may not be quite so straightforward and will probably need a lot more documentation and explanation. Then there are bespoke applications where the biometric process is integrated into something else which has value for the user. This may be the case for example within a banking-related system, or perhaps a customer loyalty program whereby the user may wish to access personal information. Such a system will no doubt incorporate a logical prompting system to guide the user through the process, but this needs to be understood and learned for future use of the system. You may be able to achieve this online with some of your users, but it is likely that a significant proportion of them will prefer to have this explained and demonstrated by a competent representative of the organization concerned. If your users are members of the general public, then you will almost certainly wish to make available some printed reference material that they can keep for future reference. This same material can usefully form part of the on-site training in order to promote consistency of approach.

Even a cursory contemplation of the above points should serve to highlight the fact that user training is actually quite important. Of course it is so for any new system or process being introduced, but particularly so for a biometric system, which can be a little intimidating for new users if they have no previous experience of interacting with such devices. It should also be apparent that this is an element we shall have to budget for within our overall project. We shall need to provide competent individuals as trainers, each of which needs to undergo a training program themselves in order to bring them up to speed with the system as a whole and the biometric front-end device in particular. The whole training exercise additionally needs to be supported with documentation and other material as necessary to achieve the objective. The trainers themselves will of course need full technical and operational information appertaining to the biometric device in question, as well as perhaps a training manual to outline the systems operation and respective benefits. The users would in most cases probably benefit from some sort of flyer that outlines the purpose of the system and how they, as users, should interact with it, plus contact information for when they experience difficulties or have any questions relating to the system overall. This may take the form of a simple laminated sheet, or perhaps a little booklet.

We have already mentioned the importance of timing in relation to communication, training and implementation, but within the training area alone there will be timing issues to address, depending on the exact nature and size of the system you have in mind. This is obviously easier in a contained system where you know who and where your users are and you can simply draw up a training schedule accordingly. However, you will not wish to train them too far in advance of the live implementation, as it is important that they can practise their new-found skills in the live environment as soon as possible. In a broader based public system this will probably be a little easier, at least once the system has been implemented, as user training will be ongoing.

## 5.7 Managing the system

Here is an area where there is tremendous scope for getting value from the system as well as tremendous scope for limiting its potential. There are several factors which come into play in this context, starting perhaps with the management of the physical system components.

Let's start at the front end with the biometric device itself. We shall assume that it has been properly and securely installed in the appropriate location. Many biometric devices have an optical or special surface that is key to the way they operate. For example, a fingerprint reader may have an optical scanning surface, an iris scanning device will have a surface through which the camera operates, the leading hand geometry device has a reflective surface which aids the image capture process. It goes without saying that these surfaces should be kept clean. This is best attended to with a soft cloth, such as might be used for cleaning camera lenses for example. However, a decision will need to made as to how often this cleaning should be undertaken, and naturally this will depend upon the environment and number of users. Whilst the devices themselves may work quite happily with a mildly dirty surface, this would be rather off-putting to the users and so this should also be taken into account when deciding upon your maintenance schedule. Whilst we are on the subject of optical surfaces, these should also be checked for abrasions and other minor damage which may affect the operation of the device. If this is the case, then a replacement should be substituted.

Whilst we are engaged with our cleaning schedule, it is a good opportunity to check the overall operation of the biometric device. If there is a keypad or card reader involved, be sure to check this thoroughly also, together with the operation of any user interface such as an LCD panel or LED displays. Mostly, we shall find that contemporary devices are fairly rugged and reliable, but certain elements may degrade over time or fail completely, damaging user confidence in the process, and so a regular maintenance check and clean is essential. No doubt you will record such checks in a log as you progress around the system.

Moving on from the device, we shall assume that the network itself is functioning (you will soon find out if it isn't) although a visual check of any interface components, routers, hubs and the like would not go amiss. Back at the server end (where applicable) you will no doubt check that the environment itself is being maintained and that the server is as it should be. You will already be running periodic data backups, so you will know that things are working OK in general terms. There may be some software maintenance to consider; for example, you may periodically pack the database, or de-fragment your hard drives. At the administration terminal, you should be checking that this is operating correctly and that the VDU and peripheral components, such as keyboards and mice are clean and functioning properly.

If all the hardware is in good order and functioning correctly, then we can turn our attention to some of the software-related issues. Of primary concern in this context is the management of the user database and associated biometric templates. We must ensure for example that if a user leaves the organization, or is transferred permanently to another office, then we should remove the biometric template and system data for that individual (you may choose to retain historic records in your personnel department, but that is a different issue). Similarly, a new employee will need to be enrolled into the system without delay and be set up for access rights etc. accordingly. There may also be times where you need to re-enrol an individual if the original template was sub-optimal, causing operational problems. If your database includes photographic images of users, then obviously you will need to take care that the image is always in sync with the template and other data. In addition to the user template, there are with most systems other parameters which may be configured on an individual basis, notably the matching threshold for the verification process itself. In addition, your system may allow for access and time zones to be set independently for each user.

Ordinarily, you will probably set the matching threshold to the same level for everybody when the system is first commissioned. Shortly afterwards you will no doubt discover that this isn't ideal as some users may struggle with a setting which seems fine for the majority. With a system which continually refines the stored template with each successful transaction, there will also be scope for tightening the threshold after a while, in order to lower the possibility of false accepts. In either case it will mean delving into the system and making changes for the individuals in question. There are some points worth noting here. Firstly, any changes you make to the threshold settings should be small ones. It is better to fine-tune this setting incrementally over time for a user than to make drastic changes which may result in unnecessary false accepts or false rejects. Secondly, the cynic in you will probably become suspicious if a particular user keeps coming back and asking you to lower the threshold for them. If this is the case, go with the user to the nearest applicable reader and watch them using it. It may be that user inconsistency is the main problem and that a little additional training will cure this without lowering the threshold to questionable levels.

With regard to access levels and time zones, you may suppose that you will set these once and forget them.  In reality, it is quite feasible that certain employees will change their working habits and location from time to time and that these parameters will need to be re-set accordingly.  Care should be taken in this respect, especially as there may in some cases need to be a transition period where the user has access rights for a wide range of access points.  If your system features a full audit trail, you will be easily able to monitor this.  If it doesn't, there may be a user-definable field that you can press into service to note such changes.  If all else fails, a manual logbook should be used to log alterations to system settings.  If your administration terminal is on the main network and you also have access to personnel records, you may like to set up some sort of automatic notification when employees change departments in order to check the settings for such individuals.

Most systems software will feature a report generation system of some description.  In some cases, this may consist of some rudimentary fixed transaction reports, while more sophisticated systems may allow you to query the database in order to configure your own bespoke reports.  Another option, if the database is in a known format, is to use a purpose-built reporting package such as Crystal Reports, ReportSmith, or similar to produce your required reports.  In any event, you will need to be clear about exactly what you need from your reports, for whose benefit and how often you need to run them.  For example, the system no doubt will be capable of producing a report of all transactions for you, but this is probably of little value.  It is more likely that you will want to know about just the exceptions where the verification process has failed, or perhaps transactions for an individual or group of individuals, and almost certainly you will wish to filter this information by date range.  If the standard software you are using does not allow for this, then you will be better served by one of the specialist reporting packages.  There will also be non-transaction related reports that you may wish to produce periodically, such as user lists or user lists by group.  If your system is using cards or tokens, you may have related information such as issue number, issue date and renewal date that you wish to produce reports on in order to manage supply of the tokens.  Then there is administration-related information such as audit trails or automatically logged system faults and so on.

In configuring your reports, you should bear in mind how you are going to analyze the resultant information.  With transaction reports for example, you may be able to establish patterns around specific verification points, users or time of day, which help you to understand issues and perhaps anticipate problems and their solutions, accordingly.  You may also be able to use such reports to analyze an individual user's transactions over a period of time and understand how performance is affected by slight physiological or behavioral changes in this context.  Indeed, this should be an integral part of managing and fine tuning the system accordingly.

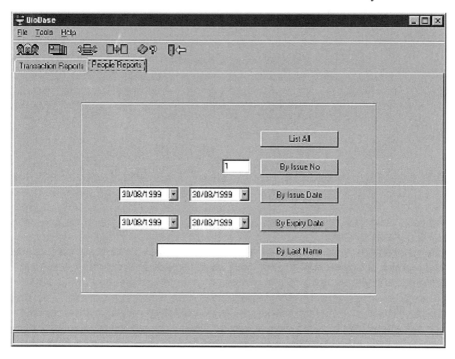

Figure 5.5 A simple but intuitive reporting methodology

These reports may also help you to understand general system performance and, if you have a number of readers on your system, perhaps be able to identify when a particular reader is performing below standard, or perhaps where there is a network connectivity problem. Certainly, a powerful reporting functionality is to be considered an asset within any biometric system. Its real value however will depend very much on how prepared you are to spend some time thinking through the reports, their precise purpose, frequency and how you utilize the data they provide. They should certainly be considered as part of the ongoing system management process.

An example of using reports positively may be in the interpretation of false reject and false accept errors within everyday transactions. Hopefully, these will be few and far between, but if you do come across instances then you should very quickly address them with the individuals concerned (in the case of false accepts, you may or may not have identified the impostor, but will at least know the identity that has been compromised). It may be that the threshold is set at an inappropriate level or that the reference template is of poor quality and the user in question should be re-enrolled into the system. In either case, some systems adjustment and related administration may be necessary. If you suddenly start to experience increased errors just at one verification point, then this would point towards a fault with that particular device, necessitating an unscheduled maintenance check. These are obvious examples of how your reports may help you in the day-to-day management of your biometric system.

## 5.8 Dealing with exceptions

In even the best planned systems there will still be exceptions, either with users, individual readers, environmental conditions, external network influences, force majeur and other occurrences. The way in which we deal with exceptions may make a significant difference to how the system is perceived by the users, and indeed in some cases potential users.

Let's consider for a moment the individual user who for some reason just cannot seem to make the system work for themselves. There may be a temptation on the part of the systems administrator to think of this person as a hopeless case who just doesn't understand technology or perhaps doesn't listen to instructions. This would be a big mistake. If an individual user is having difficulty with the system there will be a reason for it, and often a good one. This may be a physical characteristic which makes it difficult to interact with the biometric reader in the usual way. For example, an elderly person may have recurring bouts of arthritis in their hands, making it difficult to use a hand geometry reader. Someone else may have particularly weak fingerprints, making it difficult to capture a good sample for comparison. Perhaps someone using a retinal scanning device has such poor eyesight that when they remove their spectacles they find it difficult to focus on the target and keep properly aligned with the device. There may be a hundred other legitimate reasons why certain individuals have difficulties with a particular technology which aren't experienced by the majority of users.

Whatever the situation, it is important not to become impatient with, or otherwise belittle the user - in all probability the error is with the system in not being able to accommodate a sufficiently broad range of subjects. Of course, the users themselves may be becoming impatient if they do not understand why things don't seem to be working for them. The important thing is to understand why the problem exists and to be quickly able to remedy it. If the device you are using features an individually adjustable matching threshold for each user, then you will probably be able to find a setting which works for this user. Indeed, with some systems you can reduce this setting to such a point that it will accept virtually any sample. Naturally this compromises the security somewhat, but if the user doesn't know this, it may be an acceptable compromise, at least in the short term while you consider other measures. If this sort of situation is handled properly, with courtesy, understanding and a genuine desire to help the user, then it portrays the whole system and its administration in a good light. The user concerned will become a good ambassador for the system - an important point if you are dealing with the general public. On the other hand, if the user is made to feel that they are a nuisance and somehow 'different' from the norm, then this will have the opposite effect. Alienating a user will cause difficulties, even when you have a captive user base. If you are dealing with the public, it could lose you customers. Any such user-related problems you should therefore look upon as a gift, as they represent an opportunity for you to show just how good you are at handling such issues, and how important the welfare of your users is to the organization.

Not all exceptions are user-related. You may have a rogue device on the network which seems to work intermittently, causing unnecessary delays in transaction processing. Such a fault may or may not be easy to track down, but we must attend to it promptly. In many cases it may be appropriate to simply swap out the offending device and deal with the rogue unit off-line, providing of course that you had the foresight to keep a spare device on site for just such emergencies! The important thing of course will be to not inconvenience your users for a moment longer than is absolutely necessary. If you do not have a replacement device, then it may be better to fall back on a manual process in that particular area, until the system is fully operational again. Perhaps you are thinking, ah yes, but a fault may develop within the network infrastructure itself, which is perceived incorrectly as a device fault. This is of course possible, but perhaps less likely if the network was well designed and configured initially and monitoring tools are being used to watch capacity and performance. In a really critical situation, you may choose to build in some resilience in the form of duplication or alternative routes that can be switched automatically when performance drops below a certain threshold. Then there are host software related faults. You would naturally expect any serious software to be predominantly bug free, but it is hard to test for every scenario, and certain system BIOS/OS/core software relationships may work slightly differently and produce different effects under certain operational conditions. This is a tricky one, which will be sometimes hard to pin down and eliminate entirely. However, thorough testing of the system before final live roll-out should have identified any major problems in this respect.

Sometimes faults may naturally fall outside of your immediate control. Extended power outages spring to mind, although this is less likely in contemporary situations and you will no doubt have UPS systems in place which will keep the system up for a certain period in such an event. More difficult would be actual and serious physical damage to either systems components or the network infrastructure itself. This is certainly not unknown, especially when there is other on-site construction taking place. To deal with exceptions efficiently, you must have a suitable process for doing so. Part of this is around acknowledging the sort of errors that could conceivably occur and having a contingency plan in place to ensure business continuity. Part of it is also around having the right resource on hand to manage the situation. If you outsource any of this, be sure that your contract includes service level agreements accordingly.

In conclusion, there will always be exceptions, whether they be user, systems or process related. How they are managed and therefore the impact they have on the overall system, will be indicative of the amount of thought and planning that has gone into the system beforehand. A well designed and professionally managed system will distinguish itself in this respect. This in turn will create a positive perception among users, leading to more consistent and higher performance throughout. A poorly managed response to exceptions on the other hand will almost certainly have a negative impact on user perception, which, as we have already discussed, can adversely affect overall performance.

## 5.9 Implementation conclusions

In this chapter, we have discussed some of the primary issues around the implementation of a typical biometric system. Depending on the scale and precise nature of the system in question, this may be considered as a general overview or perhaps as the tip of the iceberg. One thing is for certain, the system will not install and manage itself, therefore we need some degree of forward planning, installation expertise and subsequent system management. The effort and resources that we assign to this will have an impact on the initial success and subsequent smooth running of the system overall.

It is recommended therefore that we view the system's implementation as a project in its own right and treat this as we would any other business orientated IT project. Even though there may be various degrees of collaboration with external entities such as device manufacturers and systems integrators, it is still important to manage the whole efficiently and with clear objectives and milestones in place. In the majority of cases I believe that this is best undertaken by the organization themselves, who after all will be using and living with the end result. In this respect an overall Program Manager might usefully be appointed who can draw together the various entities and maintain the complete picture at any one time. This will be important, as within any sizeable system there will be many strands to co-ordinate once implementation actually begins. For example, delivery and testing of the individual biometric capture devices will obviously need to be undertaken in good time before they are finally installed in situ and connected up to the network. In turn, the network itself obviously needs to be in place before we can start connecting things to it. These are obvious examples where a logical sequence of events needs to take place in order to install and commission the hardware and software which forms the nucleus of our system. However, there are additional factors such as communication and training which are equally important and must be carefully planned in order to coincide with the relevant phase of the systems installation.

If we agree with the above points, it will become obvious that there are various people who need to interact with our project plan, some of whom come from quite different backgrounds and disciplines. If this is not carefully planned and orchestrated then much time could be lost in misunderstanding, leading to a rather piecemeal approach to implementation. This is precisely why an overall Program Manager should be appointed to run the project and resolve any issues arising therein. Furthermore, this individual should be an experienced and skilled project manager with a track record of delivering business improvement programmes. It sounds obvious doesn't it? But sadly this has not always been the case, with some systems implementations being run by purchasing managers, security managers or whoever seems to have been standing around at the time.

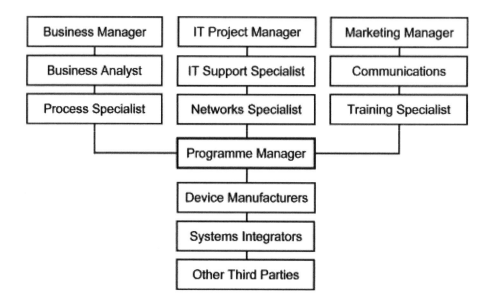

Figure 5.6 A possible project structure for implementation

The illustration in Figure 5.6 represents a possible project structure with which to implement a typical biometric system. Naturally it rather depends on scale and in some instances nothing of the sort would be required, whilst in others this might be regarded very much as a skeletal framework. The important point is that there should be *some* structure in place in order to implement the system properly and therefore realize the anticipated benefits accordingly.

# 6. Application Development

It is curious that in the formative years of what we shall call the biometrics industry there was much emphasis on the front-end capture device, or sometimes integrated devices, but relatively little on software. Perhaps this was natural as many were preoccupied in proving that the concept actually could work and that their particular device was a leading contender. Nowadays there exist a raft of biometric products targeted at the workstation/network access control function which naturally feature some sort of software integration into the operating system. However, high quality innovative software applications which feature biometric technology (or the potential to integrate to it) are still relatively thin on the ground. This may appear surprising to some people when you consider the plethora of professional software houses across the globe and the fact that biometrics are often perceived (and publicised) as representing an exciting, leading-edge technology within the broader computer science arena.

Where does that leave you if you are planning to implement a biometric system? It will naturally depend upon the nature of the system you had in mind and whether an off-the-shelf software package exists that can meet the requirement. If this requirement is a relatively straightforward one such as basic physical access control or time logging, then you may well find something suitable that you can take from a vendor and implement straight from the box. If the requirement is more organization specific or involves close integration with your existing systems infrastructure, then things are a little different as there will undoubtedly be a certain amount of custom development required. The question is, who undertakes and manages this development?

There are various ways forward in this respect including total outsourcing, whereby you simply hand over the project in its entirety to a third party, a joint development utilising the services of a trusted software house, or perhaps an in-house development project whereby your own IT staff will develop and test the proposed solution. The relative merits of these approaches will naturally depend upon the scale of the system, in-house resources and a number of other factors, but in any event it will be necessary to understand how contemporary biometric devices interface with host systems and how we might allow for them in software development terms. In this chapter we shall therefore take a look at some of the issues around application development for systems which utilize biometric technology. This may perhaps assist the reader to reach conclusions as to whether this is something that could easily be undertaken in-house, or otherwise.

## 6.1 Choosing the development tools

The choice of development tools is an area that will require some consideration. This will especially be the case if your biometric application needs to integrate with other applications, perhaps sharing databases or existing procedures, and you wish to realize the best systems performance. In areas such as data access for example, do your development tools include native drivers for the core database, or are you having to rely on some interpretation layer? In what language were your existing applications written and can you easily interact with them, even if your preferred development environment is from another source? Sometimes this is perfectly possible, and sometimes it is fraught with difficulty.

If we are considering a stand-alone application, then obviously things are more straightforward as we do not need to think about interfaces and dependencies, but even here we shall have to think about the platform on which the system will be deployed. Will it run under UNIX/AIX, Windows, OS2, Linux, or perhaps some other system? We need to ensure that the development tools we use are suitable for the deployment platform. In many cases we can probably assume the use of Microsoft Windows in some version or another at the desktop, and probably something like Windows NT Server for medium-range back-office situations. Let's assume this to be the case for our discussions within this chapter as this will help to focus our thinking. OK, so we have a 32-bit Windows environment in our theoretical organization. What are the other parameters we should consider when choosing our development tools? Well, we shall probably be relying on a database, both for user details and also storing authentication transactions, so good interaction with databases should be on our list. We may be wish to be displaying graphical information in the form of user photographs, animated displays and perhaps images of the chosen biometric itself, such as fingerprints or irises for example, so graphics should be well supported also. Naturally we shall wish to develop an attractive and intuitive user interface which is familiar in look and feel to those who will be using it, so a tool which integrates seamlessly with the Windows API and various dialogues will be required. In the case of a stand-alone application such as we are considering, many developers will naturally gravitate towards the popular Windows development environments such as C++, Delphi and Visual Basic, all of which could be suitable. Others may lean towards Java and the promise of portability across platforms, although some may have some views around relative performance in this respect.

However, before a final choice is made, we should consider which biometric device is going to be used and what is available in the way of a software development kit (SDK) to support it. Some device manufacturers may supply a DLL or two with some fairly low-level function calls for the primary functions, but still leave a fair amount of work for the developer to undertake in the form of integration and communications. Other vendors may encapsulate everything nicely in an OCX control or equivalent such as a Delphi component or package, with a minimum of relatively high-level functions for the developer to deal with. If controls such as this are provided, then naturally you will wish to ensure that your development environment can make the best use of them. Another consideration here is that of physical communication with the device, which might be via an RS232 or RS485 serial connection, or perhaps increasingly via a USB connection. If the device manufacturer has not encapsulated this within their own SDK, then the developer must consider using a comms library - another factor which might influence the decision of which tool to use. For general stand-alone application development for the Microsoft Windows environment, popular tools such as Visual C++, C++ Builder or Delphi would seem to offer a good balance between power, stability and flexibility of interaction with the sort of SDKs provided by biometric device vendors.

Let's return for a moment to the more complex applications where there is a requirement to interface to other applications. Some of these may be legacy applications that were written in a less familiar language or might perhaps be running in relative isolation from the general office applications perhaps on a middle range machine. In such a case, we shall need to understand how these were written and how we can interface with them. It may be that we can use the native programming language and call the biometric manufacturer's DLLs directly in order to provide the authentication functionality. On the other hand, this may be more complex if there is already a rat's nest of interfaces between different modules or even different programmes running in the background. This is where a little upfront analysis is required in order to understand exactly how a particular application is configured and working, so that we can ascertain the best way of integrating the biometric functionality into it and what will be required to do this. If it involves different programming languages and skill sets, then we had better appoint a project manager to co-ordinate this activity. Of course, it may not be a problem at all and we may find that a competent C++ programmer can undertake all of the necessary interfaces and application logic, whilst cleanly integrating the necessary biometric functionality. This is the whole point of this section, to emphasise the need to understand our objectives and the detailed architecture of our existing infrastructure, in order that we might choose the most appropriate application development tools for the job at hand.

So which tools are likely to be the best suited in this respect? In many cases you will already have your preferred in-house methodology and if this will meet all of the requirements, then it would make sense to use it as you will already be familiar with its operation and there will be little in the way of a learning curve, except perhaps for the various biometric-specific function calls. If you do have a free hand, then tools which have good database connectivity and functionality would be useful. Popular examples for the Windows environment would include the 'enterprise' editions of Borland C++ Builder and Microsoft Visual C++. Borland Delphi is also an extremely versatile tool in this respect and well suited to iterative RAD style development. If you are constructing your own back-end database, possibly using something like Oracle or SQL Server, then it would be pertinent to ensure that you have native high performance drivers for the correct version of your chosen database methodology. Starting off on the right foot with the right development tools is extremely important if we are to realize the best performance and functionality from our new biometric application. One can bring to mind several corporate grade applications in the IT world that have become dismal affairs with lumbering performance and poor stability, largely because they were built with sub-optimal tools in the first place and were not well considered from an architectural perspective. If you have a clean sheet of paper, then with a little foresight you can avoid this trap. If you have legacy systems and infrastructures which you have to work within, then at least spend some time thinking about these issues and try to arrive at the best all-round solution.


## 6.2 The intuitive GUI

The reader may at first find it strange that we include a section purely on the GUI, or graphical user interface, but this is a very important consideration, especially when we are dealing with technologies and methodologies that will be new to many users and system operators. Presenting these new ideas in a familiar and friendly fashion will go a long way to ensuring that users quickly grasp the principles involved and enjoy using and becoming proficient with the software.

Perhaps the first point to note here is the importance of keeping things simple. If the interface is cluttered and unintuitive, the users will struggle to find their way around and will quickly come to the conclusion that this is a poor piece of software. This could be disastrous in the context of enrolment software, where it is so important that the administrator becomes confident and skilled in capturing good quality biometric template information. It pays dividends therefore to make things easy for both the administrator and users in general. Whilst keeping things simple and intuitive, let's also try to make the interface attractive. There are lots of things we can do in this respect to ensure that each screen the user sees is neatly laid out and pleasing to the eye. Part of this is ensuring that the relative proportions of objects such as data fields and labels are well balanced and aligned properly on screen. Another factor is the intelligent use of color. Users will not wish to be distracted by outlandish color schemes just for the sake of being different, let's stick to the tried and tested conventions that everyone is familiar with. Whilst we are on the subject of familiarity, we should also ensure that objects such as menu items perform in the expected manner. For example, if the user selects 'File' from the main menu, let's present him with the options that he would normally expect to find in a mainstream Windows application (assuming we are developing for the Windows platform). Similarly, let's ensure that we use the standard Windows dialogues for printing and file maintenance. Whilst all this sounds rather obvious, one does still come across applications that are quite poor in this respect. A certain well-known corporate email client springs to mind which has users scrambling all over the menu structure looking for functions which should be obvious, even after they have been using it for many months. This approach would not help your biometric application, where we are already trying to engage the user in new processes and concepts. The last thing we want to do is make the everyday functions difficult for them. There are some areas of course where we shall have to depart from the norm due to the unusual nature of our biometric application and the functionality required of it. An example of this is menu bar buttons, for which you may have to design some obvious glyphs, but again these should be kept relatively simple and obvious as to their purpose. A simple, clear and attractive interface is therefore what we should be looking to provide. We can leave the complexity of the program out of sight, buried in the code where it should be.

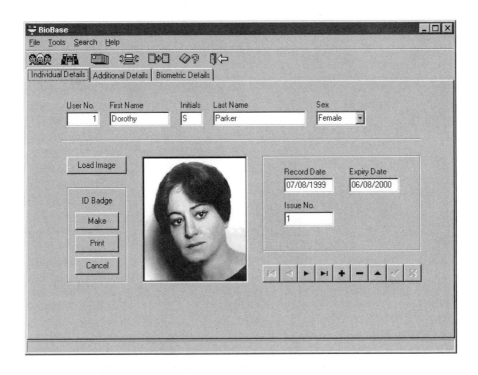

Figure 6.1 An example user interface within a biometric application

In the example above, there is actually quite a lot of functionality available from within this screen, and yet it doesn't seem over-complicated at first sight and a new user should quickly understand what is happening and how to interact with the software. Note also in this example the use of a tabbed dialogue, effectively spreading the related functions across three 'pages' or screens so as not to clutter the user interface or add unnecessary complication. This can work well when you have a number of related functions that you wish to group together in a logical manner which is also intuitive for the user. You may also decide to group related objects together on the same screen by the use of boxes or frames. For example, in Figure 6.1 you will notice that the ID badge-related buttons for creating, printing or cancelling a badge are neatly grouped together within a frame, effectively separating them out from other functions. A first time user should have no difficulty in understanding how to create or print an ID badge from this screen. Note also, that although there is a fairly significant amount of code involved in creating and formatting a photo ID badge from the user database, this is effectively hidden from the user, who only has to click on a single button in order to create the badge.

The same approach may be taken with regard to the biometric-related tasks around enrolment and subsequent verification. If this is made as straightforward and intuitive as possible, then the systems administrator will be able to undertake the task quickly and reliably from one user to the next.

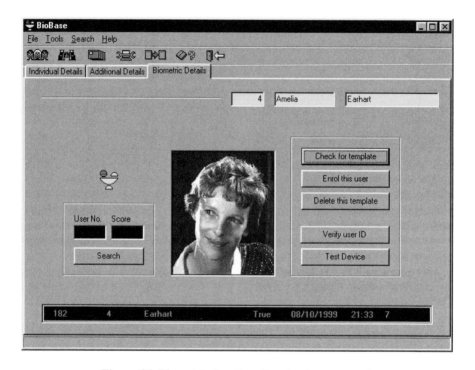

Figure 6.2 Biometric functionality simply presented

In Figure 6.2 above, there are a number of functions that can be performed. Firstly, the administrator has a visual check of the user's ID number, name and photograph. He can then easily check to see if a template is already enrolled against this index in the database. If a template does already exist, it may be simply deleted from the system. Enrolling a new user into the database and subsequently undertaking a biometric verification check couldn't be any simpler, as the administrator has only to click on the relevant button and will be guided by messages appearing in the status bar. Note also that information appertaining to the verification result is neatly displayed in its own window at the bottom of the screen. Another function available here is a search facility, whereby a user's biometric may be captured, converted into a template and compared with others already in the database - a useful check to ascertain whether an individual may already be enrolled under another name. If a match is found, the details of the individual with the matching template who is already in the database will be displayed, including photograph and a relative score of similarity. The administrator only has to click on one button to do this. All in all, there is a considerable amount of functionality available within the screen depicted in Figure 6.2, and yet the presentation is simple, uncluttered and intuitive, making it easy for a first time administrator to find their way around. Another way we can help the user is by providing simple 'tool tips' for each button which briefly display the button's function when the mouse cursor is placed over it. We may choose to make these switchable via a user preferences section within the software. The Windows 'status bar' offers another valuable way of communicating with the user and we may choose to display error messages or other information here as applicable.

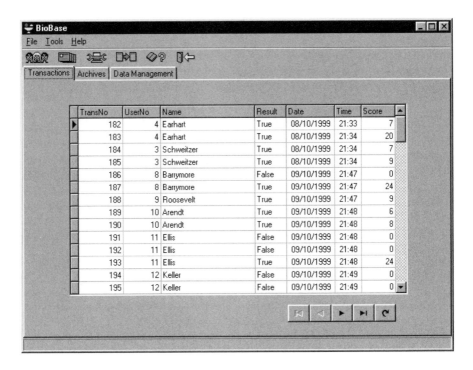

Figure 6.3 Transactions

One area where there is much scope for practising the intuitive GUI is that of transaction monitoring, where we should be aiming to present information to the administrator in a clear and unambiguous fashion that allows him to see, in real time, exactly what is happening throughout the system. This will be particularly important in situations where there are multiple readers or verification points throughout the facility. If this transaction data can include a relative 'score' of how closely the templates were matched, then all the better as this will allow the administrator to monitor individuals who may be having difficulty using the system for one reason or another.

In addition to being able to monitor transactional data in real time, it will be pertinent within most systems to provide the administrator with some sort of report generation functionality. Sometimes this might be provided via the provision of a standard report generation tool such as Crystal Reports or ReportSmith, wh ch allows the user to configure and run their own custom reports against a standard database architecture. This may suit the 'power user' very well, especially if they have prior experience of the chosen tool and know how to find their way around. However, this can be quite a complex area for someone who may not be particularly skilled in IT database methodology. Your biometric system administrator may be such an individual and therefore, if we can make things easier by providing a simplified report generation function, then this would be worthwhile.

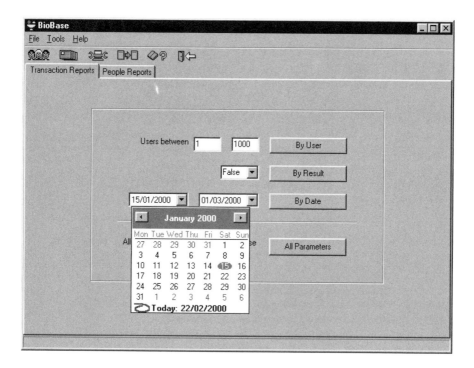

Figure 6.4 An intuitive reporting engine

A simple dialogue such as that featured in Figure 6.4 allows the administrator to easily and quickly produce reports against historic data with just a few mouse clicks. In this example, reports may be quickly produced by user, by verification result, by date range or by any combination of these parameters. This is quite powerful, but does not burden the administrator with having to construct

SQL queries or run specialist scripts in order to get at the data. Of course, there is no reason why a more powerful reporting tool may not additionally be used where this is warranted, and provided your database is in some known format then this will no doubt be a relatively straightforward matter for your LAN or IT support manager to organize.

The 'setup' section in your application should be equally straightforward and easily understood by an administrator with average IT skills. Once again, it should be possible to hide much of the complexity behind an intuitive GUI, leaving the administrator with only those choices pertinent to the high-level operation of the system on a day-to-day basis.

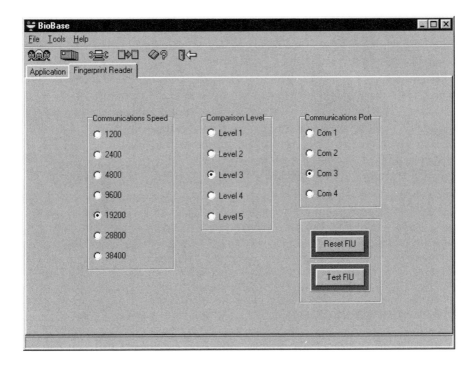

Figure 6.5 Setting the basic operating parameters

An example of this may be with regard to the connection between the biometric device and the computer where the ability to quickly select and test the physical connection without getting into too much low-level detail would be valuable. We might additionally include the ability to set any device-specific adjustable parameters (such as template matching threshold) from the same screen.

Within a typical application there will of course be many more screens and functions to those depicted in the above illustrations, but the principles outlined above would serve us well in most cases. When we are enhancing an existing application to provide additional biometric functionality, then the situation will perhaps be a little different as we shall have to blend in with the existing design and operational logic as seamlessly as possible. But even in such a case, we might still be guided by the simple and intuitive GUI.

Another area worthy of our attention is the application help file. This may be perceived as either a blessing or a curse, depending on the amount of consideration we give to this within our overall design. I am sure we have all experienced the sort of poor help file which, whilst containing many thousands of words, just doesn't seem to cover the areas most likely to be useful. Similarly, the type of help file that takes you off in an endless series of links to other sections until you have become well and truly lost is of little real value. What we need is something that is succinct and straight to the point whilst remaining easily and quickly navigable, even by a first time user. How many help files have you seen recently within mainstream applications that fall into this category? Possibly not very many as this is an area where even household names in the software industry often get themselves into something of a mess and this is such a shame as the help file represents an area where an application can really shine and be perceived by the user as one of quality. Let's ensure therefore that our biometric application help file remains sleek and intuitive and performs the function it was always intended to, i.e. to guide the user in the correct operation of the software and not to act as a part-time advertising medium.

In conclusion, the way we present information to the user and systems administrator is an important part of our biometric application. This should be considered in some detail and the GUI designed by someone who has experience in this field and understands how users interact with computers. If there is an award somewhere for the most easily understood, logically operated and beautifully presented professional software package (as I am sure there must be), then our biometric application should be a solid contender for it. If it isn't, then it is time to go back to the drawing board.

## 6.3 PC Communications

In many cases, when we utilize an SDK (software development kit) from one of the major biometric vendors, it will include the necessary communications functionality to be able to communicate with the biometric device via the computer's serial ports (or sometimes a parallel port). In such an instance the developer will not have to concern himself with the detail of what is happening behind the scenes in order to achieve this. In other cases, the developer may be interacting with the device at a lower level and may need to provide the code to communicate via the PC's ports. This may be simplified via the provision of a robust comms library designed for the chosen development environment and there are certainly some good examples of such tools available to the development community. In either case, perhaps it would be useful to briefly remind ourselves of some of the basics of serial communication, if only to serve as a starting point in understanding what will be required in this context and what sort of errors might occur.

Within the more general software development world, communications programming has often been considered as something of a black art, with many practitioners seeming to spend hours tinkering with code in their efforts to initiate or restore communications. In fact, the situation is not so bad in reality, but is often not particularly well documented, even within the popular Windows based development environments that constitute a good deal of the international development toolkit. Whilst acknowledging development for other operating systems, we shall base our discussion around the Windows environment as this will be familiar to the majority of readers. The tools available within the Windows operating system itself allow the user to configure the communication ports on the PC to a reasonable level of detail, although this functionality may remain unfamiliar to many users, some of whom will be unsure of some of the terminology bandied around. Similarly, not many developers would have had occasion to look at this area in depth if they have been concerned mostly with desktop office applications.

Let's start with the term UART. This stands for Universal Asynchronous Receiver / Transmitter and represents the chip inside your PC which handles the sending and receiving of data via the PC's communication ports. When we are discussing PC communications we are usually referring to asynchronous serial communications. Asynchronous means that the data stream we send includes start and stop bits to mark the beginning and end of each character in the stream (in synchronous communication, clocks at either end of the data link maintain synchronisation between devices). Serial means that the data bits are transmitted one at a time over a single wire (in parallel transmission bits are sent in parallel over several wires). The objective in each case being the transfer of data between applications and devices. The UART has a collection of registers, eight in fact, which enable it to communicate with your application via the Windows communications driver and the User.exe library. These registers may be thought of as a little like pigeon holes which the UART uses dynamically in order to note information about line parameters, interrupts, line status and so on. A small 16 byte FIFO (first in, first out) buffer collects incoming information until it can be retrieved by your application, ensuring that you do not lose any data. You may have noticed reference to terminology such as '9600.N.8.1' within some of your communications based programs. This is referring to the communication line parameters such as baud rate (usually interpreted as bits per second but actually means events per second), parity (a bit checking scheme which adds up the bits within a byte and then adds a final bit called the parity bit to ensure that the sum of all bits is either odd or even, as specified), data bits (a byte can contain 5, 6, 7 or 8 bits, usually 7 for text data or 8 for binary data), and stop bits (follows the data bits to mark the end of each byte, value either 1 or 2). Naturally it is important that the line parameters are set the same for equipment at either end of the line if error-free communication is to take place and we must therefore include provision within our application to match these parameters for the biometric device and the host PC. The UART will calculate the value of the parity bit (if parity is used) and raise an error if the two values don't match, indicating corrupt data. We shall need to handle this within our application accordingly. If flow control is used, then the sending and receiving of the data will be regulated automatically so as not to create bottlenecks leading to loss of data.

Having got the data into the PC, we now have to recognize it within our software application. Assuming this has been written using one of the popular visual development environments such as Visual C++ or Delphi, there are, as previously mentioned, various plug-in communications libraries available that can handle the interface between our application and the serial ports on the computer within the familiar component-based architecture. The event driven methodology will usually rely on a 'trigger' that is activated whenever data arrives at the designated communication port. Upon activation of this trigger we shall need to look at the incoming data stream in order to ascertain who has sent the message (a biometric device somewhere on the system no doubt) and what the message is telling us (probably details of an authentication transaction). We do this by analysing or 'parsing' the data stream to look for familiar information at designated points within the stream, usually identified by character position in the case of an ASCII character stream. A transaction stream from a biometric device or network master might for example have a start character, reader address, user number, result flag, tamper flag, other condition flag, parity checking and so on, all at predefined positions within the message stream. Our application code will need to extract from this stream the appropriate details and ensure that the correct response is generated within the program, from displaying information to writing a database record or whatever is appropriate. The stream may of course be encrypted in some way in the interests of data security and include an advanced error checking methodology with respect to data integrity, all of which will need to be accommodated by our application, with error handling routines incorporated as necessary. Naturally this communication is not all one way, and we shall no doubt be generating an equal amount of communication traffic back to the biometric device or network of devices. We may additionally be 'polling' the network in order to ensure that all the devices are present and working correctly.

In conclusion, data communication between the host PC and our biometric device, or network of devices, may be an area with which we do not need to get too involved if we are using the function calls provided courtesy of the biometric vendors SDK. However, an understanding of what is happening in this respect would still be useful in order to understand any external error messages that may be generated. If we really do need to get down to low-level communications programming, then the developer should be experienced in this field or quickly be able to get up to speed with the necessary knowledge to tackle this area. In most cases, using one of the available proven comms libraries will be most expedient as the learning curve will not be too steep and the functionality probably more than adequate to meet our requirements.

# 6.4 Interfacing to biometric devices

Mention was made in the last section of SDKs as provided by the majority of biometric device vendors. This is sensible as it enables external software developers to develop applications, or enhance existing ones in order to provide biometric functionality via the chosen device. Typically, the SDK will consist of a DLL (dynamic link library) containing a number of functions that may be called from the host application. The developer must naturally be familiar with the DLL model and how to use this functionality from within the chosen development environment. Some biometric vendors will go a stage further and provide an OCX control or perhaps a dedicated component for use within a development tool such as Borland's popular Delphi product. This makes life even easier for the developer as the component will effectively encapsulate the functionality required to interface to the biometric device, making for easier setup and initialisation. The various operational functions of the device such as 'enrol template' or 'match template' will be called via the DLL functions provided as part of the OCX or component when registered within the chosen development environment. This allows the developer to spend less time worrying about the device interface and more time concentrating on the operational aspects of the software being developed.

Just as finished software can be of variable quality, so can SDKs, especially with regard to their documentation and overall stability. Sometimes one may find that the SDK is fine for a particular development environment (usually the one favoured by the vendor) but may be a little more sketchy in its support for alternative environments. This is worth establishing in advance via discussion with the vendor's own development team. It may be that they are happy to co-operate in any fine-tuning required to make the SDK suitable for use with your preferred development tool, in order to broaden its overall appeal. This may be a point to consider for those looking at Linux for example.

Another issue that has been on the minds of independent software developers when considering biometrics is that every vendor seems to have its own set of rules with regard to device interfaces and the necessary function calls. This was recognized some time ago by the biometric industry and an initiative named BioAPI was triggered by a consortium of interested parties including household names such as Intel, Unisys and Compaq as well as a raft of leading biometric industry vendors. The BioAPI Consortium announced in April 1998 that it intended to develop a common biometric API standard. Throughout the remainder of 1998 and 1999 other API initiatives (BAPI and HA-API) were incorporated into the overall mix with working drafts produced towards the end of 1999. By the time you read this book, the first release of the BioAPI standard will have been issued and hopefully adopted by the majority of biometric vendors. This will make it much easier for software developers as they will be able to become familiar with a standard set of function calls, making it a simple process to port different biometric devices to their applications. This is not exactly 'hot swapping' as different subsets of function calls may be used with different devices, but it is a much better situation than has hitherto been the case and will hopefully encourage more independent software houses to develop applications incorporating biometric technology. From an end user's perspective, it can mean that they are not totally reliant on a single vendor and may perhaps incorporate devices from more than one source - a most desirable state of affairs. At the time of writing, the BioAPI working draft document was a hefty 107 pages in length, representing a considerable effort on the part of the consortium members. Future SDKs from the leading biometric vendors will hopefully be BioAPI compliant with respect to their various function calls, placing less of a learning curve on the application developer.

But what actually happens in practice and how difficult is it for the average developer to incorporate biometric methodology into an application? Much depends upon the development environment utilized. It may be a question of initialising and then calling functions within the biometric vendor's own DLL, or in some instances it may be possible to encapsulate the biometric functionality within a module, making it easier to refer to from other parts of the program.

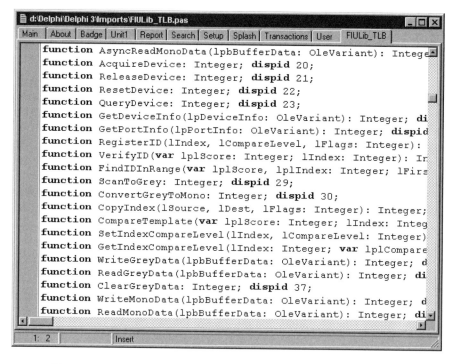

Figure 6.6 Encapsulating device functionality within a code module

In the above example, we have encapsulated all of the required device-specific functionality into a single code module which can then be referenced from anywhere else within the program. This effectively provides an interface layer between the main application code and the underlying DLL's provided by the biometric device manufacturer. Having made the link between our program and the biometric device, we still need to consider how we will translate the intuitive GUI presentation we discussed earlier with the code necessary to make it actually work. For example, the following code calls a predefined function when the user clicks on the 'Test' button within the setup screen of our application.

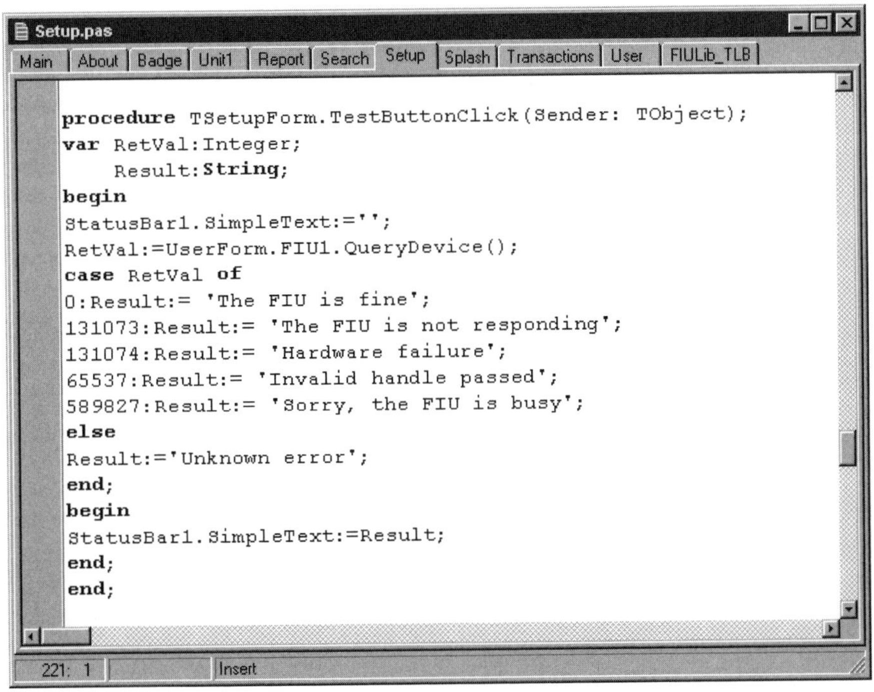

```
Setup.pas

Main | About | Badge | Unit1 | Report | Search | Setup | Splash | Transactions | User | FIULib_TLB

procedure TSetupForm.TestButtonClick(Sender: TObject);
var RetVal:Integer;
    Result:String;
begin
StatusBar1.SimpleText:='';
RetVal:=UserForm.FIU1.QueryDevice();
case RetVal of
0:Result:= 'The FIU is fine';
131073:Result:= 'The FIU is not responding';
131074:Result:= 'Hardware failure';
65537:Result:= 'Invalid handle passed';
589827:Result:= 'Sorry, the FIU is busy';
else
Result:='Unknown error';
end;
begin
StatusBar1.SimpleText:=Result;
end;
end;

221: 1                    Insert
```

Figure 6.7 Testing the biometric device from within our application

This is a very simplistic example whereby we call the function named 'QueryDevice' and monitor the returned value in order to translate it into an English language text string and write it into the Windows status bar component at the bottom of the screen. In this instance, it allows the user to quickly check that the biometric device is indeed present and communicating as planned.

Things will start to get a little more complicated when we integrate the biometric device function call with another element within our application. For example, one of the parameters which we pass to the biometric function may be derived from elsewhere in our program. This may be a temporary piece of information that the user has just typed into an on-screen field, or perhaps a permanent piece of information such as that which might be held within a database. In the latter case, we shall obviously need to reference the database in order to look up the relevant piece of information and post it into our function call as appropriate. Selecting the correct record may be more or less straightforward according to how your application is controlling the database. In our test application example, the user has already selected the appropriate record on screen and the database is therefore 'pointing' at the correct record. All we need to do is go to the database and extract the pertinent information from the correct field.

```
User.pas                                                                    _ □ X
 Main │ About │ Badge │ Unit1 │ Report │ Search │ Setup │ Splash │ Transactions │ User │ FIULib_TLB │

   procedure TUserForm.DeleteButtonClick(Sender: TObject);
   var UserNo,RetVal:Integer;
        Result:String;
   begin
   UserNo:=Datamodule1.UserTbl.FieldByName('UserNo').AsInteger;
   RetVal:=FIU1.ClearIndex(UserNo);
   case RetVal of
   0:Result:= 'Template number ' + IntToStr(UserNo) + ' deleted';
   131073:Result:= 'The FIU is not responding';
   131074:Result:= 'Hardware failure';
   -1:Result:= 'The FIU has failed';
   65540:Result:= 'Invalid index';
   65537:Result:= 'Invalid handle passed';
   589827:Result:= 'Sorry, the FIU is busy';
   else
   Result:='Unknown error';
   end;
   begin
   StatusBar1.SimpleText:=Result;
   end;
   end;

  1:  1                    Insert
```

Figure 6.8 Deleting a template from within the biometric device

In the above code example, you will see that we have gone to the database table named 'UserTbl' and selected a field named 'UserNo' in order to locate the piece of information we are looking for, in this case the unique user ID number. We can then post this into our function call as a required parameter. The part of the application we are dealing with here is the User Database section whereby the administrator has the facility to delete a biometric template from within the biometric device itself (this particular device can store up to 1000 templates internally). The administrator accomplishes this with just a single button click whilst the user's database record is selected on screen. The UserNo field within our application database is also used as the index reference for the templates stored within the biometric device, so it is a relatively straightforward task to pass this number as a function parameter. The biometric device will, via the DLL, action our request to delete this particular template and pass back the return value which we can interpret accordingly. Note that we still allow for an error type return value, which may be the case if the device did not properly receive our instruction, possibly due to some sort of communication fault or maybe a failure within the device itself. This code represents another relatively simple example of calling a function within the device-specific DLL, this time passing a parameter from elsewhere within our application and once again monitoring, interpreting and displaying the result to the administrator in simple plain English terminology. The next example will take us a stage further to actually recording the transaction within our application's transactions database.

```
begin
Score:=00;
UserNo:=Datamodule1.UserTbl.FieldByName('UserNo').AsInteger;
RetVal:=FIU1.VerifyID(Score,UserNo);
case RetVal of
0:Result:= 'The templates match - ID verified';
131073:Result:= 'The FIU is not responding';
-1:Result:= 'Alert! The templates do not match';
65537:Result:= 'Invalid handle passed';
589827:Result:= 'Sorry, the FIU is busy';
else
Result:='Unknown error';
end;
begin
if Retval = 0 then
Pass:='True'
else
Pass:='False';
StatusBar1.SimpleText:=Result;
Datamodule1.TransTbl.Insert;
Datamodule1.TransTbl.FieldByName('UserNo').AsInteger:=UserNo;
Datamodule1.TransTbl.FieldByName('Result').AsString:=Pass;
Datamodule1.TransTbl.FieldByName('Score').AsInteger:=Score;
Datamodule1.TransTbl.Post;
end;
```

Figure 6.9 Writing a transaction to the database

In Figure 6.9 above, we are looking at an identity verification transaction within our application code. Note that once again we pass the UserNo parameter to the device in order to select the right template for comparison with the live sample (the user having placed their finger on the fingerprint reader). The return value from the device will tell us not only whether the templates match within our predefined threshold setting, but will also return a relative 'score' of just how closely the templates did match. This is very useful information, especially in the initial stages of a biometric system implementation when we wish to know how easily our users are using the biometric devices and whether our device threshold settings were the most appropriate. It follows then that we would wish to record this information within our application, probably via a dedicated 'transaction' table which we could subsequently issue queries against in order to retrieve the pertinent data. This means we shall have to write the transaction details into a new record within our database at every verification attempt. In Figure 6.9 you will see that as well as allowing for communication or device errors as in the previous examples, we have also said that we shall insert a new record into the 'TransTbl' which holds all such information, add the relevant data into the UserNo, Result and Score fields and then 'post' or save the record into our database. Actually, these aren't the only fields in our Transaction database. The action of posting will also complete the user's name fields (based upon UserNo) and will additionally enter the current date and time (based upon the system clock) into the respective fields, thereby creating a comprehensive record of the transaction. This is an interesting example of our still relatively simple code controlling both the external biometric device and elements of our host application, which, bear in mind, may be a legacy application which was not initially written with biometric functionality in mind.

The previous code examples showed how we might easily interface to a given biometric device via the manufacturer's supplied DLL and integrate its functionality into our host application. Whilst the examples have deliberately been chosen to be as simple as possible for illustrative purposes, the principles remain similar for more sophisticated functionality. Provided we have an SDK (software development kit) containing the necessary device-specific DLLs, this will be a relatively straightforward process. Without this information things would naturally be a little trickier; however, the vast majority of device manufacturers have an SDK available for just such purposes and with the introduction of the BioAPI, application developers will soon become familiar with biometric functionality and how to integrate it into their own programmes.

## 6.5 Database fundamentals

Whilst we are on the subject of application development, it is probably worth spending a few moments considering databases and how we might utilize them within our biometric application. Traditionally, when databases are mentioned people tend to think of either the large corporate databases on mainframes or middle range DB2 type platforms, or the sort of desktop RDBMS systems such as MS Access, Paradox, dBase and the like that office power users like to tinker with to manipulate their decision support information. In reality, a biometric system database may be any one of these, or perhaps a combination of different methodologies, depending on exactly what we are trying to achieve. For example, we may be able to utilize an existing corporate employee database for user-related information and yet maintain a dedicated transaction database on a separate platform. Or perhaps we have access to public data as might be the case with a benefits payment system which utilizes biometric technology. At the other end of the scale, the user may effectively carry the database with them on a token such as a chip card, with only minimal data held within the system.

In any event, the issue of data and how we store it and use it within our application is one that we need to consider carefully. As a first step, it will be useful to consider exactly what data we are going to be storing. Naturally we shall be storing some information about our system users. This may be limited to something simple like a name and reference number, or may constitute a full user database with perhaps some user-definable fields for organization-specific information. If this is a commercial application, we may also be storing information (with the user's consent) about their transaction history, for example a travel system might include flight history, traveller preferences and so on. Then there is the transaction-related information to provide an audit trail of who has been verified, when and where etc., and there may even be a requirement to store responses to transactions or administrator comments. In many systems we shall want to store the biometric templates themselves, possibly more than one, together with perhaps photographic identity information. In addition to the above, there may be administration or systems-related information which needs to be stored somewhere. All in all, when you start to think about it, there is probably a fairly considerable database element to many biometric systems. In several cases, there will additionally be the requirement to interface to other external databases, either in real time or perhaps with some sort of batch process interaction and naturally we shall have to consider the data security element of any such design.

But for now, let's go back to our 'collections' of data such as user-related, transaction-related and so on. These will often fall into fairly obvious groups which we can consider as either separate databases or separate tables within the main database. Using our example application model, the latter would be the case as we were using a self-contained 'internal' database which would typically (although not necessarily) reside on the same platform as the application. In this particular (albeit rather simple) case there are two primary tables that form the core of our database. The User table which stores all the pertinent information about our users including the biometric template, and the Transaction table which stores details of actual authentication transactions. In our example application we have chosen to integrate the biometric functionality with a fairly comprehensive personnel database, such as might be used by a large corporation or government department. Because of this, our User table has a larger number of fields than would be strictly necessary for the biometric functionality. If a suitable personnel database already existed, we may of course have been able to link into this in order to reference the basic information such as name, department, etc. If our user table is likely to be very large, as might be the case in a public system such as benefits payments or border control, then we would take great care to choose the right back-end database, the platform it is running on and also to optimise the tables and related queries for the best possible performance. In a smaller system such as our example application (which incidentally could handle around two million records) we should still consider designing the tables in as efficient a manner as possible in order to optimise speed when referencing user-related information. Obviously, the less data we need to shuffle around, the less is held in memory and the better the performance. Similarly, if we create specific indexes on fields on which we wish to search the database, then this will also provide performance benefits, especially on the sort of typical desktop machine or workstation that such an application would run on.

| User | UserNo | RecordDate | Expiry Date | First Name | Initial | LastName |
|------|--------|------------|-------------|------------|---------|----------|
| 1 | 1 | 07/08/1999 | 06/08/2000 | Dorothy | S | Parker |
| 2 | 2 | 31/07/1999 | 30/07/2000 | Alice | DR | Walker |
| 3 | 3 | 14/07/1999 | 13/07/2000 | Albert | T | Schweitzer |
| 4 | 4 | 09/06/1999 | 08/06/2000 | Amelia | F | Earhart |
| 5 | 5 | 17/08/1999 | 16/08/2000 | Andrew | F | Carnegie |
| 6 | 6 | 31/08/1999 | 30/08/2000 | Emmeline | S | Pankhurst |
| 7 | 7 | 21/07/1999 | 20/07/2000 | Ernest | P | Hemmingway |
| 8 | 8 | 15/07/1999 | 14/07/2000 | Ethel | D | Barrymore |
| 9 | 9 | 04/07/1999 | 03/07/2000 | Franklin | D | Roosevelt |
| 10 | 10 | 23/06/1999 | 22/06/2000 | Hannah | H | Arendt |
| 11 | 11 | 15/08/1999 | 14/08/2000 | Havelock | R | Ellis |
| 12 | 12 | 15/07/1999 | 14/07/2000 | Helen | V | Keller |
| 13 | 13 | 19/07/1999 | 18/07/2000 | John | D | Steinbeck |
| 14 | 14 | 30/07/1999 | 29/07/2000 | Lillian | T | Hellman |
| 15 | 15 | 23/07/1999 | 22/07/2000 | Mark | V | Twain |
| 16 | 16 | 15/08/1999 | 14/08/2000 | Shirley | H | Chisholm |
| 17 | 17 | 31/07/1999 | 30/07/2000 | Theodore | T | Roosevelt |
| 18 | 18 | 31/07/1999 | 30/07/2000 | Thornton | M | Wilder |
| 19 | 19 | 31/07/1999 | 30/07/2000 | William | G | Wilder |

Figure 6.10 A section of our example User table

The illustration above shows only a small section of the fields within our example User table, which as mentioned, also serves as a primary personnel database and so also includes address details, photographs, user-defined fields and other information. However, with a relatively small self-contained system such as this we can afford to take the view that we are unlikely to have more than one or two thousand user records and can easily manipulate this amount of data within our application without notable performance penalties. We could have split this table up into two or more referential tables in a relational model, but there was little need to for our example application. In this table, the Record Date and Expiry Date are actually generated for us by the system, although the administrator can override these settings if desired. Having the system generate time and date-related information automatically is quite useful as we shall see later on. We may also choose to generate the user number automatically, unless we have some organization-specific protocol that prevents this. The advantage here is of course that the automatically generated numbers are bound to be unique. An important consideration in system terms.

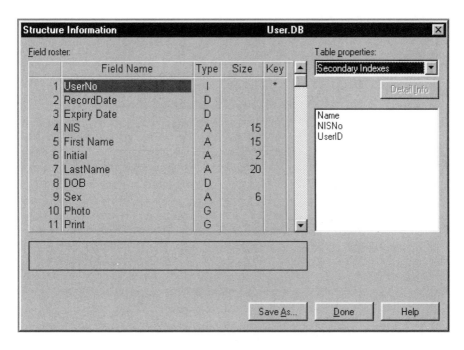

Figure 6.11 A section of the User table structure

In the illustration above you can see some of the User table structure and how this has been constructed. Certain fields, like the date fields for example, follow a fixed structure determined by the database methodology in use. With other text-based fields we will be able to limit them to a certain size in order to prevent our individual records from becoming unwieldy. We should also choose our numeric field types carefully in order not to waste space unnecessarily by using long integer or double field types when it is not necessary to do so. Notice that in the above example, in addition to the key field which acts both as an index and a reference to other tables, we have constructed a secondary index on certain other fields that we know we shall be searching against within our application and given these indexes meaningful names so that our code is easily understood.

Even within a straightforward self-contained application such as the one we have been using as an example, it still makes sense to pay a little attention to the database fundamentals in order to ensure a reasonable level of performance when the application is run on average level hardware. This becomes especially pertinent when we need to 'look up' data, perhaps from more than one table in order to complete a real-time transaction. On the subject of transactions, our transaction table should be especially streamlined and optimised in order not to add an unnecessary overhead to the biometric transaction process. This naturally becomes more pertinent as the number of concurrent users increases.

| Transaction | TransNo | UserNo | Result | Date | Time | Score |
|---|---|---|---|---|---|---|
| 1 | 182 | 4 | True | 08/10/1999 | 21:33:57, | 7 |
| 2 | 183 | 4 | True | 08/10/1999 | 21:34:03, | 20 |
| 3 | 184 | 3 | True | 08/10/1999 | 21:34:29, | 7 |
| 4 | 185 | 3 | True | 08/10/1999 | 21:34:36, | 9 |
| 5 | 186 | 8 | False | 09/10/1999 | 21:47:19, | 0 |
| 6 | 187 | 8 | True | 09/10/1999 | 21:47:40, | 24 |
| 7 | 188 | 9 | True | 09/10/1999 | 21:47:57, | 9 |
| 8 | 189 | 10 | True | 09/10/1999 | 21:48:11, | 6 |
| 9 | 190 | 10 | True | 09/10/1999 | 21:48:17, | 8 |
| 10 | 191 | 11 | False | 09/10/1999 | 21:48:27, | 0 |
| 11 | 192 | 11 | False | 09/10/1999 | 21:48:39, | 0 |
| 12 | 193 | 11 | True | 09/10/1999 | 21:48:54, | 24 |
| 13 | 194 | 12 | False | 09/10/1999 | 21:49:10, | 0 |
| 14 | 195 | 12 | False | 09/10/1999 | 21:49:18, | 0 |
| 15 | 196 | 12 | True | 09/10/1999 | 21:49:30, | 24 |
| 16 | 197 | 13 | False | 09/10/1999 | 21:49:46, | 0 |
| 17 | 198 | 13 | True | 09/10/1999 | 21:49:59, | 24 |
| 18 | 199 | 13 | True | 09/10/1999 | 21:50:02, | 24 |
| 19 | 200 | 14 | True | 09/10/1999 | 21:50:19, | 3 |
| 20 | 201 | 14 | True | 09/10/1999 | 21:50:25, | 14 |
| 21 | 202 | 15 | False | 09/10/1999 | 21:50:45, | 0 |

Figure 6.12 The Transaction table from our sample application

Consider the table in Figure 6.12 above. In this instance, the data within the TransNo, Date and Time fields is generated automatically by the system. All we are passing between the biometric device and the system software is the user number reference, the binary result and the score. The result is a single digit translated automatically by the system into a 'True' or 'False' text string and the user number is stored in a short integer format in this example. An individual record may therefore be written very quickly indeed to this table and processed for on-screen display with an absolute minimum of perceptible delay. For reporting purposes we can include this streamlined table in a relational model with other tables in order to provide whatever level of detail we are looking for. With indexes on all tables and properly constructed queries our reports will zip through these tables with no trouble at all and return the pertinent data almost instantaneously if the tables reside on the host machine. Even with remote tables being accessed from elsewhere on the network, we shall be adding very little overhead to the overall transaction.

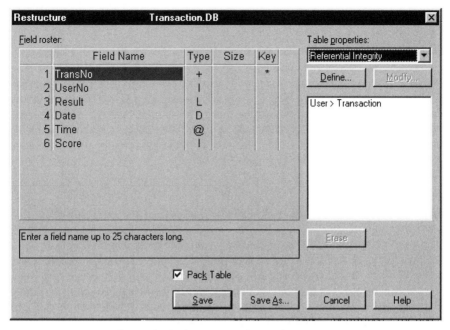

Figure 6.13 The Transaction table structure

Figure 6.13 shows the minimalist data structure of our example Transaction table. Earlier on in Section 6.2 of this chapter, The Intuitive GUI, we showed a straightforward report generator whereby the user simply had to select from drop-down boxes to quickly generate a fully formatted report against the system data. What the user was actually doing, was constructing a parameterized SQL query to run against our efficiently constructed tables and return the required information. On our test system and with just a few hundred transactions, this was producing a fully-formatted on-screen report in less than one second - not a bad performance. Naturally, with several thousand transactions and a larger user base it would take a little longer, but would still be within acceptable limits.

In conclusion, it pays to spend a little time considering how the database element of our biometric application should be constructed. Those familiar with relational database theory and the SQL query language will be able to design an efficient database structure to sit either within our overall application, or externally on a server elsewhere on the network, depending upon the scope and architecture of the application in question. In fact, there is no reason why we should not design a database which is scaleable from a stand alone workstation to a true client server model. The biometric application developer should therefore be alive to the various database-related issues and possibilities and ensure that they are not forgotten among the more exciting biometric device-related code. This is the reason for including a small database section in this chapter. Interested developers may like to reference some of the excellent books on the subject. Some of the Oracle Press publications may represent a good starting place.

## 6.6 Wrapping it up

We have covered quite a lot of ground in a relatively short chapter on application development and naturally each of the issues referred to deserves more consideration than space permits within this book. Hopefully we have raised some interesting points, though, and perhaps provided the reader with some food for thought in this context. Let's recap on some of the key points in order to conclude this section.

Firstly, the importance of how the system actually looks and feels to the user (in the case of host software this is going to probably be the system administrator) should not be underestimated. Some of the early software from biometric vendors drew criticism in this respect, not because there was anything wrong with it operationally, but because it was sometimes unintuitive and clunky in its execution. These days, users are used to seeing slick and well-presented applications for everyday business/office requirements and will expect the same from your biometric application. In the case of a systems administrator for a large public system, this individual is going to have enough to think about without worrying about how to find his way around the software. We therefore need to make things as easy and intuitive as possible whilst presenting the overall program in an attractive manner. If the administrator loves the software, he will feel a little more enthusiastic about the overall concept and this will in turn rub off on those being enrolled into the system. Enthusiasm is infectious. So, unfortunately, is frustration. In this respect, a well-presented, intuitive high-performance host application should be our objective.

A related element is general connectivity and how easy it is to get the system up and running initially. The end user is not going to be too interested in undertaking complex surgery on his host workstation, just to get your system running. He also won't be too keen if he has to call you in for chargeable support because he cannot get the system to run properly. Naturally the depth of this question will depend very much on the size and type of system being implemented, but even with a low-cost straightforward application such as the one used as an example in this chapter, we need to ensure that the biometric device and host connect simply and that everything is well documented. If there are network components involved, perhaps in a multi-reader system for example, then these should also be brought into the overall picture, with everything designed as a whole and designed to interconnect perfectly first time around. We should not assume that the person responsible for implementing the system necessarily has a detailed knowledge of these issues and therefore ensure that we document everything relative to the correct functionality of the system, even if this entails covering items not directly supplied by the biometric vendor, but for which a certain level of understanding is required. This clear architecture and connectivity should also extend to a logical and well-documented troubleshooting model that can be easily followed by the average internal IT support function within a typical organization. Vendors who pay attention to such matters will find that their investment pays dividends in terms of customer satisfaction.

This brings us on to questions of software stability and general performance. Sometimes things happen within the operating environment, either globally or on the host machine, that the application developer cannot always predict. However, he can ensure that his application has robust error catching and reporting code so that if and when the worst happens the application can withdraw gracefully and inform the user of the situation in plain English. Some of this may be undertaken automatically by elements within the database engine or elsewhere, but it is a good idea to allow for the worst for user-generated actions, perhaps within a 'try - finally' code block which allows an exit route where applicable. We should also ensure that a forced reboot on the host machine doesn't necessitate some complex re-initialisation. All of this will be basic fare to experienced developers who will also know how to optimise their code in order to extract the best performance. Speaking of performance, it should be acknowledged that the machines used within the development environment may be rather different from those expected on sites where the finished application will be deployed. This is particularly the case with respect to desktop PCs where the end user may wish to utilize existing hardware. The developer should therefore clearly specify the level of hardware required for acceptable performance, including processor type and speed, memory requirements, graphics adapter specification where applicable and any required network methodologies or protocols. Furthermore, if an overall systems performance is specified, then it should be clearly stated with what hardware this specification was derived. Once again, let's not assume anything, but spell out exactly how the system works and what hardware is required to facilitate this desirable state of affairs.

A similar philosophy should be applied to network-related issues, although this is a much more complex area, especially within large organizations. However, if the biometric application being considered is designed to sit within an existing network structure and pass information across it, then we must develop an understanding of how this might impact the current situation. Does the network in question have sufficient bandwidth to accommodate the additional load we shall be placing upon it? If we are anticipating large numbers of transactions against a central database, does our server have sufficient processing power to handle this in addition to other processes that may be running? Do our data storage and backup procedures have sufficient spare capacity to absorb the extra load? Whilst these are questions that only the end user can answer, it would help a great deal if the systems integrator/vendor can supply the necessary information relevant to the system under consideration. The end user's capacity planning people can then do their sums and come up with suggestions accordingly.

Finally, having developed our biometric application we should consider a robust and thorough testing exercise before we commit it to live implementation. It may have run quite well within the development environment, but this may be a relatively protected environment compared with typical on-site conditions, especially within a public or multi-tenanted area. The developer should ideally try to replicate as many worst case scenarios as possible in order to understand what it takes to make the system fall over. Yes, we all know that proper testing costs money, but so do failed systems and disillusioned users. It is far better to invest a little upfront effort in order to deliver a robust system that functions as expected on day one and continues to do so. There may be a little good humoured bantering between the engineering and sales functions within the supplying vendor organization in this respect, but test, test and test again is a pretty good motto to adopt, especially with any large-scale bespoke system. With such a system, we should of course be just as pedantic about understanding on-site architectural issues and ensuring that we have all the answers we need before the system is installed. With off-the-shelf 'generic' systems, having conducted our testing we should state clearly exactly what is required for the system to perform as designed and expected.

# 7. Moving on

In this chapter we shall take a little diversion and consider some potential futures for biometric and related technologies. Whilst it is acknowledged that this is a somewhat risky exercise, I believe there are certain trends emerging that nevertheless make it an interesting one and pertinent to the overall theme of the book. Time alone will tell whether such projections are realistic.

## 7.1 A biometric world

One can imagine a situation, perhaps not too far in the distance, whereby routinely using biometrics within everyday processes will be as familiar to us as using a plastic card is today. With more and more people in the world and more services being offered both publicly and privately, the subject of personal identity verification is one that can only grow in importance. Naturally there will be those that will wave the privacy and civil liberties banner, and in some cases with very good cause. However, it is important to distinguish between the technology and its application. Biometric technology in itself is not evil. The application of biometrics, as with any technology, needs to be considered from both an ethical and practical viewpoint. The key to successful applications is in providing benefits to the user, not in imposing a strict methodology that nobody wants on behalf of an administrative function. Having got that point out of the way, let's turn our attention to some of the areas where this technology may prove to be useful.

These days, it seems that you cannot pick up a newspaper or watch a television program, or have a business conversation without some reference to the Internet popping up. Like it or loathe it, one has to acknowledge that the rise in use of the Internet has been phenomenal. There are dangers associated with this as unscrupulous organizations may systematically remove their publicly available support on the street, forcing people on to the net where the opportunity to deal with a 'real' person is removed, together with a large portion of accountability. If you have ever tried to contact a real person within a large multi-national organization with a support issue via the net, you will know how difficult this can be. The largest software companies (no names) and banks are a very good example of this disgraceful behavior, reminding us that we live within a greed culture where accountability and support is simply not on the agenda. I mention this not to be negative but to make the point that really smart organizations will strike a balance between offering their services via whatever channels are most appropriate to their customer's wishes, one of which will naturally be the Internet. If we follow this thread of providing customer or user benefits, then it is clear that in the case of Internet transactions two areas which are of particular importance are ease of use and security. If I am to be persuaded to engage in online banking for example, first of all I want to be assured that only I can access my account details across the net (the traditional PIN is hopelessly inadequate in this respect) and secondly, I want the process to be fast and intuitive with the minimum of time spent online. On the latter point, this will be up to the banks and financial institutions to provide a slick and attractive site. On the former point, I would be very happy indeed to use a biometric in order to verify that it is indeed me attempting to access my private information - note that this is a case of biometrics *promoting* individual privacy.

Imagine that my computer keyboard has a small fingerprint reader integrated into the surface. When I apply for the first time for a secure online service such as Internet banking, in addition to vigorous security checks I can also register my biometric against this account. The biometric template may be held locally (i.e., not on the bank's database) and perhaps integrated into some sort of PKI encryption in order to provide secure access. If we wanted to get really secure, we may advise that the individual visits the local bank branch in order to verify the biometric before online activity is permitted. There are various levels we could consider. Another approach might be to store the biometric template on the bank card, where it could be originally registered at a local branch at the time of issue after suitable security checks have been undertaken. If the price of chip card readers comes down to the point where they could be economically integrated into a standard keyboard, then this might be an attractive solution. With such a system, I would feel a lot happier about the prospect of accessing my financial accounts online.

Of course the same principles apply to any online transaction. Suppose I wish to purchase something online - I simply insert my chip based credit card into the keyboard and place my finger on the fingerprint reader also on the keyboard, and away I go - secure identity-authenticated transactions straight from my desktop with the minimum of fuss. If such a methodology were to become popular, there would be no reason why it should not be operable with a variety of compatible tokens such as customer loyalty cards and so on, which would automatically provide the account-related details such as account number, expiry date and so on, making the whole process as simple as possible for the user. This comes back to the point made earlier about providing benefits for the user. Smart organizations may encourage authenticated transactions (which are also in their interest) by offering additional benefits to users who have purchased goods in this manner. For example, if I have bought an item of software over the Internet, perhaps I might qualify for a special higher level of support; after all, the vendor knows exactly who purchased the software and who it is registered to, ensuring that support is not being falsely claimed. There may be additional marketing-related benefits for both sides in this context.

Having discussed the Internet, it is a logical progression to move towards mobile communications and the similar phenomenon we have seen in the uptake of the mobile phone. Having reached a certain market penetration, the mobile communications companies are obviously keen to introduce new services to maintain the momentum, one of which is Internet access from mobile phones. This is undoubtedly on its way and may indeed be a reality by the time you read this book. However, its value to the individual will depend on what services can reasonably be provided in this context. Some websites are a nightmare to navigate even on a 17inch or larger desktop monitor. Compressing the same information into a format that can be sensibly read on a few short lines of an LCD display may be something of a challenge, especially if we were to offer online transactions via this medium. A while ago, there were several examples of integrating a mobile phone and a PDA (personal digital assistant) which seemed a fairly logical idea, although some of the implementations were a little expensive. Maybe something along these lines would be the answer for mobile Internet access. Imagine a PDA that could fit in your pocket, but had a decent sized screen, say 60 characters by six lines. A slot in the base of the device would accept a standard chip card, and a fingerprint reader would authenticate the user (or we might implement voice verification for applicable services). The PDA database would store all your telephone numbers, email addresses and favourite websites, together with incoming mail messages and other information. Naturally, this data could only be accessed by the bona fide user after supplying a biometric (assuming that is what the user wishes). The whole might be integrated with PKI functionality into the bargain.

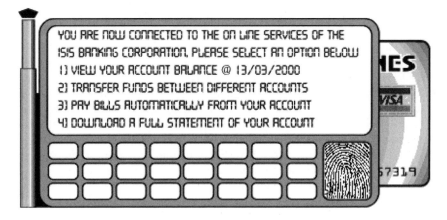

Figure 7.1 A future mobile communications device

Surely a device such as that depicted in Figure 7.1 would be feasible to supply in the not too distant future at an attractive price? We already have all of the component technology parts, it is simply a matter of putting them all together and providing the background service that makes it all possible. If I had such a device now, I would happily be using it for all sorts of things that at the moment tie me either to a PC, a telephone or both. Once again, thinking through the benefits to the user is undoubtedly the way forward in this respect. One could foresee a variety of such devices available at different price points depending on memory capacity, display quality and so on.

Whilst we are considering biometric-linked cards and tokens, let's consider some of the other applications for such technology. A health card for example could hold information about various public or private health schemes you are a member of as well as your specific medical history and details of any unusual conditions that preclude the use of certain drugs. Perhaps this health card is issued in conjunction with a credit card company which facilitates its use to purchase general medical and prescription items under an authenticated transaction scenario. Or maybe such a card could be issued by the local authority and combined with other functionality such as a national ID card or driver's licence. Once we have absolutely tied the token to the individual via a biometric, it opens up windows of opportunity to a whole raft of potential applications where additional benefits may be provided to the user, because we now have a high degree of confidence as to their true identity.

## 7.2 Biometrics in business

This is an area which will naturally be of interest to many over the coming decade. How exactly can businesses benefit from the introduction of biometric technology, either internally or as an integral part of their customer services? Is this a technology that businesses should be looking at now, and if so can it help to provide any competitive advantage? There are many things that can be achieved with biometric technology, but the fact that they are possible doesn't necessarily mean that they are desirable from a business perspective. We need to be sure of our objectives and where biometrics might fit within the various processes that make up our daily business activities. We should also bear in mind that most organizations do not have unlimited funds available for such projects and therefore the business case needs to make sense and should be considered in detail before we get too far down the road with our biometric thinking. It is worth mentioning this point, because it is easy to get carried away with enthusiasm for any new technology and think of a thousand and one possible applications, but this approach will more often than not lead to disappointment if there is not a strong commitment from the business in the first place. Any biometric project should be business-led, with clear objectives and expectations of the benefits to be delivered. The fact that there is a biometric facet to it should be incidental. Biometrics may be considered in this context as an enabler for enhanced functionality or processes within an existing operational strategy. With that thought in mind, let's consider some of the areas where the technology might usefully be deployed.

Many organizations these days maintain a 'call center' where potential customers can make contact to enquire about goods and services offered, support programmes or perhaps place an order. Sometimes these call centers are a dedicated in-house function and sometimes they are outsourced to specialist organizations who have proven expertise in this area and can represent your organization accordingly. When an existing customer phones the call center number, it is naturally useful to have all of that customer's details and transaction history quickly available. Currently, many such operations achieve this by asking for an account number, post code or other such information. This is fine and works well enough although it is perhaps a little impersonal, especially if your question was a generic one which doesn't really need to reference this information. There is also the question of whether the caller really is the account holder, or whether it is someone who just happens to know the criteria asked for. Molly Clackett might call in and order some goods against an existing account number, get them delivered to an alternative address and then mysteriously disappear. Although there are various safeguards and checks that can be made, it is nevertheless nice to know that you are really speaking with the right person, especially if you can offer some additional personal service or incentive as a result of their loyalty status. Now this may be an area where voice verification can be deployed to good affect. Imagine that I call the number of my favourite software supplier to enquire about a new program. The phone is immediately answered by an automated response which welcomes me and asks me to speak my name or account number, which also happens to be the biometric password. Within a short time the call is automatically routed to an available operator who already has my details on screen, can welcome me by name and make intelligent observations around my request based upon previous history. They may know for example that I run an operating system that isn't suitable for the application I have enquired about and can therefore check this point with me prior to accepting the order. Now I am receiving a truly personal and useful service, even though the operator has probably never spoken to me before and doesn't even work for the supplier organization. They may actually be responding from another country, it doesn't really matter, as long as I can get the information I am seeking and place an order for the goods I need.

We might take this idea a stage further and integrate voice verification biometrics into a totally automated system which also makes use of speech recognition technology. Supposing for example I am a regular flyer with Global Airlines and have accumulated a certain amount of air miles over the last few months. I would like to take a short break in Europe and wonder if I have enough air miles to accommodate this, or at least contribute significantly to the cost. I phone the Global Airlines call center and receive an immediate welcoming message asking for my account number and name (which acts as my biometric 'password'). The automated response then asks me whether I would like to access flight information, air miles status, special offers or speak to an operator. I simply state "air miles" and the system has enough information to retrieve the current balance from my account and enunciate this clearly to me, without any human intervention or lengthy waiting times. Global Airlines and I are both happy for this personal information to be divulged automatically because they have a high confidence level as to my true identity. In fact, almost certainly a higher level than if they had a live operator asking me a shopping list of questions in order to confirm my identity. The biometric verification check may be taking place on the servers within the call center, or maybe it is being undertaken on my mobile communications device into which I have inserted my frequent flyer card which contains my biometric template and can be updated with my current air miles status so that I have a date-stamped record of this information.

In the scenario mentioned above, we have provided for two sets of benefits. Firstly and most importantly, to me as a customer, as I can access personal information quickly and securely from wherever I am, and perhaps automatically be notified of special flight offers and other information that may well be of interest to me, all without waiting for an operator. Secondly, to the business, as it can automate many of the common enquiries, providing a faster but still personal service to customers while utilising its live operators for the more exceptional enquiries. Let's extrapolate this further. Supposing I did have a frequent flyer chip card with my voice template on it. Maybe the same token could accommodate a second biometric, perhaps a fingerprint or hand geometry template for example, which could be used in other synergistic systems such as automated border control, fast lane access at car hire centers, in room check-out at participating hotel chains and a host of other systems where there are benefits to me as the user and additional benefits to the organizations offering privileged levels of service, because they know exactly who I am. Now my Global Airlines frequent flyer card is *really* worth having and not just another piece of plastic taking up room in my wallet.

Earlier on we mentioned the Internet and touched upon the topic of secure transactions facilitated by biometric user authentication. But there may be several other areas where the fingerprint reader integrated into my computer keyboard could be useful in relation to my Internet activities. Suppose for example that I regularly visit a large site such as the Microsoft website. There will probably be a few key areas on the site that I am familiar with and like to visit from time to time in order to keep updated of developments, perhaps the Visual C++ or Windows 2000 sections for example. However, there may be other synergistic areas that would be of interest to me that I am simply not aware of, and maybe some areas that require me to register with Microsoft for access. Now supposing that when I access the site next time, I provide my biometric which identifies me as an individual to the Microsoft site and takes me straight to my area of interest. The website knows that I am interested in development tools and operating systems and can therefore highlight or suggest other pages which I might like to browse. In addition, it can allow me direct access to privileged areas without having to go through the irritating rigmarole of remembering and entering a password, or perhaps registering my full details all over again in order to get into a synergistic area of the site. I appreciate that this is something of a sketchy idea and would need to be developed, but an Internet site that offered this sort of interaction and intelligent profiling could be quite interesting, especially when there are privileged support areas or similar that not everyone is entitled to access. The same idea may be of interest to government departments and research agencies who have some information on their sites which is suitable for general public access and other information which should only be accessed by individuals of a certain status. In this scenario, passwords and PINs are really not suitable as they can so easily be compromised, but a biometric provides that extra level of identity verification that enables such functionality, together of course with other security measures. Such sites could be designed so that certain links, objects and facilities are only visible to those who logged on with their biometric, and may require periodic user re-validation to prevent them timing out, depending upon sensitivity levels.

Now let's turn our attention to a completely different area, the automotive world. Some automobile manufacturers have already toyed with the idea of using in-vehicle PINs and keypads as a security device to enable the ignition. You may have seen some French cars with this facility. Obviously biometrics could be introduced here and in a way that provided much more than just an extra layer of security. Suppose Frankie and Johnny share a car fairly frequently and that this car is equipped with a biometric 'control panel' conveniently located beneath the standard audio device.

Figure 7.2 The automobile biometric control panel

Unfortunately, Frankie is very slightly built and Johnny is exactly the opposite, requiring the seat and steering wheel to be reset when either drives the car. But by selecting her name on the control panel and placing her finger on the reader surface, Frankie not only enables the ignition, but the seat adjusts automatically to her preferred setting and the steering wheel aligns itself accordingly. If we really wanted to get fancy, we might select her favourite radio station for her and adjust the volume to her normal listening level. Perhaps we also adjust the air conditioning. In other words we can automatically personalise the in-car environment for Frankie whilst additionally providing considerably enhanced security. This functionality would be enabled by the original purchaser, who may like to enrol several members of the family into the automobile biometric system, so that any may drive the car. Supposing we extrapolate this thinking to larger vehicles such as buses and trucks. In the case of a truck, we could not only activate the vehicle only for a given set of drivers, but we could also integrate this into the tachograph, ensuring that accurate records are produced of driving time for each individual. Perhaps if we also enabled this with chip cards, we could maintain the tachograph record for drivers while swapping from one vehicle to another, simply by taking the data with them on the card. Perhaps for bus drivers we could integrate this into route planning and traffic control systems, predefining the driver's weekly schedule and ensuring that the correct information is automatically available within the vehicle, even if the driver has to change vehicles due to mechanical breakdown or other situations beyond his control. Clearly, from a business perspective there are many opportunities for vehicle manufacturers to consider the use of biometrics and how they may offer added value to their customers accordingly.

Another man and machine related application for biometrics may be in the control of complex or hazardous machinery which should only ever be operated by individuals who have been properly trained and subsequently assessed as to their ability. This may be in a factory or heavy engineering environment, a process control environment, or maybe something as simple as a fork-lift truck operating in a dangerous area. Furthermore, if the operator is required to be periodically re-assessed as to his ability, then we could time-stamp the enabling technology accordingly. Maybe nuclear power plants and other potentially dangerous installations could usefully adopt an operational methodology based on something along these lines. This would ensure that unqualified individuals didn't inadvertently activate a dangerous chain of events. If you are in a business where such personal training and safety-related issues are important, then maybe there is an opportunity to evaluate biometrics in this context.

Whilst we are considering physical situations, perhaps we should visit the area of physical access control. Biometrics are already used fairly extensively in this application area, but are we really taking advantage of all that the technology can offer? We may be able to do a little more than simply open a door somewhere within our corporate headquarters. Imagine that when I join the organization and register my full details with the human resources department, I am enrolled into a central biometric database. My access privileges into distinct physical areas are predefined as are the time zones that I would ordinarily be on site. When I arrive each morning and enter through one of the main entrances, my record is tagged to indicate that I am on site. I may be trained in emergency first aid or as a company fire warden, in which case an administrator can quickly and accurately produce a report of who is actually on site at this moment and falls into one of these categories. This information may be integrated with a messaging system which automatically calls the physically closest qualified individual when there is such an emergency. Similarly, we may integrate the biometric into a softer messaging methodology which enables me to access strategically placed terminals throughout the facility and pick up any urgent text messages or priority labelled emails, even though I am not at my desk or anywhere near my normal office location. Of course, we could also seamlessly integrate the biometric authentication into a time and attendance monitoring or flexitime system. Depending on the biometric chosen and the number of on site employees, we may be able to do all of this without the use of tokens or PINs, providing a high level of convenience for me as a user, together with valuable functionality for the organization. Supposing I am visiting one of the organization's overseas offices for the first time. My biometric data could be sent ahead of me in order that I be configured for the appropriate privilege levels at the remote site in advance. In addition, personnel (and security) at the remote office who have never met me before, can have a high level of confidence as to my true identity. This may be important in some circles.

Certainly there is potential for some adventurous thinking as to the use of biometrics in house.

Many biometric vendors have concentrated their efforts towards workstation and network access, no doubt seeing this as an obvious application of the technology and certainly a biometric-based security model is considerably more robust than the PINs and passwords we currently rely on in this context. But even here, there may be opportunities to broaden the concept and derive more value accordingly.

Imagine a Government department dealing with sensitive international or defence-related issues. It will already have in place some sort of hierarchical information security model that restricts documents and files on a need-to-know basis. Perhaps we could construct a file access level structure and assign individuals to the appropriate access levels according to status, ensuring that they are authenticated via their biometric at each transaction. Documents and files could then simply be tagged with the appropriate access level at source (naturally there would be additional encryption and other measures involved). This would be a good deal easier than trying to assign access individually to every file. The same approach could be utilized in the corporate environment. Research and development departments could ensure that all of their work-in-progress documentation and records are assigned to a unique access code, preventing unauthorised or otherwise inadvertent access by those outside of the department. There are of course ways of achieving this now with traditional methods, but perhaps the implementation of biometrics offers an opportunity to rethink this a little and come up with some innovative, elegant and highly secure solutions which are also straightforward to administer.

Another area which may affect certain Government departments and other organizations is that of secure voice and data communication. By this, I am not referring to the technology used for encryption or other 'scrambling' techniques, but the fundamental question of who is really at the other end. Is 'our man in Brazil' really the person feeding information to you, or is it someone else who can impersonate him? Even if there are passwords and procedures involved, these could be compromised. There are many circumstances in the commercial and governmental sectors where misinformation could have a dramatic impact on a developing situation. Now suppose that our man in Brazil used a mobile communications device that incorporated a fingerprint reader, perhaps linked to some sort of encryption that enabled the communications channel. For voice communications perhaps we additionally implement biometric voice verification to ensure that our man not only initiated the call, but is actually the person speaking. OK, there may be duress situations to account for, but this could easily be accommodated by an appropriate procedure. Such a system, utilising both local fingerprint verification and remote voice verification would not be difficult to implement and would perhaps provide a somewhat higher level of confidence as to the true identity of the speaker than we currently enjoy. A similar approach might be taken to remote data communications where the combination of a biometric and secure encryption would provide a high confidence level of authenticity. This concept could in fact be taken much further, depending on just how secure we want to get and of course the usual law of diminishing returns.

Getting back to the everyday commercial scenario, there is much dialogue currently about business-to-business e-commerce and how if there is not an 'e' in front of every procedure in your organization you will be bankrupt by next year etc. As usual with rapidly developing concepts such as e-commerce, there are some genuinely useful ideas floating around amid all the consultant's hype for those who can separate them out. Take the purchasing function for example. In many organizations there will be significant savings that can be made in this area due to automation and business-to-business direct data communication. In some instances, minor automobile parts supply perhaps, you may be happy to totally automate the process. In others, you may still wish to have some authorisation procedures in place. The trouble with all this automation is that, assuming you have been driven to it by the potential to reduce headcount in your purchasing department, it is now harder to assign accountability in instances where things don't look quite right. If the supplying organization receive an order for 100 grade A widgets when you would usually order 70, no doubt they will happily supply them but is this correct? Has somebody pressed the wrong key? Have the records been altered? Will such a discrepancy pass unnoticed? If it is noticed 90 days later when you are due to pay the invoice how do you really know who initiated this particular transaction? Are the extra 30 widgets still on site or have they miraculously disappeared (and no one noticed because you had enough (70) to meet your demands)? Accountability and individual identity verification become even more important in the e-world. Biometric authentication linked to (particularly large value) transactions may not be a bad idea in this context, especially if you are already using the technology for workstation and network access.

This brings us neatly to the point that in data processing environments there are greater opportunities for utilising biometrics than just network access control. This is where it would be nice to see corporate IT vendors picking up on the concept. Take your financial systems for example. Who currently may access the general ledger, accounts payable, accounts receivable etc., and how exactly do they do this? Via a password no doubt. Does everybody in the department have access to all modules? How is access to the finance LAN controlled? Is there an audit trail? Is it based upon passwords? Perhaps some of the vendors offering corporate finance packages may like to consider the integration of biometric verification as an option. Similarly with your HR systems. This information is very sensitive and deserves to be protected: what better way than via a biometric? Do you use a centralised project management system? If an individual knows the correct password, can they access details of all the projects currently running within your organization? Maybe the vendors of these systems can see some advantage to offering biometric functionality, especially as it could so easily be included as an additional module to the core system. As more organizations start to use biometrics for workstation and network access, they will increasingly wonder why the same functionality isn't seamlessly integrated into some of the core enterprise systems that form the 'digital nervous system' of their organization, especially when they already have the necessary hardware. Simply enabling the executable file is not enough, there are far more interesting possibilities for the mainstream vendors to consider.

The banking industry is of course an area where people have expected to see implementations of biometric technology and certainly there have already been some interesting trials undertaken in various parts of the world. Having the facility to use a biometric at the ATM machine has obvious benefits for both the user and the bank, especially if it is implemented in a manner which allows the template to be under direct control of the user, perhaps on a chip card for example. Wouldn't it be nice if the banking and credit card giants could agree on a standard which allowed users optionally to enrol their biometric onto the card in a standard manner and then choose when and where to use it? Enrolment might be undertaken under supervision within a local bank branch, or perhaps even at an ATM machine within a strict time period after issue. Once successfully enrolled it would be impossible for the user to tamper with the template in any way or to re-enrol, except under strict supervision at the bank. Early adopters might perhaps be offered incentives such as higher credit limits or other associated benefits. Considering the obvious synergy with financial transactions and the banking industry, it may seem surprising to some that the major banks have not already embraced this technology enthusiastically, and not just for card related transactions either. However, the banking industry is sometimes a little slow to adopt technology and to be fair, in most cases it would involve a huge and costly project to implement on any sort of scale. Having said that, it is perhaps inevitable that sooner or later we will see biometrics used in this context. The danger here is perhaps one of standards. The longer the major banks sit on the fence, the greater the opportunity for smaller concerns to start implementing the technology, no doubt each in a completely different manner. This would lose one of the principal potential user benefits, that of portability and control over just how their biometric is used. Perhaps one of the banking associations should take a lead on this issue. The sceptical may suggest that 'user benefits' are simply not on the priority list of banks, but the smart banking organization that gets this right may win a lot of friends among both private and corporate clients. The turning point will come when they stop concentrating on costs of implementation and start concentrating on all the additional services and benefits that could be offered to the consumer (both private and corporate) with some intelligent thinking and marketing applied to the biometric opportunity. Again, there is much more to this than just the use of ATM machines and the imaginative reader can no doubt think of dozens of areas where high-confidence personal identity authentication in relation to financial transactions would be extremely beneficial. At the beginning of this book, I mentioned the ancient Egyptians and how they used biometric principles in association with financial and important business transactions. Perhaps the 21st century banking fraternity has some catching up to do. They are a few thousand years late, but there are still some exciting opportunities to be explored in this area.

Now let's engage in a little lateral thinking and turn our attention to the entertainment industry, specifically the creation of content such as music and video, much of which is created and/or edited under studio conditions. Much of this nowadays is produced digitally. Analogue die-hards who affectionately reminisce over 2inch multi-track audio tapes and celluloid, will no doubt concede that there are certain advantages to digital when it comes to editing and production (even if the argument about absolute quality lives on). Accordingly, whole organizations have been built upon the provision of digital tools and equipment to facilitate this operation. If producers and artists are involved in the production of digital content, could not a digital signature (in the form of a biometric) be also assigned to the resulting software? Imagine two or more recording studios in different countries collaborating on a project and exchanging audio files over an ISDN link. Is there a possibility of confusion over exactly who produced what, what copyright exists and who should receive royalties accordingly? No doubt there are existing mechanisms in place to handle this, although one does hear of the occasional dispute where copyright and contract lawyers seem to have a field day. Suppose this concept were carried further into databases where finished content encoding is assigned absolutely to the individuals who were really involved with the production of the work. Subsequent public performance such as radio/TV play could be automatically monitored via the encoded information and royalties assigned to the bona fide individuals accordingly. It could work like this. Well-known music producer Charlie Brown spends 75 hours in the studio working diligently on the production of a new song by a well-known artist. Session musicians are brought in and at the final run-through all those involved have their biometric ID encoded onto a control track of the master according to an accepted formula of apportionment. This control data also includes a unique encrypted ID for the work itself. All such control data produced in this studio is collated and batch-loaded weekly to an independent copyright protection agency who maintains databases of relevant information. Each time the song is played via any media channel an automatic monitoring system (maintained by the copyright protection agency) picks up the unique encoded ID and logs the event. A subsequent 'play list' can be periodically produced and royalties paid accordingly. Now, suppose that the song Charlie Brown produced is unexpectedly successful and breaks all records and there ensues a dispute over who actually worked on the original session and in what capacity. The independent copyright protection agency can simply produce the original control data with a high level of confidence as to its accuracy. Furthermore, individual claimants may be checked against the biometric information thus contained. This idea needs some thinking through, but maybe there is some potential here for significant administrative savings together with enhanced benefits to the users, in this case the artists and producer of the original work. An example perhaps of how biometrics may be integrated into a not so obvious process. In fact, if we consider the video and audio studio production environments, there are a wealth of areas where individual identity verification can be very important, not only from the overt commercial perspective, but perhaps in areas where privacy and authenticity of high profile individuals is paramount. Vendors supplying into this area may like to give the biometric concept some serious consideration.

## 7.3 Overall conclusions

In the preceding section we have looked at some obvious and perhaps not so obvious potential applications for biometric technology. It is clear that the more you look at a particular sector of activity, whether governmental, academic or commercial, the more you realize that personal identity verification is an important factor in just about any transaction (and the world revolves around transactions and interaction). We have not even scratched the tip of the iceberg in the examples given above. The question is not so much where can we use biometrics, but where can we not use biometrics in the context of identity verification. Naturally there will be areas where we really do not need the high confidence levels provided by biometrics, in which case their use would be superfluous, but there are countless other areas where the use of the technology can provide real and undoubted benefits. Furthermore, the technology is now relatively mature and easily implemented. It is not perfect and will probably never be so, but it does offer a degree of confidence in individual identity verification unattainable by other more traditional methods.

There are some factors of contemporary society that conspire to make the issue of individual identity a thorny one. One of these is that the population of the world continues to rise at a time when efficient global communication perhaps raises expectations of a lifestyle which will only be enjoyed by a percentage of the population, leading to a have and have-not regional and global society. Such a model inevitably leads to rising crime and opportunism among those wishing to get ahead or 'beat the system'. These are not necessarily archetypal villains in striped jumpers and masks, but could be anyone from shopkeepers to politicians. Another factor which complicates this is the relative ease of mobility that many enjoy today. This naturally means that those of dubious intentions will migrate to where it is easiest to defraud the administration or engage in whatever other activity they have planned. Then there are those who maintain multiple identities, sometimes in the same area, sometimes across several areas, usually with intent to defraud in some capacity or other. For all of these people (and sadly there seems to be an ever growing number of them) positive identity verification, either absolutely or in relation to a specific transaction, is something they would rather not see implemented or even discussed. An interesting paradox appears here as to whether positive identity verification using biometrics may be against the interest of the individual as an infringement of privacy, or actually in the interest of the individual as a means of substantiating a genuine identity claim.

There are of course those who are genuinely concerned about privacy issues and fear that if biometric systems are implemented, the state, or perhaps large commercial organizations, would use this personal data against the interest of the individual. Whilst one in principle has every sympathy with this view, it should be understood that there are ways of ensuring that the biometric template is stored in such a manner that the original biometric (fingerprint, iris pattern etc.) cannot be recreated from the template data. Furthermore, in most cases it would be possible not to store it remotely at all, but to let the user manage it via a portable token. When one looks at the situation in this way, it is hard to imagine what extra mischief the state could get up to with this information, compared to the volumes of information they already hold on you - except of course to accurately assign you to such already held information. If you are a law-abiding citizen, you may not be too concerned about this, although your natural suspicion of politicians may be a healthy one. In a commercial situation you will always have the choice of not dealing with an organization if you don't approve of the way they are managing your personal information, biometric or otherwise. On balance, my personal view is that I would be very happy indeed to use biometric verification techniques in situations where I was accessing my own personal information, such as at a banking terminal, or perhaps conducting an online transaction of some sort, or as a convenient alternative to the plethora of passwords I have to remember to access networks and applications in the course of my job. If I happened to be working in a relatively hostile environment I would also be very happy to use a biometric based physical access control system.

In conclusion, there are a wealth of possibilities for the deployment of biometric technology within contemporary society. The viability of many such implementations may depend very much on the perceived benefit to the users. When the emphasis switches firmly towards user benefits as opposed to technological possibilities, I believe we shall see a dramatic upturn in the adoption of this technology and I further believe that we shall see this within a very few years. The technology is there. The potential applications are there. What has perhaps been missing to date is sufficient quantities of imaginative thinking and first class systems design. But those elements will surely follow.

# 8. Running a biometric pilot scheme

The preceding chapters of this book have hopefully provided the reader with a good background into biometric technology, how it has evolved and where it might be going in the future. We have even looked briefly at application development and the integration of biometrics into other processes. For many organizations however, having discovered the technology and considered potential applications within their particular sphere of operation, the next logical step would be to conduct some sort of trial or pilot scheme in order to prove the concept prior to a more ambitious implementation. The problem for many will be that this is a relatively new technology and that consequently they may not have a high level of in-house expertise or experience on which to draw. Furthermore, they may or may not be too enthusiastic about sharing the detail of their future plans and aspirations in this context with third party organizations, at least not at this stage. So how on earth do we go about setting up, running and evaluating a biometric pilot system? Well, hopefully this book will be of value in this respect as this chapter will be devoted to precisely that subject.

In order to facilitate a meaningful discussion, we shall assume a hypothetical example of a banking organization named County Bank. The County Bank management have been aware of biometrics and the potential for enhanced user identity verification for some time, but have been a little uncomfortable with the overall business case for implementation, especially in the areas of actual cost (which is more than just the cost of providing the technology) and user acceptance. On the latter point, whilst they have no evidence to suggest that their customers would not like at least the option to use biometrics, they are also conscious that they would not wish to turn potential customers away or to upset existing customers, if the introduction of such technology were to bring with it any negative associations with respect to individual privacy. There are no easy answers to these questions, but clearly some sort of voluntary participation pilot scheme would provide a wealth of practical and pertinent information on which to base further decisions.

The management at County Bank have concluded that any such pilot scheme should go further than simply integrating a biometric into ATM machines if it is to provide the sort of information they are seeking with regard to identifying further opportunities for this technology within their operational processes. They have therefore decided that some sort of third party collaboration would be useful in order to broaden the benefits for participants within the scheme and also to understand what would be involved if they sought strategic associations of this kind in the future. Obviously such a project would need to be kept contained and carefully monitored and any collaborating partners would need to agree to this principle and be prepared to commit the necessary resources in order to work closely with the project team throughout. After careful consideration the County Bank project manager has developed the following plan for the pilot.

♦ County Bank will provide a suitable token in the form of a chip card, which will contain the biometric template and other relevant information. The card will also contain a conventional magnetic stripe in order that it be compatible with other systems which do not offer the advanced functionality of the pilot scheme.

♦ The County Bank card may be used in a selection of participating branches' ATM machines within a given geographical area wherein additional benefits will be available to participants in the scheme.

♦ The card may also be used in conjunction with the County Bank online banking service and a suitable project partner will be sought who can provide customised computer keyboards which incorporate both the chip card reader and biometric capture device.

♦ Envisaging simplified and secure online purchasing as a major customer benefit, a limited number of project partners will be sought who will agree to incorporating the County Bank methodology into their own on line purchasing model. These partners should be chosen so as to represent typical areas of interest for customers.

♦ Other related opportunities may be considered if identified in the course of detailed planning for the project.


The project is to be led and managed overall by County Bank, but with a strong input envisaged from the participating partners. Each participating partner will be responsible for their own direct costs in relation to the project, although County Bank will absorb the cost of providing both the chip cards and the necessary hardware such as the ATM machine modifications and computer keyboards, together with any enabling software as required. Each participating partner may promote the pilot scheme within their own channels, provided that all such text or advertising material is submitted in advance to County Bank and authorised accordingly. This is in the interests of continuity and accuracy of information as it is imperative that potential participants are not inadvertently misled as to the objectives and operation of the scheme. Each partner will have an important part to play within the overall scheme and regular progress meetings will be encouraged in order to gauge and understand both public response and the day-to-day operational requirements of such a business model. With the scene thus set, let's now turn our attention to the project in earnest and consider how it might be planned and orchestrated towards its successful conclusion.

## 8.1 Setting the objectives

As with any important project it will be necessary to set down the objectives in advance and ensure that these are well understood and agreed by all those involved in the project. This is particularly the case with a biometric project as there may be a tendency to either subsequently think of all manner of additional facilities and functions which weren't part of the original requirement, or perhaps to compromise on the way the project is physically implemented due to expediency, misunderstanding or lack of experience among one or other of the partners. The latter point may be attended to by a robust project plan, but this in turn must be derived from a well-documented set of objectives which are clearly communicated throughout the participating partners and associated vendors where applicable. Furthermore, these objectives should be considered from all perspectives if a realistic project is to emerge. In this case, we shall group these objectives into (a) the overall project objectives from the County Bank perspective, (b) the objectives from a potential user perspective and (c) the objectives from the participating partner's point of view.

From County Bank's perspective the main objectives of the project are fairly clear and straightforward. Firstly, they wish to evaluate biometric technology and its current viability within a commercial operation. This will include both the performance characteristics of the chosen biometric capture device and matching algorithm as well as the total system performance. In addition, they will wish to carefully monitor the associated costs in order that these be properly considered in any subsequent business proposal which includes the use of biometrics. Secondly, they wish to gauge user reaction and form an opinion of whether a larger scale implementation would be acceptable to the majority of customers. This will entail not only the detailed analysis of participant feedback, but also the understanding of any user-related problems that are experienced and what effect they might have on user perception of the overall service. Thirdly, they wish to evaluate the potential for strategic partnerships and understand what co-operation they could expect from organizations should they decide to market the idea on a broader scale. Fourthly, and very importantly, they want to understand the effect that implementing such technology might have on their overall brand profile and perception in the market place. Will they be perceived as innovative and bringing new benefits to their customers through the use of advanced technology? If so, there are clearly implications for future marketing initiatives. On the other hand, will they be seen as being intrusive and expecting too much from their customers for their own benefit? Much of this may depend on exactly what benefits are offered to customers in this respect and how genuinely useful they are. This is an important distinction. It is one thing to offer a brace of additional 'facilities' which actually aren't particularly useful to anyone and another to offer something which clearly benefits the user in a manner that hasn't been possible previously.

From the user's perspective, initial research has shown that firstly, participating in the pilot scheme should be fun and emotionally rewarding. No one wants to give their time to something which is either overtly security orientated or otherwise too serious and demanding for the voluntary participants. Secondly, whatever operational methodology is adopted should be easy and intuitive in use. If the whole thing is too complicated to remember or involves a host of additional processes which are potentially confusing, then participants will quickly lose interest and revert back to the traditional mode of operation. Thirdly, the application procedure for potential participants should be straightforward and clearly communicated in order that they understand exactly what is involved and what they will need to produce when being enrolled into the scheme. Fourthly, there should be tangible benefits for those participating in the scheme, beyond that of general interest, ensuring that they remain enthusiastic about the concept and use it as much as possible.

The objectives from the participating partner's perspective are obviously based primarily around commercial considerations. Firstly, they wish to understand whether the adoption of such technology has the potential to attract new customers and additional revenue. Secondly, they would like to gauge whether biometric technology is mature enough to be used in front-line transactions and whether this is likely to be acceptable to customers. Thirdly, they want to understand the potential for higher user authentication confidence levels within secure transactions and what impact this has from a business perspective. Fourthly, they would like to understand precisely what is involved in the integration of biometric technology into their existing operational processes and what additional technological demands this places upon them, if any.

As mentioned earlier, it is important that with any significant biometric pilot project we carefully consider and openly discuss the objectives of all concerned right at the start and understand the potential benefits, to whom and at what cost. The author has seen several potentially interesting pilot schemes fail to deliver anything of value, simply because there was not enough understanding and planning undertaken in advance, or there were too many vested interests and egos around to develop a clear picture of objectives and follow these through to their natural conclusion. Another important element here is one of timescales. It is important to understand not only the overall project objectives, but also what the key deliverables are and when they can be expected. You would think that most projects of this nature would adhere to some sort of formal project plan with milestones that can be baselined and measured accordingly. Amazingly, this doesn't always seem to have been the case with biometric pilot schemes. Perhaps people get carried away with the technology, or maybe there is not enough central project management and control.

Fortunately, our mythical organization County Bank have done their homework in this respect and understand what the objectives are from everybody's point of view. Furthermore, they have discussed this at length with all of the commercial participants and have additionally undertaken consumer research within their branches in order to gauge the likely response from prospective participants. This has all been carefully documented and presented to the participating partners at a special workshop where full agreement from all concerned has been confirmed. This means that County Bank can now move forward with some confidence into the more detailed planning stage. They have also recognized the importance of providing the project with an identity of its own right upfront and have accordingly introduced a logo and some sample cards for the participating partners to take away with them and use in their own internal discussions.

Figure 8.1 The County Bank Smiley Card

The design of this card has deliberately been kept simple and cheerful in concept in order to create an instantly recognisable token to associate with the project. This is an important psychological point, both for the participating partners and subsequently the participating users as it provides focus for discussion and a vehicle with which to promote the project. It also represents an early indication of the commitment from County Bank to the project overall, and an encouragement for the other commercial participants to move forward with their plans.

In conclusion, setting the objectives and demonstrating commitment to them is an important starting point for any significant biometric-related project. Furthermore, these objectives should be well documented and communicated among those involved with the project, ensuring that everybody has the opportunity to raise questions and observations accordingly. When the refinement process has concluded and we have an agreed and understood set of objectives, these should be published together with a high-level project plan setting out the relative timescales and identifying the key milestones. This will then form a template for a subsequent and much more detailed plan to be developed and maintained by the project office which in our mythical example will be run by County Bank.

## 8.2 Choosing the project team

Those who have worked on a variety of projects across different industry sectors will appreciate the difference that can be made by a really good project team whose performance is often greater than the sum of the parts might suggest. Sometimes this may result from a happy accident or coincidence of selection, but more often than not it will be the result of careful orchestration by the project director or leader who understands this point. This is a relatively complex area as it deals with human emotions and personalities, but is well worth spending some time on if we are striving for a successful outcome.

In our example project, before we can select individual team members, we must first identify and engage the collaborating partners. County Bank decided that one of the areas they particularly wanted to investigate was the potential for using the Smiley Card for web-based transactions and so, after much deliberation they have decided to work with the following collaborators.

2XS are both an Internet and store-based company selling entertainment software including videos, CDs and electronic games. They have agreed to provide a streamlined web-based transaction model for Smiley Card holders as well as a range of benefits and discounts via both the web and in-store channels.

WebWorm are an Internet-only company selling books and related gifts via the web. They have also agreed to provide special benefits and a streamlined transaction process for Smiley Card holders.

Tranquil Tours are a holiday company who sell via both the Internet and traditional high street channels. They are very enthusiastic about the project and have agreed to provide a special web experience for Smiley Card holders which enables them to easily purchase their flights and holidays with a streamlined no-nonsense interface. Furthermore, via interfaces with other systems, Tranquil Tours' Smiley Card customers can confirm their own seats and check their air mile status and other related information either via the web or at special in-store and airport-based kiosks.

CashCo are a currency exchange company who operate at most international airports and additionally offer an in-flight cash exchange service in association with certain airlines. They will offer a special service to Smiley Card holders whereby they will guarantee to buy back unused currency at the purchase exchange rate within a limited time period. The project also coincides with an idea of their own around the installation of special unattended cash kiosks within the arrivals area of certain airports, allowing passengers to purchase a limited amount of local currency via credit card. The Smiley Card project will enable them to integrate biometrics and offer additional benefits, including a higher cash limit, to Smiley Card holders.

KeyOptics are a computer peripheral manufacturer who have agreed to produce a limited production run of special computer keyboards incorporating both a chip card reader and fingerprint-based biometric capture device. As they were already designing such a product, the Smiley Card project provides them with an ideal opportunity to gauge user reaction to such a device, especially with regard to web-based transactions which they perceive as the primary application. They have also agreed to produce the necessary background software to integrate with the popular web browsers and to share this with the other project participants in order for them to create the necessary processes and procedures within their own website software and accommodate Smiley Card holders accordingly. This latter point is somewhat vital to the success of the project as it is the enabler for all the web-based functionality.

As County Bank will be leading the project they will set up and run the central Project Office which will function as the hub of the operation throughout the entire project life cycle. The personnel involved will be as follows. Overall responsibility for the project will fall to the project director. The individual chosen for this post should be from a high-profile management background and have the necessary authority and experience to steer the project through to completion. He or she needs to have a broad technical understanding but doesn't need to understand the fine detail of every element of the project. Similarly, they must have an understanding of project management principles and tools, but they won't be performing the role of a project manager in the accepted sense. What they will be doing is acting as the overall co-ordinating force and being the public face of the project. They will also be the ultimate decision maker for issues which need to be resolved and will also be the conduit to the County Bank board of directors.

The second person in the County Bank team will be the project manager. This individual, as the title suggests, will be responsible for managing the practical implementation of the project using proven principles and project management tools. They will be primary creator and ultimate custodian of the project plan and responsible for the practical co-ordination between all participating elements. The project director and project manager will share a project secretary who will take care of all the administration and communication in relation to the project as it progresses.

The County Bank team needs strong representation, in the form of a competent individual, in the following additional areas.

- ◆ Technical. This individual must have a complete understanding of the County Bank operational systems and be able to liaise with their counterparts within the other participating organizations. Whilst they may delegate much of the actual development work to others, they must nevertheless have a complete grasp of the situation.

- ◆ Process. This person must be an expert in all of the County Bank operational processes and know exactly what happens and why within all the systems and interfaces. They will work closely with the technical representative as well as their counterparts in participating organizations.

- ◆ Training. The training representative will be responsible for understanding the training requirements for both internal staff and County Bank customers and designing the necessary training programmes accordingly. They will also be responsible for implementing these programmes and will need to work closely with the project manager in order to ensure that time scales and schedules are met. They will also need to understand exactly how the various systems are working and will therefore need to work closely with all the other departments.

♦ PR/Publicity. This person will be responsible for developing and publicly communicating an overall image for the project as well as producing all the attendant publicity material and managing the application process. They will also manage media attention and be the focus for all external enquiries in relation to the project. It will be necessary for them to liaise closely with the Project Office at all times and also the training representative with whom they will design and produce the relevant training aids and associated materials.

This seven-strong team will form the nucleus of the County Bank project effort although they will of course be assisted by various individuals within the organization as necessary in order to fulfil their project obligations. It will be the project director's task to put this team together and in doing so, he will be highly conscious of individual personalities, striving to create a team which is both highly talented and harmonious in operation. It will also be the project director's task to motivate and lead from the front, maintaining an air of enthusiasm and excitement throughout.

Having established both the central project team and the Project Office, the project director will recommend a minimum project structure for the other participating organizations. This is very important indeed as good peer-to-peer communication and collaboration will be crucial to the success of the project as it progresses through the various phases. The recommended structure will include an overall project manager as well as representatives from both the technical and operational process areas within each organization. In addition, all media and promotional initiatives will need to be co-ordinated via the County Bank Publicity department who will require a suitable contact within each participating organization.

With all personnel identified across the participating organizations, it will be a good idea to get everybody together for a relatively informal project launch at an off-site location. This will give the project director the opportunity to present the project concept and explain exactly who is doing what, and what the key milestones are along the way. The PR/Publicity representative can also use the event to introduce the public image and perhaps offer a presentation of how users will be invited to participate in the scheme. This should be followed by a general question and answer session where everybody has the opportunity to make observations or raise issues accordingly. After the formal presentations and questions, the remainder of the time may be spent informally whereupon people from the participating organizations can meet and get to know each other, perhaps over a buffet lunch. This may seem a little extravagant, but it is well worth spending some time and effort arranging an official project launch event in order to start everybody off on the right foot and with a crystal clear understanding of who is doing what and when. It also provides an opportunity to distribute copies of the detailed project plan together with any other pertinent information.

## 8.3 Choosing the technology

It goes without saying that choosing the right technology will be a key element of success in such a scheme. It is all too easy to be swayed by an accommodating vendor or consultancy who seem to have all the answers, but this is an issue (or to be more correct, a collection of issues) which should be considered and decided upon by the organization running the project, albeit with help and advice from the collaborating partners. In our example case this is County Bank.

One of the first steps will be to decide which biometric methodology will be best suited to the project. There are many factors to be taken into consideration in this context, including ease of use, accuracy, template management, operational issues and environmental issues. Whatever methodology is chosen has to fit comfortably with the type of application envisaged, particularly with regard to ease of use and acceptability from the user's perspective. For example, if were thinking of a situation such as spectator access control for a sports stadium, we want something which is capable of fast and intuitive operation with low incidents of false rejects. In a prison visitor system, we may place the emphasis more heavily on accuracy and be less concerned about absolute speed and user convenience as it will be operating within a facilitated environment. We must also balance the requirements of absolute accuracy against the potential of user frustration if false rejects are too high. In a straight one-to-one verification situation, we may choose to compromise slightly on the accuracy front, if it leads to an enhanced user experience. It all depends on the application under consideration and the objectives thereof. This is one of the reasons why a pilot scheme is so valuable, as it provides the opportunity to experiment with some of the variables before rolling out the application to a wider audience. However, even within the context of a pilot scheme, the choice of methodology is an area that deserves careful consideration and should not be taken lightly.

In our example scheme, County Bank wanted something which was fairly intuitive and easy to use and that would be easily and unobtrusively integrated into other equipment such as their ATM machines and the special-issue computer keyboards mentioned earlier. This integration issue was a key one as they didn't want a situation which demanded several pieces of loose equipment for the user to grapple with, it had to appear as homogenous and natural as possible. Another key factor was that the biometric template should fit comfortably within the available space on the Smiley Card chip card, together with some other related information. In this case, after a certain amount of deliberation the choice was fingerprint biometrics as the methodology was well suited to the operational scenarios envisaged and was also seen to be cost effective and relatively straightforward to implement. Facial recognition was considered but it was felt that at the current time the technology on offer was not as well suited to the project requirements and may not be as intuitive to the user. Whether users would have strong views about the use of fingerprints in this manner was one of the questions that the project would hopefully answer. So, for County Bank, this was a relatively straightforward decision. In a different project, things may not be quite so clear cut and a decision may be taken to trial more than one biometric.

Having chosen the methodology, there may be several vendors who can supply a suitable biometric capture device and another decision will need to be made as to whose device will be used. In many instances, this may be decided upon by a pre-project in-house evaluation in order to quantify the accuracy and ease of use of all the devices under consideration. In the case of the Smiley Card project, this upfront evaluation has already been conducted by KeyOptics who have chosen to integrate a particular sensor into their keyboard. This raises an interesting point. Within a potentially large-scale project, the ease of integration of a given biometric device will be of some importance. For KeyOptics, they needed a capture device that could be provided simply as a sensor component with the necessary SDK in order to integrate the device seamlessly into their own hardware and software. This OEM approach will often be the case and will naturally limit the choice of available devices. However, it also provides the opportunity to fine-tune the user experience and the operation of the application in question. For our example project, we shall assume that KeyOptics have satisfactorily undertaken comparative tests of the available components and have chosen to use the most appropriate device for the application at hand. In other projects, the choice may be more complex, especially if there are several devices which would all in theory be suitable. In this case, questions around available SDK's and support, the relative stability of the vendor organization, actual costs and so on, will all come into the equation.

We have discussed the biometric device, but there are of course other areas of technology to consider, supporting devices for example. In our mythical Smiley Card project we have decided to use chip cards as a means of managing the biometric template and also giving visibility to the project overall. County Bank will therefore have to choose a suitable card and also the chip card reader which will be integrated into their ATM machines. KeyOptics shall also have to source, or design a chip card-reading element for their special keyboard. The requirements in both of these cases will be different. On the one hand, County Bank will wish to have a reader that can read both chip cards and their existing magnetic stripe stock, as well as fitting physically into the available space and integrating with the existing ATM electronics. KeyOptics will be looking for something which is physically compact and can be easily integrated into a conventional-looking keyboard. Once again, components from different vendors should be evaluated as to their suitability to the project in question. With any significant project, the two areas of durability and repeatability are key. We shall naturally be looking for high levels of reliability from any associated hardware, but we also need to feel comfortable that the vendor can supply the quantities we need and maintain both further supplies and support accordingly. For our project, the supply of the Smiley Cards represents an interesting opportunity to evaluate not only the relative durability and usability of the cards, but also the service supplied by the vendor. In this context, it may be interesting to deliberately source the pilot scheme stock from more than one vendor in order to gauge the support and service received accordingly, and this is precisely what County Bank have done.

There may be a host of supporting hardware in certain cases. For physical access control applications for example, there may well be turnstiles or door locking equipment to source, user displays and other equipment. All of this needs to be carefully considered and should not be chosen simply on a cost basis, but should be designed to provide the best overall solution and complement the objectives of the project as a whole. As with most systems, the weakest link in the chain will break soon enough and remind you of the importance of attention to detail. This is particularly the case with biometric projects as there will be a tendency to concentrate on the front-end technology at the expense of the supporting equipment necessary to make the system function properly. The system should be designed as a whole from the ground up, with due attention paid to every element which forms part of the operational jigsaw.

This brings us on nicely to the supporting infrastructure. In many cases, it may be tempting to just consider the existing infrastructure and how the biometric system overlays on to this. However, we should really be asking the question of whether the existing infrastructure is the best infrastructure to support our objectives. In certain cases we may have no choice as the legacy structure may not lend itself to change or enhancement, at least not at this point in time. At the other extreme, if we have a clean sheet of paper we can design the best supporting infrastructure and architecture from the ground up. Somewhere in between will be where many pilot schemes fall and there may exist the opportunity to subtly enhance certain aspects of the infrastructure to better support our objectives. This may be particularly pertinent in situations where we are dealing with central databases and require an optimal level of capacity and bandwidth. This question of course also extends to the various interfaces and dependencies between synergistic systems and the best way of accessing or passing data between them. It is an area that is easily underestimated if the project team gets carried away with the biometric technology and the user application layer, but must be properly considered if we are not to experience some nasty surprises downstream. In the case of our Smiley Card project, County Bank have looked carefully at the existing infrastructure within the geographic area of the pilot scheme and are confident that the Smiley Card functionality will not impact this adversely. They have also looked carefully at their existing online banking system and how this can be enhanced to fit in with the project requirements. The merchant settlement schemes applicable to the participating partners are hardly affected as from the point of transaction authorisation onwards, nothing will change, although County Bank will be looking to add a flag somewhere to Smiley Card transactions in order to monitor these as exceptions. This may be accommodated within the card number itself, ensuring that no fundamental change is required to the clearing system or process.

For the Smiley Card project there will be operational and process changes required within the web technology of the participating partners and this will need to be co-ordinated in order to offer a consistent experience to the participating end users. Furthermore, enabling software shall need to be developed and supplied to users together with the special keyboard in order to ensure that their client web browsers and operating systems can offer the appropriate functionality. This is an interesting example of how the overall infrastructure may reach right to the user's desktop. Within a more self-contained closed-loop system, there will be a different set of factors to consider, but the principle will be the same.

Choosing the technology for our biometric pilot scheme doesn't stop at the biometric device. We have to consider the total system, how this operates and what the external influences are. We should then ensure that we have the correct technology in place at each functional layer.

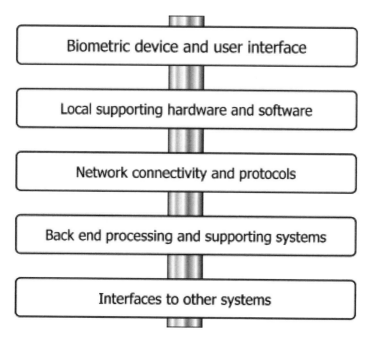

Figure 8.2 Considering the functional layers within the total system

The diagram above represents something of a simplification in this respect but perhaps usefully illustrates the importance of thinking about the total system at the outset and not just concentrating on the biometric device. When the project is up and running, the realized performance will be the product of the total system as required to perform the transaction and not the performance of the biometric device in isolation. We must therefore always be considering the system as a whole at each phase of the project, including when we are initially choosing the technology. We may choose not to change the supporting infrastructure or certain physical components, but this should be a reasoned decision based upon a complete understanding of the total system architecture, processes and functionality.

## 8.4 Working with vendors

This is a topic which could probably fill several books quite easily and represents an area which may swing between managed success and a recipe for disaster depending upon the initial understanding between vendor and client, the expectations on both sides and how well the relationship is managed. Within this book, we shall simply highlight some of the important areas and bring the subject to the attention of the reader as an integral part of running a biometric pilot scheme.

As with any business relationship, it is important to start off on the right foot with a crystal clear understanding of what the project entails and what the expectations are on both sides. When something goes wrong in the relationship between vendor and client, it is often because neither party really took the trouble to get the fundamental requirements and scope established and agreed right up-front. Both sides have a responsibility in this context. The client has a responsibility to produce and manage a robust project plan and ensure that this is adequately communicated. The vendor has a responsibility to ensure that he can deliver what is required when required, has the necessary expertise to do this and does not exaggerate his company's capability. Both sides naturally have a responsibility to be truthful and ethical in their dealings. Once again, biometric projects are especially vulnerable as there exists considerable potential for misunderstanding, especially with regard to factors such as device performance and ease of integration. It is easy for a vendor sales person to roll off theoretical performance specifications out of context, or to assume that because there is an SDK available, it will be easy to integrate the device into a larger process. Similarly, it is possible for the client to underestimate the complexity of the existing infrastructure. However, no relationship should be entered into unless there exists an unequivocal understanding of the requirement on both sides.

The first step for the client is to understand to what extent they require the services of third party organizations. Hopefully, it will just be for the supply of the relevant hardware and software modules necessary for the client to design and build the total system. On some occasions, the client may decide to outsource the whole project to a third party consultancy. This will in some cases almost certainly be a big mistake and end up costing several times what it should and the client should consider such a move very carefully indeed. However, the client may choose to use the services of different third party organizations for different elements or phases of the project if applicable. The important point here is that it should be the client who designs the project, produces the detailed project plan, specifies the hardware and software requirements and manages the implementation. Nobody knows the client's business better than the client himself and nobody has a better understanding of the client's systems architecture with all its attendant interfaces and dependencies than the client's own internal IT support personnel. If these fundamental elements are outsourced, much time and effort will be wasted while the third party strives to understand the necessary detail, which in any case, he can only obtain from the client. It is precisely in this area that things can start to go wrong with the third party relationship. The recommendation then is that the client firmly manages all aspects of the project, including the decisions over which vendors will be used and how the relationships with them will be managed. In our example project, County Bank understand this point and have a firm grasp on the project accordingly.

Having decided upon the external vendors who will be supplying goods and services to the project, it will be necessary to precisely determine and agree the scope of their involvement with each of them. For example, for the chip card suppliers in the Smiley Card project, County Bank will provide an exact specification for the card including artwork, the quantities required and when, the address to which they should be delivered, the method of delivery and so on. The costs and payment details will also be agreed and adhered to. All of this will be properly documented and agreed by both parties. There will be no deviation from this agreement without mutual consent, which shall not be entered into unless there is a genuine unforeseen circumstance which makes compliance impossible. Neither party should enter into the agreement unless they are absolutely confident of their ability to fulfil their obligations accordingly. It all sounds rather official and binding, but this is by far the best way to work within a project of the nature we are describing. Scope must be clearly defined, understood and fully agreed for every relationship within the project.

The next important point to establish and agree is that of schedule. When a robust and detailed project plan has been produced, there will be a large number of dependencies between individual tasks and phases of the project. The project manager will have built in a certain amount of contingency for unexpected delays, but not too much. Therefore if a critical component is delivered late, it may well have an impact on the project overall. It is vital therefore to communicate these critical time scales to all concerned and ensure that each third party vendor understands where they fit into the overall picture, what they are expected to deliver and when. If sufficiently detailed information is produced and circulated, there can be no misunderstanding or reasons for delay. This is better for both sides in any such relationship.

In addition to the fine detail of individual tasks and their dependencies, there will be some major project milestones along the path to success. Again, these should be communicated to all concerned in order that participating partners and third parties can work towards them with a high degree of co-ordination. Once again, the project manager will be key in setting these milestones at an achievable level and managing the project towards each one. Depending on the size and scope of the project, it may be useful to hold some sort of informal event to celebrate the achievement of each key milestone, providing the opportunity for everyone involved to get together again and discuss the next phase.

Part of managing the project is managing the third party, and, in our example case, participating partner relationships. On a day-to-day basis this will be undertaken largely by section leaders in each of the key areas described in 8.2, Choosing the project team. However, there also needs to be an agreed mechanism and process for escalating any arising issues in order to ensure that they are swiftly resolved. This should be decided upon by the project director after due consultation with the parties involved and it will be the project director who is the final arbiter for issues that cannot be resolved at a lower level. If this process is well designed, communicated and understood, it will help to safeguard the project against unnecessary delays due to misunderstanding or misinformation. Here lies another good reason for holding periodic 'celebratory' events, as they provide the opportunity for individuals to discuss any issues or concerns with their peers and ensure a close working relationship. The project director will additionally hold regular meetings with the key managers from each area to monitor progress as the project develops.

In conclusion, working with third party vendors and suppliers should not be a problem if the project as a whole is properly designed and planned and expectations are clearly communicated on both sides. With scope and schedules firmly agreed it is naturally important for both sides in any relationship to stick to their part of the bargain. This includes vendors delivering on time and clients paying on time. Disputes between clients and vendors are negative, time wasting and frequently costly to either party or both. They should be and can be avoided with a little planning and consideration.

## 8.5 The test environment

This is a complex area that will vary greatly between projects of different sizes and operational design. With a relatively straightforward project where everything is neatly contained within a single closed-loop environment, it is an easy matter to consider the requirements and construct the most appropriate environment accordingly, especially if you are starting with a clean sheet of paper. Many projects however are far more complex than this and may be spread across several user environments (as with our hypothetical Smiley Card project) with a complex set of dependencies and interfaces. There are some key parameters which are nevertheless applicable to both and may serve as a good starting point when considering the test environment.

First of all, let's define what a test environment actually is. In most IT circles this will be defined as the necessary hardware and software to run the system, implemented separately from the organization's core infrastructure and therefore incapable of interfering with it or adversely impacting it in any way. Generally speaking, unproven concepts or software will be run in a test environment during an evaluation stage before being transferred to the 'live' environment at the time of final implementation. This makes a lot of sense for any project involving new or previously untried technology and should certainly be the case for a significant biometric pilot scheme. Of course, it may be necessary to interface to real-time operational systems in order to extract data or feed into existing databases. From an operational perspective, the test environment will be the actual physical environment in which the user interacts with the system. In our example case, there are several environments in which the user may be utilising the Smiley Card and its attendant services, from inside a bank, a store, an airport or even sitting at home in front of their personal computer. The combination of the information technology and operational environments together constitute the overall test environment for our biometric project.

The reader may at first wonder why we draw attention to this factor within the book and might imagine that the environment is something we have little influence over, or conversely, has little influence on our project. In fact the environment can have a huge influence on the results of our biometric pilot scheme and is therefore something that has to be considered carefully and therefore should come under the influence of the project designers and project managers. Precise details of the test environment, both technical and physical, should also be noted and logged for consideration at the end of the project when the results are evaluated.

Let's first consider the technical environment. In our example Smiley Card case, many of the technical processes are already in place, such as the retailer transaction and settlement schemes, the ATM transaction management, the third party websites and so on. Wherever these can be used transparently they will continue to be so. Any additional processes will be separated out as much as possible in software modules in a way that does not impact the core functionality for non-Smiley Card holders. In addition, the County Bank project managers have arranged for a batch feed of all Smiley Card transactions to be run nightly into a physically separate server in order that they may be analyzed off-line with no impact to the normal day-to-day business reporting activity. The software developed by KeyOptics for the client side web access will maintain the biometric matching algorithms and transaction logs on the client machines, thus impacting the participating vendor's services as little as possible. This information will be uploaded every time the Smiley Card user accesses the County Bank online banking facility (which they will be encouraged to do at least weekly) and written to a separate database within the County Bank online system, before being batch copied to the project server on a nightly basis. The County Bank project team have taken the view that as long as they can extract the relevant data from the real time operational systems, they can then analyze or otherwise manipulate this off-line via a physically separate local network for the purposes of the project. In a different scenario, if we didn't need access to real-time operational systems, then we could have operated the whole system in isolation. However, part of the County Bank requirement is to evaluate the feasibility of integrating biometric technology into existing processes, and so this is a highly relevant approach. From the participating service partner's perspective, they will need to add an additional module to their web based systems in order to accommodate Smiley Card holders. As this takes the user into a quite separate mini loop for the biometric authentication before returning them into the main process, this can be isolated from their existing process and have little or no impact upon it. One function of this additional module will be to log all Smiley Card transactions for their own analysis. County Bank will already have identified the transaction by the card number and can thus sort by merchant code etc. In conclusion, from the technical environment perspective the goal will be to impact existing systems as little as possible by the use of existing processes where available, and carefully constructed interfaces into unique processes or functionality. In addition, any project-related use of the subsequent data should be undertaken off-line, with no possibility of interfering with the main line databases.

Now let's turn our attention to the physical operating environments. These are key, not just from the point of view of overall performance, but also to understand the user psychology and how they interact with and accept different ways of working with the technology and associated benefits. In our Smiley Card project, there are several areas where this factor needs to be considered. Starting with the County Bank ATM machines, as these are already in a known and accepted environment, the main task here is to integrate the Smiley Card functionality as seamlessly as possible. County Bank have chosen to do this by using a chip card reader that can also read magnetic stripes in place of the usual ATM device, thus rendering the system suitable for all users. The biometric fingerprint reader is automatically backlit when a Smiley Card is inserted and user prompts and instructions are provided via the existing VDU.

Figure 8.3 The County Bank Smiley Card ATM

The County Bank ATM machine has deliberately been changed as little as possible in order that non-Smiley Card holders will not be disadvantaged or disorientated in any way. However, in order to draw attention to the project and provide a welcoming and attractive environment, there will be significant in bank displays and promotional material. This is a very important aspect of any biometric pilot scheme. Potential users must know where they can use the service and must have no difficulty recognising participating sites - in this case selected County Bank branches. This is also where the benefits of a catchy and colorful logo start to be appreciated. If the site is contained within a larger area, such as an airport terminal for example, then this becomes all the more important as users must be able to recognize it (and be attracted to it) from a distance. In cases where multiple verification points are to be provided, then we must also think about user comfort and convenience, ensuring that they are not too cramped and that operating instructions are clearly displayed. County Bank are fortunate in this respect as the ATMs have been carefully sited and of course already incorporate a VDU display that can be used to guide the user through the verification process.

The other main user interface for County Bank is the portal into their online banking facility. This needs to be designed to offer an intuitive operation to Smiley Card holders while not inconveniencing other users. They would like to make it obvious that there is such a pilot running however, partly to see how many additional enquiries they receive about the scheme from non-participants. Therefore the Smiley Card logo will be reasonably prominent.

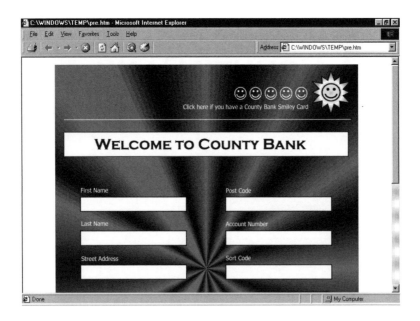

Figure 8.4 The County Bank welcome screen with Smiley logo

Visitors to the County Bank home page will immediately notice that there is an alternative route for Smiley Card holders which obviates the necessity of filling in the user details form. When the Smiley Card holder clicks on the Smiley logo, he or she is then invited to provide their biometric via the special KeyOptics keyboard sensor which is only activated when the Smiley chip card is inserted into the reader.

Figure 8.5 The user is invited to supply their biometric

The verification process is actually undertaken at the client end and the result passed back to the County Bank website to be processed accordingly. Naturally, the user will be guided by appropriate error messages if the verification process is not undertaken correctly and, as a last resort, the system will fall back to the conventional mode of operation if the user's identity is not verified by the biometric process. However, as all participating users will receive comprehensive training, this is considered an unlikely occurrence.

Having progressed to this second screen, the Smiley Card holder is now in a somewhat privileged position and can interact with the system in a very personal way, as a result of having the Smiley Card and the special KeyOptics computer keyboard. There is a psychological factor at play here as we are engaging the user far more positively than would be the case if they were simply browsing the site or were a non-cardholder. This immediately gives us the opportunity to customise and personalise our response in such a way that it makes for a pleasant user experience. This can be as simple as addressing the user by name, to offering information based upon the user's particular profile and transaction habits. Importantly, we can do this without the user having to enter a PIN or completing any online forms.

Figure 8.6 The County Bank automatic personalised response

The Smiley Card holder may now complete their online banking transactions with the minimum of inconvenience within a secure environment whilst the County Bank web server has a high degree of confidence as to their true identity as this has been verified against the template on the Smiley Card, a far more reliable method than the use of PINs and passwords. In fact, this represents a good example of using biometrics primarily for user convenience, whilst simultaneously introducing a far more robust security model.

In setting up the test environment, County Bank need to ensure that the end-to-end process functions as expected and is suitably robust. Furthermore, the biometric pilot system should not have any adverse impact on the core system behavior in any way. This is quite a challenge as the system inevitably requires links and interfaces to parts of the main County Bank operational systems. It is a similar story for the participating partners who must find a way of seamlessly integrating the biometric pilot scheme into their mainstream activities without any risk to the core processes or adverse impact on the performance of their existing systems. The Tranquil Tours, WebWorm and 2XS webmasters are confident of their ability to provide a loop out of the relevant pages on their websites to accommodate the Smiley Card verification process and return the user to the appropriate section. If any errors are encountered, the system will simply fall back to the standard mode of operation. They will also wish to feature the Smiley Card logo and pilot scheme heavily on their sites.

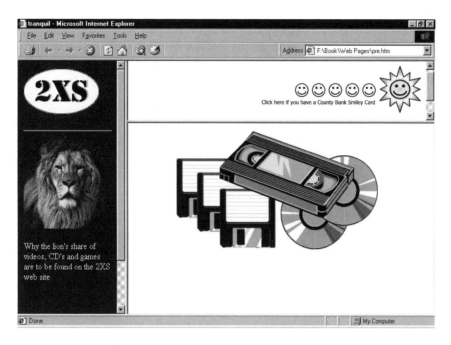

Figure 8.7 The 2XS website with Smiley Card logo

As one of the participating partners in our example pilot scheme, CashCo will also be setting up a test environment, although in their case things are a little different as there is no online facility to worry about. Instead, they will implement the Smiley Card functionality within the new cash machines they are installing in airport arrival lounges and also offer an enhanced service to Smiley Card holders at their manned kiosks. As the cash machines themselves constitute a pilot project, the biometric functionality will simply be incorporated into the existing plan. There will of course be some point-of-service promotional material to organize and CashCo will also draw attention to the pilot via leaflet distribution at strategic points within the airports they serve. This is all part of creating the test environment as users need to be informed of the pilot, and the points of service where these facilities are available need to be obvious and welcoming in order that Smiley Card holders can easily use the system. Naturally, for the unmanned cash machines there will need to be special instructions for Smiley Card holders to guide them through the verification process and offer a highly personalised and intuitive interface.

It may be considered that KeyOptics have little to worry about with regard to the test environment, but in fact they will be liaising heavily with the other participating partners and also the supplier of the chip cards, to ensure that the right numbers of fully working and tested keyboards are available for the Smiley Card holders.

In conclusion, creating the right test environment can be a complex issue as the environment contains technical, practical and even psychological elements, all of which need to be considered and addressed. Technically, we need to ensure that we separate as much of the pilot scheme as possible from our core operational systems and that there is no adverse impact on those systems as a result of the pilot scheme. Practically, we need of course to consider ergonomics and the user experience, ensuring that operation is as intuitive as possible and that the enhanced functionality offered via the Smiley Card is delivered smoothly and reliably at all times. Psychologically, we should be aiming to provide an enjoyable user experience for every Smiley Card transaction, no matter what the mechanism and process of that transaction is. Part of this may be provided by the physical environment, which if in a public place, should be high profile, clear and welcoming. In providing the best overall environment within our power and documenting it accordingly, we shall then be in a position to produce and understand some meaningful data within our pilot scheme, which in turn can be referenced to the environmental conditions of this particular project. The project manager should ensure that sufficient time and resource is allocated to designing and putting in place the overall test environment, including all the necessary interfaces.

## 8.6 Marketing and communications

There would be little point in putting together a biometric pilot project if no one outside of your team knew about it. Clearly, there is much to do in co-ordinating the technical design and implementation with a suitable marketing and communications program to ensure that participants are available and fully aware of the scheme at the right time. Furthermore, this marketing and communications requirement is not restricted to external customer-facing areas, but is highly relevant within your own organization where many departments and individuals will need to be informed of developments in a timely manner.

Let's consider some of the internal requirements. We shall assume that the project has been approved by the relevant authority within the organization and that the project director, together with the representatives from the training and PR/publicity areas will be responsible for identifying and orchestrating the various marketing, communications and training requirements. Internally, it will be important that awareness is created among the right people at the right time. There is no point in prematurely flooding other departments with information which is simply irrelevant to them at that particular point in time. In our example project, County Bank have decided to adopt a dual layer approach for internal communications. At the generic level, they have constructed an Intranet site which provides a good background into the project, its purpose and the expected outcomes. It also provides information as to who is doing what, together with the appropriate contact details and an evolving list of frequently asked questions. As the project approaches the launching phase, this site will carry an electronic newsletter which may be downloaded or printed straight from the site. Reference to this will be made in the company's printed internal magazine, together with a feature article prior to launch. At the more specific level, they will target various internal departments with presentations and workshops as and when required in order to advise on both the project and its impact on the department concerned. This activity will be supported by eye-catching literature which succinctly covers the project and its aspirations.

Figure 8.8 The Smiley Card internal flyer

The customer-facing staff within the area that the pilot scheme is run will naturally need to receive training prior to the project launch, as will customer support call center personnel. The technical support department who looks after the County Bank branches involved with the pilot shall also need instruction and training with respect to the new components in the ATM machines and their precise functionality and interaction with the host. Similarly, those supporting the online banking facility will also need a thorough understanding of the functionality and operational processes involved. These various support functions will also need co-ordinating and an issues/event log will need to be put in place and vigorously maintained. We have mentioned County Bank, but of course similar requirements will exist for the participating partners and this will all need to be managed within the overall project. The internal marketing and communication requirements are therefore both extensive and significant in relation to the success of the project overall and this is an area that needs careful consideration and planning.

The external marketing and communication requirement is no less vital to the success of the project. Decisions need to be made as to what is the optimum time to reveal that such a project is being undertaken and to invite participants accordingly. Furthermore, there is the question of exactly who should be invited to participate and how best to reach them. For the project to be meaningful, it is important that we have a fairly broad cross section of participating users and also that we know who these users are in terms of demographic information. In our example project, County Bank have fairly extensive information on the profile and buying habits of their customers and it is therefore not difficult for them to randomly select likely participants from different sectors. They also have a ready-made information distribution channel via their monthly statements which are mailed directly to users. It would of course be possible to invite participants via in-branch displays or online information, but this would be a little indiscriminate and County Bank are confident that they will receive a sufficient number of applications via the direct mailing route. The other participating partners must also consider this question carefully and propose a suitable plan accordingly.

Naturally, the timing of any such communication is very important. There needs to be sufficient time to answer any questions from prospective users and arrange training sessions prior to the project launch, if we are to start off with a reasonable number of participants. Once the project is under way, additional participants may be enrolled as required. The precise content of any such communication is also very important. In addition to explaining the obvious items such as how the scheme works, what its objectives are and so on, we should explain in suitable detail exactly what is happening with the biometric data, how it is being stored, what happens with it during enrolment and subsequent verification transactions. Very importantly, we should also state quite clearly that this biometric template data will not be used in any way outside of the pilot scheme and will be destroyed at the end of the pilot. We may also like to make some sort of statement as to the anonymity of individuals within overall test results and various reports which might be generated in this context. It is very important to cover these issues in advance and have a clearly stated and unambiguous policy around user privacy issues and the use of biometric data. This is all part of the marketing and communications requirement and needs to be planned and co-ordinated as a key element of the overall project. In addition to project objectives and matters of policy, we also need to communicate to the users all of the potential benefits offered within the pilot scheme. In our example project there are many such benefits from easier use of ATM and online banking facilities, to personalised and simplified online shopping via the participating partner's websites, special offers and privileges only available to Smiley Card holders and of course the greatly enhanced security in relation to personal transactions. This will give our

PR/publicity representatives plenty of scope to produce some attractively presented and informative material for distribution to potential participants. Exactly what we say at this point and how we portray the benefits associated with our scheme will tend to shape the users' initial views about biometric technology and its applicability to everyday processes such as those included in our scheme. Naturally it is important to emphasise the benefits and portray the concept as user friendly and intuitive. The public perception of biometric technology has sometimes suffered due to it being portrayed as either a security methodology or as a highly complex technology which will only be understood by boffins. Our marketing and communications initiative gives us the opportunity to dispel these ideas and portray biometrics as a user-friendly, user benefits-oriented technique that is both exciting and eminently useable.

Communication to the users shouldn't stop with the invitation to participate. There are many points where timely additional information needs to be available. This is particularly the case during and leading up to the enrolment process, where it is important that activities are co-ordinated and that the user experience is positive. We need to allow sufficient time for each participant to be enrolled into the system and issued with their personalised Smiley Card. We should also anticipate that there may be some additional questions from the user at this time and these need to be dealt with efficiently and courteously with no pressure placed upon the user to 'move along'. This means that the enrolment of a given number of users (County Bank are aiming for 3000 users within the pilot scheme) needs to be carefully planned and co-ordinated. In our example project, users will be invited to visit their nearest branch of County Bank at a specific date and time in order to be enrolled into the system and receive both their Smiley Card and an information pack outlining its use and benefits. The information pack will have been designed in collaboration with the participating partners and will include details of the various options and special benefits available to the Smiley Card user.

Even after the user is enrolled into the system, there still exists valuable opportunities for communication in relation to the project. County Bank have decided to produce a bi-weekly newsletter that will be distributed by mail to each participating customer. This will provide details of how the project is running, numbers of participants, related transactions etc., and will also carry information of additional offers from the participating partners and other news. In addition, participants will be able to write in to the newsletter with any interesting views or experiences for general publication among the Smiley Card community. There is a little psychology at play here, as people generally like to feel part of an exclusive group and discuss relevant topics accordingly. This will have a positive effect on the project overall, especially if those views are listened to and responded to by those responsible for the project. The project director will thus have an important part to play in the overall marketing and communications area.

The use of graphics and visual aids within all of this communication is also important and it is well worth spending a little time and effort to get this right. In our example project, County Bank have decided that they want to portray a friendly and 'fun' image for the project in order to generate enthusiasm, but at the same time they are highly conscious that it also needs to have an air of professionalism and efficiency. Everything must be perceived to run like clockwork from the user's perspective. They have therefore chosen to use a relatively friendly logo (the Smiley on the Smiley Card) but will take pains to ensure that all associated material is professionally presented, succinct but informative, consistent in its design and delivered at just the right time. The visual themes will be repeated inside the participating banks, other customer-facing areas and on all the relevant websites. This will require some co-ordination among the participating partners and in our case this will be managed by the County Bank PR/publicity department.

In conclusion, it may be tempting to underplay the marketing and communications element of a biometric pilot scheme, especially when your chief accountant is counting the cost and looking for economies. However, I would argue that it is a very important part of such a project and should be considered as an integral element in the same way that the front-end enabling technology or architectural structure is. If the marketing and communications function is hopelessly wrong or just plain non-existent, then the project as a whole will suffer tremendously as a result. Having decided to undertake a pilot project at all, it is important to provide the very best chance of obtaining good quality meaningful data from it. To do this, you need the right number of the right profile of users with the right attitude towards the project. This requires conscious planning and good communication throughout, both internally and externally. If this is done well, you will be able to turn your attention to the operation of the scheme and the analysis of the resultant data with some confidence. If it is poorly undertaken, you will be at a disadvantage from day one.

## 8.7 The enrolment center

The physical appearance, configuration and operation of the enrolment centers will play a significant part in the initial user perception of the pilot project. The goal should be that participating users leave the enrolment center feeling highly enthusiastic and looking forward to their first unsupervized transaction. Indeed, the opposite effect is easily achieved if sufficient attention is not paid to the provision of good quality enrolment centers and this would have a direct effect on the realized performance of the biometric pilot project.

The first rule of thumb in this respect is that the enrolment centers should be highly visible and easy to find. It is interesting that in the case of certain previous biometric trials this hasn't been the case, leading to a great deal of user bewilderment and associated lost opportunities as potential users search in vain for the enrolment centers before finally giving up. This situation may be helped by timely and good quality communications explaining clearly the whereabouts of the enrolment centers and the times of day that they will be operating.

Figure 8.9 Making the enrolment center visible

The next important point is that the enrolment center should be immediately perceived as a friendly, welcoming place where users can be totally at ease and enjoy the enrolment process. This means having trained personnel on hand who can step the users through the process in a professional, but unhurried manner. The appearance, physical design and comfort of the chosen environment is also very important. If we use a spare empty office which has the appearance and ambience of a Police interrogation room (as the author has seen with at least one such project) then we shall be at an immediate disadvantage as the user will never relax or feel absolutely comfortable with the process. In addition, this sort of approach is very impersonal and shows a certain disrespect for the user, who is after all volunteering to help us with our pilot scheme. No, we must take the opposite approach and make the environment as friendly, comfortable and inviting as possible. I can visualise the accountants wringing their hands in despair at the thought of spending money on such a thing, but it is actually a very wise investment if we are to achieve a worthwhile pilot scheme that points to future opportunities for the organization in question.

Imagine you are an individual who has been invited to participate in the scheme. You have received by mail an invitation to attend your nearest enrolment center on a specific day and at a specific time. You were pleasantly surprised that a County Bank representative telephoned you personally to ask if the appointment was still convenient and if you needed any directions to the bank or any other information. Upon arrival, it was immediately clear where the enrolment center was, as a prominent and colorful sign indicated the area. Upon entering the enrolment area you are immediately greeted by a friendly, smiling receptionist named Sally who welcomes you and offers you a coffee while she explains the various facilities within the center and advises on the enrolment procedure. You sit comfortably for a few moments awaiting your turn and finishing your coffee, whilst reading the laminated enrolment guide provided by the receptionist. After a very few minutes Sally introduces you to Tom, the individual who will guide you through the enrolment procedure. Tom welcomes you and explains exactly what you will be doing to enrol and informs you that you will have plenty of time to practice the as yet unfamiliar process before you leave the bank and that you will also be given a full information pack. You already feel quite comfortable and enthusiastic about the whole thing. Tom takes great care to explain exactly how the system works and carefully steps you through the enrolment procedure, which turns out to be much more straightforward than you expected. After issuing you with your new personalised Smiley Card, he then suggests that he shows you exactly how to use it at one of the enabled ATMs within the branch. You decide to try obtaining a mini statement from the machine, a process which works beautifully without you having to enter (or remember) a PIN. Having tested the new functionality of the Smiley Card-enabled ATM, Tom takes you over to a comfortable-looking desk with a PC and special Smiley Card keyboard. The PC is running a special interactive tutorial which explains exactly how to use the special keyboard for Smiley Card-enabled online transactions and enables you to practise as many times as you wish. Tom explains that this is a stand-alone PC used solely for practise purposes and that no data is retained within it. He adds that you can stay there as long as you like and asks whether you would like another coffee. When you have finished experimenting with the practice system, you report back to Sally at the reception point, who hands you a full information pack and briefly explains the contents of it. She asks if you have any other questions that you would like to ask at this stage, to which you answer no as everything has been so clearly explained. Sally thanks you for participating in the scheme and stresses that you are welcome to revisit the enrolment center as often as you like if you have any questions or would like to spend some more time on the tutorial system. You leave the center feeling both enthusiastic and confident that you will have no trouble using the Smiley Card.

The above illustrates how the enrolment process should work. With some previously undertaken pilot schemes not nearly enough attention has been paid to this activity, leading to variable quality enrolments and a good deal of confusion among users who leave, still not really knowing what a biometric is and how best to interface with the system. The irony here is that good quality biometric templates are vital to the subsequent success of verification transactions. Good quality templates are a product of good quality enrolment procedures. Good quality enrolment procedures ensure that the participating user has a good understanding of how the system is operating and how they should use it. It follows therefore, that anything other than good quality enrolment procedures are likely to have an adverse effect on the realized performance of your system overall. This is precisely why we must pay attention to this most important aspect of the biometric pilot scheme.

It starts by ensuring that we have an attractive and pleasant environment with adequate space and facilities in which to conduct the enrolment process. This should be complemented by both a waiting area, with comfortable seating and coffee facilities, and also a practice area with interactive tutorials and the chance to test the new functionality (in our example case the Smiley Card) before leaving the enrolment center. It sounds like we are issuing an open invitation for the user to spend the entire day with us, but in fact, the more comfortable and intuitive we make the experience, the faster users will be able to undertake the process and get on with their other business for the day.

We should pay particular attention to the personnel who man these enrolment centers. They should be experienced customer facing staff who are pleasant, friendly and professional in their attitude. They should also be smartly dressed and knowledgeable about the system, how it operates, why the pilot is being run, the science of biometrics and the benefits of being a participant in the scheme. In other words, they should be fully briefed and properly trained for the task at hand. Do not simply allocate the task to whoever happens to be around and looks like they have some time on their hands (often some poor hapless security guard) as this is unfair both to the individual concerned and the users wishing to enrol in the system. Furthermore, it will almost certainly result in sub-optimal templates, with the attendant effects on subsequent transaction performance.

Full documentation should be provided at every stage. This can start with the original invitation and confirmation of appointment at the enrolment center. In this way, the participant already has a reasonable idea of what is involved before arrival at the center. Users should be handed a step-by-step guide to enrolment before the event in order that they have something to refer to. Upon successful completion of the enrolment process, they should be given a proper user pack, detailing exactly what facilities are available to them, how to use the various services and who to contact if they have any problems or questions. All such material should be professionally produced with an attractive, consistent design theme running throughout and firmly establishing both the concept and identity of the project in question.

Facilities should be provided which enable the newly enrolled user to practise off-line, before they leave the enrolment center. This way, if they find that they do have difficulty using the system, this can be immediately addressed and if need be they can be re-enrolled or re-trained in the use of the system components. This should be an extremely rare occurrence, especially if we have paid proper attention to the enrolment process. However, human beings do tend to be a little variable and sometimes there may be genuine difficulties which need to be addressed. The best time to do this is right at the start.

The participating user is a key element within your biometric project and should be treated as a very important person at all times. Every opportunity should be provided for them to ask questions or make observations concerning the use of the system. Furthermore, any such questions or observations should receive an immediate response. It is these participating individuals who are really doing all the work in testing your biometric system. You should take pains to look after them and listen to what they have to say.

Another factor with the enrolment centers is the technical construction and architecture. Obviously we shall need the necessary biometric and related components in order to capture and register the biometric templates, but we shall also need appropriate supporting software and a method of collating enrolments from more than one center where applicable. In our example project, County Bank have decided to implement a wide area network connecting the enrolment centers to the central administration unit. Each successful enrolment is given a unique identifier and logged both on the local computer and the central host machine. All chip cards carry a unique number and are referenced to the user within the system. Dual mirrored systems are provided at each enrolment center, ensuring that the functionality remains in the event of one of them failing. In addition, replacement biometric sensors and chip card readers are held on each site, facilitating fast turn-around should a failure occur.    Naturally, all the enrolment PCs and tutorial machines are subject to the usual security measures themselves and there is a designated technical support person on hand at each enrolment center who has a hot line to the central administration unit for ultimate backup and support.

The individuals conducting the enrolments should of course be fully trained in the use of the attendant software.  Ideally, this software should provide some measure of enrolment quality, perhaps in the form of a 'score' for each enrolled template which will guide the enrolling officer as to whether the template is of suitable quality for subsequent use or whether the user should be re-enrolled. This process should be made as intuitive as possible, leaving no room for border-line cases or other ambiguities.

As we have discussed, the enrolment centers and enrolment processes offer us the opportunity to capture good quality biometric templates which in turn will give us the highest probability of successful transactions, provided we pay attention to the factors mentioned above.    But there is another, equally important consequence of having the right enrolment environment and process in place, and that is the psychological effect upon the participants. There is an opportunity here to generate an air of enthusiasm and confidence which can have dramatic affects on the subsequent performance of the system when used in earnest.   We must therefore strive to get this absolutely right and ensure that the design and configuration of the enrolment centers, together with the attendant processes feature strongly within our project plan.  Similarly, we must also ensure that this element of the project is properly funded and provided for and not just included almost as an afterthought.   If this element of our biometric project is properly conceived and professionally implemented, it will set the scene for what follows and participating users who have undertaken the enrolment process will be of the opinion that this is indeed something special.   An interesting and exciting development which they are privileged to be playing a part in. That is the desired effect. If on the other hand, the enrolment environment and process is perceived as low budget and poorly conceived, this also sets the scene for what follows and participants will probably feel that the organization is not really taking this seriously, so why should they?

In conclusion, this is an absolutely vital element of any biometric pilot scheme, the output of which will have a direct effect, not only on actual system performance, but importantly how participating users perceive and therefore react to the project overall. Cutting corners in this area is not to be recommended. We must provide the absolute best we can in terms of user convenience, comfort, organization and an intuitive enrolment process. Our professionalism in how we interact with the participants must also be first class, as should all accompanying documentation and subsequent communication.  Remember, we shall not have a second chance to make a first impression. Let's ensure that it is the right one.

## 8.8 The kick off

When putting together the original project plan, our project director and project manager will have configured several milestones along the way, including the all important one of going live with the system and formally launching the pilot. Let's consider some of the requirements leading up to the launch date.

First of all, we need to ensure that all of the primary systems components are in place and have been properly calibrated and tested. This should have been undertaken according to a documented process to ensure that we know exactly how the system has been set up. In our example project, County Bank will have decided upon a particular configuration of the biometric capture devices within the ATM machines and special KeyOptics keyboards. They will also have documented a test procedure for the chip card readers in order to ensure correct operation. For the equipment within the bank branches and enrolment centers, the County Bank technicians will also have ensured that sufficient spares are on-site and tested in case component failures are experienced. This testing and calibration/fine tuning also extends to the software components before final release and implementation.

Apart from the individual component testing, there is a requirement to test the operation of the system prior to launch in an end-to-end manner, to ensure that the user expectations will be met. In our example project, this will mean close collaboration with the participating partners who will make available a test environment in order that the County Bank project managers can undertake systematic tests of all the available functionality, both at the physical points of service and also online via a dedicated PC using a modem and the PSTN network. All of this testing needs to be carefully co-ordinated prior to the official launch. In addition, it needs to be properly documented with each element signed off by the test team as to its readiness for live implementation. Sufficient time should be allowed for this function in case any unforeseen developments or technical issues need to be addressed. It is a function which also demands close collaboration and communication among the participating partners. Indeed, in our example project County Bank have decided to make this a mini project in its own right, with a dedicated testing project manager whose final deliverable is a complete pilot scheme infrastructure certified as ready for live implementation. This individual will liaise closely with designated colleagues within the participating partner organizations to ensure that everything is covered prior to launch. Of course, there will always be subtle differences between a test environment and the live environment, but with intelligent design and a thorough understanding of the live environment and its performance characteristics, this should not present any real problems.

Another thing to check is whether sufficient quantities of user components and accessories are going to be available for the launch date. For our Smiley Card project, this includes the special KeyOptics keyboards and associated software, the Smiley Cards themselves and all of the documentation for both the enrolment process and the hand-out user packs. This is another area which will require collaboration across the board, both between participating partners and also between different functional areas such as PR, training, technical and so on. Not only does the availability of the various components and supporting material need to be assured, but also the quality. This means that physical components and software needs to be checked and that all published material needs to be checked for accuracy of content.

Earlier in the book we referred to the importance of the enrolment environment and associated procedures. The planning around this is very important, as whilst we shall certainly be enrolling individuals after the initial launch, it is also important that we have a suitable number of participants enrolled prior to the launch date in order that the project kicks off in some meaningful manner. There is a PR element involved here as we shall want to be seen to have thought this through properly and be launching a viable pilot scheme which is of considerable interest to our targeted audience. Once again, collaboration between departments and the participating partners is important in order to agree on the numbers concerned and how this will be organized.

The above-mentioned considerations and no doubt many more, should all have been included in our detailed project plan at the start of the project. This is why in our example project, County Bank decided to put in place a properly structured and cross functional project team with clear lines of communication and equally clear objectives. In this instance, all of the participating partners and the various departments knew well in advance of the targeted launch date and what they needed to do in order to prepare for it. As the designated day approaches, the relevant project managers will be busily ensuring that everything is in place and well co-ordinated. In extreme circumstances, if any one element is not performing properly or is proving to be inconsistent, then it may be appropriate to delay the launch slightly in order to get this attended to. However, this should certainly not be the case with any well-planned project as sufficient time will have been allowed to configure and thoroughly test every element prior to launch. County Bank, confident in their preparations, are bang on schedule and will launch on the designated day. The joint project teams have agreed that all functionality will be switched on just after midnight the day before, with a last round of testing taking place in the early hours of the launch day, leading to final sign-off as a live system by 07.00.

When the County Bank project team decided to absolutely confirm the launch date, they authorised the PR/publicity department to initiate preparations for a suitable launch event. This is important, as we shall want to ensure that there is a degree of public awareness of our biometric pilot scheme, both as a PR initiative and also as a vehicle to gauge reaction to the concept overall. The County Bank team have arranged for a co-ordinated event to take place in the participating bank branches and the Tranquil Tours and 2XS retail outlets. They have invited the local media, including radio, TV and press to one designated branch of each of the above, in order to cover the project launch completely. In addition, they have made arrangements with a local Cyber Café to demonstrate the online functionality of the project. Participating partner representatives will be on hand at each location and the previously enrolled participating users will be invited to the launch areas in order to take part in the occasion and share their views accordingly. There will be a variety of commemorative tokens and hand-outs to celebrate the occasion and attract further applications to participate in the pilot scheme. The designed and generated ambience will be one of good humour and excitement over what is seen as a step towards the future for consumer transactions.

It goes without saying that such an event needs to be very professionally organized and conducted in order to be successful, with the right calibre of individuals in charge. This is another area where cost cutting will prove to be a false economy. If we are going to do anything at all, let's do it properly. Of course, different projects will have different requirements in this respect, some wishing to remain relatively low key while others will perceive a PR benefit in a higher profile launch. In our example project, County Bank and the participating partners are very keen to promote the project as an example of them looking ahead and testing technology that offers the potential for a new wave of customer benefits. They are equally keen to gauge customer response to the concept overall and understand the likely adoption of any such services that they might subsequently offer in this context. To do this, they must ensure a certain public visibility for the project, and whilst there is an element of risk in so doing, it is considered that this risk may be effectively managed via quality project management and a professional attitude throughout.

If we picture ourselves at such a launch event for a moment and then look back over the sections of this chapter, the relevance of strong project management and good design in all of our processes becomes clear. If we are to embark upon any biometric pilot scheme, we should think all of this through in advance and agree on the level of our commitment to the project overall. Whilst in many cases it will be a question of scale, within that scale we should obtain full commitment, including the appropriate funding, to cover all of these areas, leading to a professionally organized and successful project launch. This is the day that all of the individuals involved in the project, including those from the participating partners and suppliers, should be able to hold their heads high and be proud of what has been achieved in getting to this point. This success should also be celebrated and in the case of our example project, the County Bank project director will be organising a special meal for all concerned, at which individuals will be recognized and presented with a small memento of the occasion. This will provide a little light relief and re-energise people for the tasks ahead associated with actually running the pilot project.

## 8.9 Gathering data

This is an interesting area. Having got our biometric pilot scheme up on its feet, we shall naturally be interested in how it functions and what information we can gain from it. But this won't happen automatically, we shall need to think carefully about the data we require, how to produce it and how to interpret it. In a well-planned project, we will have arranged for someone with proven analytical skills to help clarify the requirements and undertake the subsequent analysis in close co-operation with the project managers, leading towards a final report.

Before any of this can take place, we need to have ensured that our systems architecture and infrastructure allows us to easily obtain the raw data. As explained earlier, in our example project County Bank will be gathering Smiley Card transaction details by interpreting the card number and this information will be batch-loaded nightly to the project office. In addition, every time the user accesses the County Bank online banking system, specific details of their biometric transactions such as pass, fail and score will be uploaded from their personal computer log to the County Bank system, which will in turn batch-feed these into the project office server on a nightly basis. Similar information from the ATM machines will be captured and sent accordingly. Transaction data from the retail premises of Tranquil Tours and 2XS will be stored locally and batch fed to the project office on a nightly basis, provided there is something to send. We thus have three main pools of data. The primary transaction data, which tells us how many Smiley Card purchase transactions have occurred, through what channels, and their relative value. Smiley Card non-purchase transactions via the online banking service. And lastly, the individual verification transaction data such as pass, fail and score. In short, we have identified what data we wish to receive and how we are going to obtain it.

This data will all be collected on to a main server within the project office, from where those wishing to analyze the data can access it via their client computers. Having configured the systems infrastructure in such a way that we are getting the relevant data into the central project office, it is important that we have in place procedures to preserve and backup the original data in an unaltered form, whilst any analysis or reporting is undertaken from copies of the data. Perhaps we may arrange this via some sort of data warehouse where all the data is copied and from where reports may be run for analysis purposes. The original data will be stored separately. This must of course be configured and undertaken within a secure and self-contained environment and subject to well-defined and adhered to policies. This is an important point. The project must be run within a clearly understood and documented framework which includes policy statements around the use of any transactional data. This policy should be clearly stated within the information packs given to participants at the time of enrolment and their attention should be drawn to it, ensuring there are no misunderstandings in this respect. You may preserve individual anonymity within some of the analysis, such as verification scores for example, but certain information will be closely linked to the individual user and we must be clear on how this is used.

We have already mentioned the importance of having the right personnel to undertake the data analysis. It is equally important to understand what we need to be measuring and why. We may start off measuring numbers of transactions and related demographics such as selling channel, user profile and so on. We shall almost certainly wish to record biometric verification errors, especially false reject rates and maybe numbers of tries per transaction. It would also be useful to capture individual transaction scores where the software allows for this, and understand if and how these vary over time. The important point here is to agree in advance exactly what we shall be measuring and why. We can then document this and issue a procedure for how the analysis is to be undertaken and in what format the results are to be tabulated. We should also agree in advance how this information is to be used and distributed. In fact, this will form an important part of our privacy policy and it is important that this is clear and unambiguous. As the Smiley Card project is a joint initiative, it is reasonable that the participating partners should have access to this information and the project office shall distribute a weekly report directly to the individuals concerned on the understanding that this is confidential data and not for a wider distribution.

Separately from the internal communication of results, the project office shall produce a regular summary for the PR/publicity department which is suitable for public distribution. This shall be at a relatively high level and shall concentrate on numbers of users and numbers of transactions. The PR/publicity department may decide to augment this with some user-related stories and interviews where appropriate. In fact, general communication issues represent another factor for careful consideration. Naturally, people will be curious about the project and will want to know how many Smiley Cards are issued and to what extent participants are using them. They may also wish to know details of systems performance, especially with regard to the biometric functionality. However, the project office will decide in advance what information will be shared and what is for internal use only. There may be a commercial element here, as you may or may not want your competitors to know every detail of your project and its relative performance, especially if you think that there is a possibility that you might subsequently roll out something similar for all your customers. This is another topic which, within a professionally run project, will have been discussed fairly early on in the project life cycle and conclusions reached accordingly.

Lastly, we need to think about how we shall log and store the test results. Having set up our data warehouse and the automatic feeds into it, we shall probably design a series of easy to understand standard reports which can be produced on a regular basis by the project office analysis team. The content of these reports and how they relate to the original project objectives will have been agreed in advance with the project director and representatives from the participating partners. This is important, as there would be little value in having a random collection of disparate reports which mean different things to different people. Our lead data analyst will play a key part in designing these reports and explaining how they should be interpreted. It is also important that, once defined, the format and structure of these reports remains constant throughout the project, enabling a clear comparison to be made between any two points, such as before and after any fine tuning of system parameters or device threshold settings.

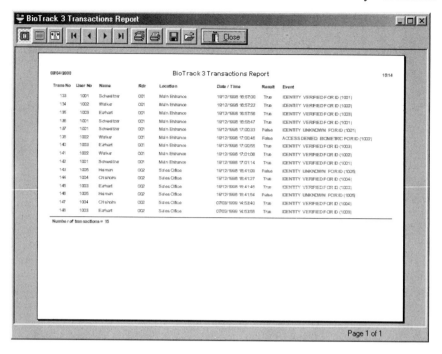

Figure 8.10 Producing standard reports from the transaction data

It is also important that the reports be kept as simple as possible and therefore easy to interpret by any of the project team or participating partners. This will necessarily mean that they represent the results at a fairly high level, although more detailed information will of course be available via the project office if required. A standard reporting tool may be the best way to produce this information, assuming that the data is stored in a common format that can be easily read by such a tool. Alternatively, a custom reporting tool may be designed and built especially for the purpose, an example of which is illustrated in Figure 8.10. A custom reporting tool may be pertinent if the data is deliberately stored in a custom format or encrypted in a proprietary manner. It may also be designed as a more elegant, streamlined and more intuitive tool as it will not need to be burdened by unused functionality. Having configured the report format and decided upon the distribution and frequency of reports, it will be a good idea to ensure that all such reports are saved and backed up for future reference. Naturally, the raw data within the data warehouse should also be backed up and stored safely, at least for the duration of the project. When the project has been finalised and conclusions drawn accordingly, you may or may not wish to keep this data. This is of course a matter of policy and will have been decided upon early on in the project life cycle and also communicated to participants. This policy should therefore be adhered to absolutely and procedures put in place to ensure that it is.

## 8.10 Making adjustments

Within any biometric pilot scheme, it may be considered necessary to make minor adjustments once the project is running and test data is being produced. This could be for a variety of reasons, but would most probably be connected with the user verification experience. In a commercially orientated project such as the Smiley Card example, we would be anxious not to reject valid users when they are undertaking the verification process. Even though we will have adjusted the verification threshold parameters (assuming this is adjustable with our chosen methodology) to what we consider to be the optimum level at the start of the project, it is conceivable that in isolated individual cases, or from a broader systems perspective, this may still require a little fine-tuning.

Capturing this requirement is an area for consideration, as we may rely on user feedback (not all users are equally forthcoming in this respect as they may perceive this as an operational error on their part) or we may deduce this from careful analysis of the test data. Similarly, we must consider the logistics of making any such adjustment. This will be easy enough within the retail or bank branches, but will be a little more involved when we are dealing with an individual user's personal computer. In this instance, the adjustment might usefully be made remotely when the user logs on to the online banking service. Alternatively, we might allow the user to make the adjustment themselves, although there are certain issues around this. In any event, we must accept that occasionally adjustments of this type may be necessary and will have to be accommodated. This should not be regarded as a failing but an acknowledgement of the way the technology works.

Not all adjustments will be user related. In our example project, we have decided to team up with participating partners in order to offer various online Smiley Card facilities. After they have gathered some experience in this respect they may discover ways of fine-tuning the software in order to increase performance or offer an enhanced user experience. The same might be true of the ATM machines or point-of-service terminals used in the retail environment. Once again, we must acknowledge the possibility of such a requirement and ensure that we have documented procedures in place to deal with it.

For any such changes, there are certain things which should be included in our procedures. Firstly, the individual undertaking the changes should carefully note and document the existing settings (or code block detail) before changing anything. The resultant changes should then be carefully noted and this information should be logged in a record and time and date-stamped accordingly, together with the location of the changed equipment and the name of the engineer concerned. This log will of course note the reasons why such a change was made, referring to a change request reference issued from the project office. The change request and changes made log should be centrally maintained and accessible to all relevant project personnel on a need-to-know basis. In our example case, the project office will produce regular reports on this activity and distribute them as appropriate, ensuring that the current situation is well understood.

Having undertaken such changes, we shall naturally want to know if they have been successful in their objectives. The project office should therefore be responsible for monitoring this and producing a 'before and after' report for each change made. This can then be considered by the relevant department and conclusions drawn as to whether any additional changes are required. In practice, this should be a very straightforward process, undertaken between the relevant personnel as required. The important point here is to ensure that everything is properly documented and accounted for and that any changed settings can be easily restored to their previous state if necessary.

In conclusion, it will occasionally be necessary to make fine adjustments to various elements within our biometric pilot project. This should be allowed for within our overall project plan and proper procedures put in place and communicated in order that everyone concerned knows how changes are to be undertaken and reported. The change request and changes made log should be accurately maintained by the project office and backed up accordingly. With these precautions undertaken, we can manage the inevitable fine-tuning requirements of our project and incorporate the changes intelligently within our analysis.

## 8.11 Concluding the pilot

Perhaps one of the first questions that people will ask in this respect is whether the pilot will be concluded at all or whether it will mature into a real-time operational system. The recommendation here is that it should definitely conclude, even if some of the devices and processes are subsequently incorporated into a larger system. The whole idea of running a pilot scheme is to use it as a test bed, not only for the chosen biometric technology, but also for your own ideas about how such a system might function. Assuming that we learn some valuable lessons from the pilot project, it is unlikely that a subsequent real-time system will be exactly the same. For one thing, the scale will be entirely different and you will probably integrate the functionality into your core operational systems in a slightly different manner. In addition, you will want to produce a far more comprehensive documentation and reconsider the ongoing technical support requirements.

If we accept then, that the pilot scheme should definitely conclude after a certain period of time, then we should specify the end date early on in our project. In a well planned and executed project this will not be difficult, as we will have carefully considered our milestones along the way and will have a good understanding of how long we shall need to gather the data we are looking for. If for any reason it looks like an extension to this date would be required, the project manager will spot this early on and be able to adjust accordingly. It goes without saying that we would have to communicate any such changes to all concerned, including the participating users. There would be costs associated with this and therefore any changes to schedule would ordinarily be avoided.

There is in fact a broader communications challenge as it will be necessary to distribute news about the forthcoming closure of the pilot scheme, preferably in a series of messages counting down to the final date. There is both an internal and external requirement in this respect. Internally, we shall need to communicate to all of those involved in the project and ensure that there is a co-ordinated approach to wind-down and final closure. In our example Smiley Card project, Tranquil Tours, WebWorm and 2XS will need to agree with County Bank precisely what messages will be posted on their websites and when, advising Smiley Card holders that the service will soon be coming to a close. There may be some interesting transaction activity when these messages start appearing, depending upon just how useful participating users have found the scheme. Externally, in addition to messages posted on the websites and also on County Bank's online banking service, all participating users will be sent a mail shot thanking them for their support and advising on the exact date of the pilot scheme close-down. There will also be point-of-service brochures at the banks and other public-facing areas such as the CashCo booths and 2XS retail outlets. It is vitally important that this activity is fully co-ordinated and that everyone is aware of what is happening and when. This is another opportunity to communicate with our customers in a professional manner and demonstrate our levels of customer service and commitment. As such, it shouldn't be missed.

We must also consider the technical implications of winding down and closing our biometric pilot scheme. Apart from the obvious need for synchronisation among the participating partners, we also need to understand exactly how the closure is going to be achieved in each area and what happens to the data. In this context, the project office might usefully produce and circulate a recommended high-level procedure as to removing functionality from software at the right time and ensuring that no data is lost. County Bank will have much to do at this point in time as they will need to co-ordinate the participating partner activity as well as ensuring that all data is finally captured within the data warehouse. This will take a little time with our Smiley Card project as the biometric transaction history data will need to be captured from the user's personal computers and for this to happen they need to log on to County Bank's online banking service - another area for communication and co-ordination. When they are sure that all relevant project data has been captured into the data warehouse and backed up accordingly, then the batch load feeds into the central project office servers may be removed. In parallel with this activity, the biometric functionality at the ATM machines and other physical points of service will need to be decommissioned and a schedule initiated and managed to do this. In our example project, we also provided special computer keyboards to the participating users and these will need to be collected. This may be easier said than done in some instances, but as this was part of the user 'contract' to take part in the pilot, this should be managed without event. It will be important to recover these keyboards as we will want to examine them closely for signs of wear and tear on the critical biometric sensor and chip card reader components. As for the Smiley Cards, these may be returned to the bank at the user's convenience (we may provide a pre-paid mailer) as they will not be valid after the cut-off date. We shall also want to gauge the durability of these cards and understand if there was any difference with the cards from different suppliers.

Part of the wind-down and final closure of the project will be to provide an adequate customer help line for the inevitable barrage of questions around what they should do now that the pilot scheme is ending. This may mean additional trained personnel for a period at the call center. Customer-facing staff within the bank branches and retail outlets will also need to be advised on how to deal with these questions and handle any associated issues. In fact, this support service will be required for a certain period *after* the project has officially closed. Once again, this will have been detailed within our original project plan and resources allocated accordingly. There will also be a related PR/publicity requirement as many people will be interested in how the project progressed, what lessons were learned, how it was accepted by participating users and of course, whether any similar scheme will be introduced for all County Bank customers in the foreseeable future. These sorts of questions will need to be very carefully considered and no information should be divulged other than via the agreed central PR/publicity department route.

As we started the project with a special launch event, we might also consider a special closing event in order to celebrate the success of the project and thank our participating users. We may once again utilize particular bank branches where special receptionists can welcome Smiley Card holders, take back their cards and peripherals and reward them with a small gift. This would also represent a wonderful opportunity to sit down with them (over a glass of wine perhaps) and capture their experiences and overall impression of the pilot scheme. This is very important, as we shall want to carefully analyze user feedback and see how it correlates with our transaction history for the period. Individual project members should also take part in these events and take the opportunity to meet with participating users face to face and understand the situation from their perspective. In our example project, the County Bank project director will no doubt organize a special celebratory event for the project team also, where they can compare notes and enjoy getting together after all the hard work put into making the project a success.

Once the pilot scheme is officially concluded and we have removed the associated functionality, it will be necessary to also partly disband the project team. We shall of course still need the data analysts and a core management team of perhaps the project director and representatives from the participating partners, although even these positions will probably be on a part-time basis. The other team members may now be released to carry on with their usual duties. This needs to be handled gracefully and, as the resource requirements would have been covered in detail within our project plan, there will be no surprises in this respect. With our project now concluded at least from the operational perspective, we may now turn our attention to what has been learned from the exercise.

## 8.12 Learning points

One of the primary outputs from our biometric pilot scheme will be a full report documenting the exercise, reaching conclusions and making recommendations accordingly. However, before we can produce any such report we must first carefully analyze the data and make sure that we understand what it is telling us.

As mentioned previously, our project director and the data analysts will have already sat down and decided upon a set of parameters which they believe are most important to capture. However, this information will still be subject to interpretation in some respects. Certain information, such as the number of Smiley Card transactions and their distribution across a date range may seem straightforward enough, although we may still wish to form conclusions with regard to average transaction values and whether we think these are above or below the typical spending patterns of our user base. In our example project, County Bank may or may not wish to analyze these transactions against user profiles in order to understand whether particular groups of individuals are more or less likely to take advantage of this technology and embrace any additional functionality offered as a result. Then there is the question of which channels were most used and whether this indicates that the technology is more or less suited to certain buying activities. This all sounds rather mercenary I know, but part of understanding the potential benefits of implementing biometrics is undoubtedly entwined with the cold hard business case for doing so. Hopefully, the majority of organizations considering the technology will come to the conclusion that offering tangible user benefits also makes good business sense.

Within our example project, the participating partners will also wish to see conclusive evidence as to the feasibility or otherwise of implementing biometric user authentication and will be keen to study the results produced by the central project office. They will probably also have put in place some sort of monitoring system themselves and will have a good idea of how often Smiley Card holders accessed their websites using the biometric log in. When all of this information is available, the County Bank project director will organize a workshop where representatives from all the participating partners may meet and discuss the results. This in fact, is part of the data gathering process as it will be important to the project initiators to understand how the participating partners viewed the project and whether there may be scope for future collaboration of some kind. All of this will be building towards the project director's final report and recommendations.

The other side of the picture which needs careful analysis is of course the technical performance of the pilot scheme. This may usefully be divided into two elements. Firstly, the fundamental performance of the biometric authentication process and secondly, the impact on overall performance of integrating biometric functionality into existing systems and processes. Taking the first point, we must be confident that we have gathered all of the biometric transaction data available from the user's computers, ATM machines and other point-of-service terminals before we apply any analysis to this data. We may then identify the most obvious criteria such as number of false rejections and the numbers of verification attempts per transaction as well as the number of failed or aborted transactions. Digging deeper, we shall want to understand any patterns associated with these errors, such as user profile, time of day, selling channel and point of service (user's PC, ATM, in store etc.). A little deeper still, if we have been capturing relative 'scores' for the successful verification transactions, then we shall wish to analyze these quite closely across the timeline in order to establish any patterns, again referencing these to user profiles if applicable.

Turning our attention towards overall systems performance and the impact of integrating biometric functionality, the individuals within each participating partner organization who track performance and capacity issues will have been tasked at the start of the project to produce 'before and after' reports accordingly. These should cover parameters such as average transaction time, network performance, bandwidth usage, application stability and others deemed important in each area. In addition, we shall want to form a view of how easy it was to integrate this biometric functionality and whether with hindsight we would have done it any differently. In our example project, County Bank will be particularly interested in analysing systems and network performance during the trial period.

What will all this analysis tell us? To start with it will provide a picture of just how enthusiastically the concept was embraced by the targeted users. If there was a much lower than anticipated actual use, then obviously we have something more to learn about our users. If on the other hand we found a healthy level of usage and perhaps even an increase on average user activity and interaction (either administrative or direct spend), then this will start to look quite exciting. Further categorisation into user profile and operational channel will provide some useful information for our respective marketing departments. Moving on from here, the analysis of the biometric verification transactions themselves should tell us much about the feasibility or otherwise of offering this functionality on a broader scale. It will also indicate the relative maturity of the technology in general and the robustness of the chosen physical devices for such a task. If we have encountered a higher than expected proportion of errors, then a little investigative work may help us to understand why and suggest how these errors may be reduced. If on the other hand there have been a fewer than anticipated number of errors, then this also tells us something about the specific configuration chosen for the pilot scheme. A pattern may also emerge as to the distribution of errors on average between the ATM machines, point-of-service terminals and home computers, indicating where further work may be required at the user interface. There is a psychological factor at play in this last point as users will presumably be more relaxed and confident in their home environment than down at the bank or at the shopping mall and we should try to understand the effects of this. From the technical perspective, we should have learned a good deal from this pilot scheme, especially in the important area of integration. Our systems engineers will now have a pretty good idea of what it takes to integrate biometric technology into a mainstream operational system and the best way of going about it. This is invaluable information and one of the major benefits of running the pilot scheme. We should also now have an understanding of the relative impact from a networks perspective and whether the requirements are substantially different for this sort of application. All of this data and the conclusions drawn from it should be carefully documented for inclusion in the final reports.

There is yet another aspect that many organizations may like to consider and this is the PR and marketing value associated with running such a pilot scheme. This is a very real issue as the scheme will have undoubtedly generated much public interest (assuming the scheme was run in the public sector, as with our example project). This represents a golden opportunity to speak with our customers and potential customers and try to understand how we can best meet their future needs. Furthermore, it does so within a relaxed atmosphere as we are focusing on the pilot scheme. We may have found that the existence of the scheme actually generated enquiries from people we would not have ordinarily reached, in which case there is a value associated with this. There may also be PR and marketing value in the participating partners being seen to strive forwards to find ways of enhancing the customer experience. All of this should be analyzed and quantified accordingly to build towards the final conclusions.

Once we have gathered, analyzed, discussed and drawn conclusions from the wealth of data generated by our biometric pilot scheme, the project director will now be in a position to produce the final report for the initiating organization and representatives within the participating partners will no doubt do likewise. The content and presentation of the report should be carefully considered and will probably be closely aligned with the original project proposal. Typically, an executive summary will be produced to highlight the main findings and their suggested relevance to the organization in question. The executive summary will also provide conclusions and recommendations for further implementation if and where applicable. This may be followed by a more detailed section which collates the information into logical areas and provides statistics to support the conclusions. Finally, an appendix which provides all of the necessary data for those wishing to understand this in fine detail, or perhaps future project teams who wish to use this material for reference. A separate internal document may be produced in order to capture learning points from the exercise which may be useful for future projects. This will include information about project structure, timescales and any areas which were considered particularly strong or weak. It may also draw conclusions around working with collaborative partners and the best way to conduct such relationships. An important point here is to capture and document as much information as possible in relation to the pilot project. Those directly involved with the project may have this fresh in their minds at the time of writing the report, but six or nine months down the line when the project team has been disbanded things may not seem quite so clear and a large part of the value of such reports is for those who read them after the event. When we have analyzed the results from our project and reflected these in well-considered reports which paint an accurate picture of our experiences and make intelligent recommendations as a consequence, we may like to reflect upon a job well done and a successful biometric pilot scheme. This will no doubt be cause for celebration among the participating partners and project teams, who will probably richly deserve the moment! At least, they will do if the project has been properly organized and orchestrated from the outset with clear objectives and attainable milestones along the way. Designing and running a biometric pilot scheme is not difficult, but it does require serious consideration of all the issues involved and should be initiated and run along proper lines as would any important project within a corporate or governmental organization. There is sometimes a tendency to underestimate the importance of such a project and place inappropriate limits on resources, timescales and funding accordingly. In the author's view, this would be a big mistake as the conclusions reached from a half-baked project will be equally half-baked and inconclusive in their appraisal of the future potential for this technology within the organization concerned. If we are going to do it at all, let's do it properly.

# 9. Overall conclusions

We have covered a lot of ground in this book. More perhaps than would ordinarily be expected in a work focusing on a single enabling technology such as biometric identity verification. We have looked at the origins of the concept in the ancient world and how the idea of using anatomical and behavioral characteristics in order to identify an individual has seemed logical to different cultures at different times. We have also briefly touched upon developments in the field of electronics and how these have made possible the automation of biometric identity verification in a cost-effective and realistic manner. We have even looked at typical applications for biometrics and of course have explored the various popular methodologies and their particular characteristics as might have been expected. Perhaps slightly less expected were the sections on application development and the setting up and running of a biometric pilot scheme. However, these are very pertinent issues, especially at this stage in the overall development and acceptance of biometric technology in relation to everyday processes.

One question that arises repeatedly when discussing the pros and cons of biometrics is that of user acceptance. Have we really reached the point where ordinary citizens will accept the use of biometrics for processes in which they have a choice of participating or not (unlike for example prison systems where the user may be positively required to use the system)? The answer is almost certainly yes, provided they can see an associated benefit for themselves in doing so. This is a point that has often eluded practitioners in the field of biometrics. Perhaps too much emphasis has been placed upon the potential for enhanced security that the technology allows, without considering the user proposition in sufficient depth. If all the technology were to achieve is a more robust security model, then certainly there is benefit in that alone for some situations. But seeing biometrics only in this light would be like seeing the wheel as something that is good for rolling down hills. In both cases the real potential is as an enabling technology for other processes. Allow me a moment to explain. Automated biometric identity verification can open the door for the provision of a host of user-related services which would otherwise not be feasible. If such services can be configured to provide undisputed and additional benefits to users (customers) then it is likely that they will be accepted, provided of course that the operation and user interface is intuitive and reliable. One could imagine many instances; for example, where the automated access to personal information could provide a greatly enhanced user experience in an unattended environment, perhaps via a kiosk, over the Internet, or maybe via the good old telephone. One could also imagine situations where the higher than usual confidence levels as to user identity offered by biometrics might promote a wider level of online transaction functionality and associated benefits. In short, whenever the question of user acceptance crops up, the view of the author is that vendors and systems integrators should concentrate a little less on providing benefits for the organizational process and a little more on providing benefits to the user. It is unrealistic to suppose that users will embrace a technological paradigm that seems at first glance complicated and possibly a little intrusive, if there are no particular benefits to themselves in doing so. This may be OK for benefits payments, border control, driver's licences and other official areas where the user has no choice, but if we wish to see the use of biometric technology mushroom out beyond these areas, then we need to start viewing the world from the user perspective and generate some innovative thinking around the provision of tangible benefits that in turn create enthusiasm for using the technology.

Another hurdle to the broader acceptance of biometrics has been the way the technology has sometimes been portrayed by vendors and some of the rather ambitious, if not questionable performance claims made in this context, many of which have simply not been realized in real-world operating conditions. Whilst not all vendors fall into this category (indeed, certain vendors are particularly open in discussing performance and testing issues and are very knowledgeable on the subject), it is an unfortunate fact that those that do, tend to generate a rather negative perception of the industry among end users who have tried their products and found them wanting. Fortunately, in the last few years this has been acknowledged with industry associations and others being keen to promote best practice in testing methodologies and published performance criteria whilst accepting that real-world implementations bring with them a host of variables which simply cannot be described or predicted within the scanty product specifications provided by device manufacturers and vendors. This is not necessarily a failing on the part of vendors per se who naturally wish to portray their products in an attractive light, but an acknowledgement of the difficulty in predicting performance across multiple situations of which they have no particular knowledge. This factor should really be addressed within product literature and advertising. Having mentioned it here, the improving performance of biometric devices and increasing familiarity with their implementation will no doubt help to make this less of an issue in the future.

OK, so the biometrics industry is cleaning up its act and the devices are getting better all the time, but where is all this leading to and are we really going to see a sudden increase in the use of biometrics in everyday life? This is the question that many industry observers have been asking for some time now. The answer lies (in the opinion of the author) in the provision of intelligently conceived and genuinely useful applications which have real user appeal, coupled to the practical and low-cost integration of capture devices into familiar user interfaces such as computer keyboards, mobile phones and public devices such as kiosks and ATMs. The technology is virtually there bar a few points of fine tuning. What might take a little longer is thinking through and providing some of the applications, although one would expect to see a significant step upwards in this respect within the next two or three years. One would also expect to see some sort of biometric functionality provided for or within software development tools and eventually included as a matter of course at operating system level. When this happens, there will be no shortage of implementation ideas together with the necessary skills to bring them to fruition.

We have already mentioned some of the obvious applications for biometric technology such as in banking, benefits payments, network access and so on, but there probably exists a whole range of specific applications within a typical organization which could easily be addressed when the means of doing so become easier and more widespread. Imagine for example the wealth of related functions around the central accounting area which require authorised access and an audit trail. Apart from the general ledger and management reporting functions, there are areas such as purchasing, payroll, accounts receivable and possibly a number of externally linked operations from remote offices etc., where you would like to be sure that individuals accessing this information are who they claim to be and are authorised to do so. Then there are the increasingly important e-commerce and various business-to-business functions, all of which introduce additional personal identity verification and audit trail issues which might usefully be addressed. This isn't to say that biometrics are necessarily the answer to all our prayers in this respect, but they do offer some useful tools for our IT toolkit. Marketing departments in customer-facing organizations and indeed, perhaps in government, might usefully look at the possibilities of providing higher levels of user functionality and automation as a result of higher confidence levels as to user identity. There are a thousand and one ideas in this context that spring to mind. The question is how easily are they verified and ultimately implemented. This is precisely why we have covered application development and running a pilot scheme within this book. All of this is quite feasible today and will become even easier as time passes and we see the introduction of new tools and devices.

In conclusion, automated biometric verification and identification technology has been around (in a useable form) for over a decade, with many interesting claims and predictions made as to the relevance of the technology to everyday situations and the acceptance rate among the general public. Industry observers and cynics will have noted that throughout the nineties, every year seemed to be the year that biometrics would sweep all before them, banishing cards and PINs forever and revolutionising the way we interact with other systems and processes. Within that period, vendors have come and gone, established security electronics and physical access control companies have dabbled with biometrics and not really done anything particularly exciting with them (with a few exceptions) and potential end users have watched with bewilderment at the antics of the biometric industry at large. Whilst this all sounds a little messy, we should acknowledge that such a situation is not unusual with an emerging technology as it struggles to find its feet in the big wide world. There is inevitably a period of rationalisation as (hopefully) the better products and ideas gravitate towards the surface and position themselves in order to provide genuinely useful benefits to the users. The question is, have we reached that point in time with this particular technology? It is the authors view that we have reached that point in terms of product usability and some of the available matching algorithms, but the presentation of the whole in terms of applications and user interfaces still needs a little fine-tuning. In this respect, we are at a particularly exciting cross roads where we have some tremendously interesting tools at our disposal and virtually a clean sheet of paper on which to design some equally interesting applications. One would like to see a little more third party involvement, whether in the form of independent software houses or potential end users themselves, as this would undoubtedly drive forward the common understanding of where this technology can be genuinely useful and why. In this respect, one would welcome the encapsulation of biometric functionality within development tools (or indeed the operating system) in order to provide wider access for the development of ideas. Initiatives such as the BioAPI are perhaps a step towards this with their praiseworthy attempt to provide a common interface. Whilst there will always be a place for the specialist biometric integrator, one can't help feeling that we need to broaden the application design activity if we are to see a rapid increase in biometric implementation. The first few years of the new millennium will undoubtedly see some very interesting developments in this context.

Biometric technology is here with us today, it isn't going away and we shall certainly be seeing a great deal more of it in the near future. The author has really enjoyed his involvement to date with biometrics, a methodology which is very much entwined with user interaction and psychology, making the subject a particularly interesting one. Perhaps the reader will also enjoy exploring the potential of this technology as we move forward into an increasingly connected and automated world. I sincerely hope that this book has provided a starting point for such a journey of exploration and may even become your guide as you consider ways in which biometric verification and identification can provide real user benefits within your organization or sphere of operation.

# Index

# The accompanying CD

Attached to the cover of this book is a CD containing some interesting utilities and sample programs, all of which are designed to run under 32-bit Microsoft Windows operating environments such as Windows 95, Windows 98 and Windows NT. Each of these sample programs has its own installation utility and may be installed separately. Furthermore, each of them has an un-install feature and may be removed cleanly from your computer via the Windows Control Panel 'Add/Remove Programs' dialogue if and when you so desire.

To install any of these utilities simply run 'Setup.exe' from within the appropriate folder. For example, double clicking on *\BioTrack\Setup.exe where * is the drive letter for your CD drive, will install the BioTrack program. Be sure to read the help files for each program before using them, as these will explain any necessary setting-up procedures.

An overview of each application is provided on the document named 'Software.pdf', which you will find in the 'Documentation' folder on the CD. To view this document you will need the Adobe Acrobat Reader. If you do not have the Acrobat Reader installed on your PC, a copy is provided in the 'Acrobat Reader' folder on the CD. Simply double click on ar405eng.exe to run the installation routine.

I hope that these programs prove useful to you, if only as food for thought as you explore the exciting world of biometrics.


Julian Ashbourn

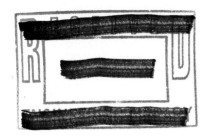